ENCYCLOPEDIA

OF

Technology and Applied Sciences

ENCYCLOPEDIA

OF

Technology and Applied Sciences

1

Abacus – Beverages

Marshall Cavendish
New York • London • Toronto • Sydney

Cover illustration: illustration of a communications satellite
Title page illustration: 40-ft (12-m) fans in a wind tunnel.
Roger Ressmeyer/Corbis

Marshall Cavendish Corporation
99 White Plains Road
Tarrytown, New York 10591-9001

© 2000 Marshall Cavendish Corporation

Created by **Brown Partworks Ltd.**

Library of Congress Cataloging-in-Publication Data

Encyclopedia of technology and applied sciences.
        p.   cm.
        Includes bibliographical references.
        Contents: 1. Abacus–Beverages—2. Bicycle–Codes and ciphers—3. Color–Engine—
4. Engineering–Gyroscope—5. Hand tools–Leather—6. Light and optics–Military communications
and control—7. Military vehicles–Plant hormone—8. Plastics–Sailing—9. Satellite–Tank—10.
Technology in ancient civilizations–Wood and woodworking—11. Indexes.
        ISBN 0-7614-7116-2 (set)
        1. Technology Encyclopedias, Juvenile. [1. Technology Encyclopedias.]
T48.E52   2000
603—dc21
                                                                                    99-14520
                                                                                        CIP
        ISBN 0-7614-7116-2 (set)
        ISBN 0-7614-7117-0 (vol. 1)
Printed in Malaysia
Bound in U.S.A.
        06 05 04 03 02 01 00   54321

ABOUT THE ENCYCLOPEDIA

The *Encyclopedia of Technology and Applied Sciences* contains a thorough coverage of all the major technology and applied science topics. Articles, arranged in alphabetical order, are written to be interesting and accessible to people who do not have a strong background in science as well as those who do. Describing and explaining phenomena that you see around you every day, these articles also include information on the cutting edge of science and help you understand theories and discoveries that you may see reported in the news. Each volume has its own index.

• The entries are lavishly illustrated with full-color photographs, diagrams, and historical black-and-white prints to enhance the concepts covered. On the first page of each entry you will find a DEFINITION, which gives an orientation to the topic, and ideas for making CONNECTIONS within technology and the applied sciences. Articles more than one page long also include a list of CORE FACTS, summarizing key information from the article.

• Throughout the entries, there are special color-coded box features with more detail on topics of particular interest. These include: **A Closer Look**; **Wider Impact**; **People**; **History of Technology**; and **Looking to the Future**.

• Each entry ends with SEE ALSO cross-references, citing related entries in the encyclopedia, and FURTHER READING, which gives a list of books or magazine articles with more information on the topic.

• The INDEX in volume 11 will help you find references to specific subjects. There is a general index, as well as indexes on specific topics such as computers and communications; engineering; manufacturing and industry; and medical, military, and transportation technology. Volume 11 also includes useful tables, further readings, a glossary, a time line, and a list of scientists and their inventions.

CONNECTIONS

● **Connections** boxes connect the topic in the main text to other areas of science.

● Words written in **CAPITALS** indicate other entries within the encyclopedia.

SPECIAL BOX FEATURES

A Closer Look boxes focus on a particular aspect of the subject discussed in the main text and give more in-depth information. For example, in the entry on Antibiotics you can read about Alexander Fleming's accidental discovery of penicillin and how it was synthesized by Howard Florey; in the entry on Acoustics and Sound you can find out how reflected sound is used to detect submarines.

A CLOSER LOOK

People boxes are about scientists and inventors whose discoveries changed the world. Turn to the entry on Anesthetics and find out about how William Morton struggled to obtain credit for the discovery of anesthesia, or turn to the entry on the History of the Automobile to find out how Henry Ford helped put the world on wheels when he developed the Model T.

PEOPLE

Wider Impact boxes highlight aspects of technology and the applied sciences that relate to everyday life. For example, in the entry on Accidents and Disasters you can find out how the people of Seveso, Italy, were affected by an explosion that blew up a chemical plant in 1976. In the entry on Antenna and Transmitter, find out how satellite technology has revolutionized news broadcasting.

WIDER IMPACT

History of Technology boxes look at how past ideas in technology and the applied sciences have changed our lives and how particular areas of technology have developed. For example, turn to the entry on Baking Industry and find out how modern baking techniques originated in ancient Egypt and were further developed by the Romans, who invented the first mechanical dough mixer.

HISTORY OF TECHNOLOGY

Looking to the Future boxes look at how ideas in technology and the applied sciences are being implemented and how particular areas are developing. For example, turn to the entry on Aircraft Design and Construction and find out why passenger aircraft are being constructed to carry as many as a thousand passengers, and why military aircraft will be made small enough to be pilotless.

LOOKING TO THE FUTURE

AUTHORS

Jonathan Adams
Susan Aldridge
Timothy Allman
Michael Ameigh
Sarah Angliss
Misha Barmin
Frank Barnaby
Patricia Barnes-Svarney
Tom Barnes-Svarney
Roger Brownlie
Michael Callahan
Sherri Calvo
Claudia Caruana
Martin Clowes
Mary Coberly
Malcolm Dando
Roger Dennett
Beth Dickey
Jennifer Donovan
Michelle Dorsett
Patricia Dwyer-Hallquist
Greg Faulkner
Tom Finch
Simon Fletcher
Mike Flynn
Jackie Fox
Joan Froede
Kathy Gill
Leon Gray
Hayden Griffin
Don Gwinner
Charles Hagedorn
Feona Hamilton
Barrett Hazeltine
Ian Hogg
Sarah Houlton
Brian Innes
Robert Jones
Vincent Kiernan
Lorien Kite
John Lohr
David McMordie
Peter Macinnis
Stuart Nathan
David Owen
John Paul
Blake Powers
Timothy Scott
Mike Sharpe
Antony Shaw
David Shoup
Roger Smith
Giles Sparrow
William Steele
Joann Temple-Dennett
Pearl Tesler
Colin Uttley
Patricia Weis-Taylor
Art Western
Ian Westwell
Harvey Wichman
Mel Wiener
Philip Wilkinson
Chris Woodford
Robert Youngson

BROWN PARTWORKS
Managing editor: Anne O'Daly
Project editor: Andy Oppenheimer
Development editor: Richard Beatty
Sub editors: Martin Clowes, Kathy Gemmell, Leon Gray, Tom Jackson, Will Kragh, Sally McFall, Amy Prior
Art editor: Colin Tilleyloughrey
Illustrators: Richard Burgess, Mark Walker
Picture researcher: Jenny Silkstone
Project administrator: Tim Mahony
Indexer: Kay Ollerenshaw
Bibliographic researcher: Valerie Simmons

MARSHALL CAVENDISH
Editorial director: Paul Bernabeo
Project editor: Marian Armstrong
Editorial consultant: Beth Kaplan

CONTENTS

VOLUME 1

Abacus	11
Abrasive	12
Accidents and disasters	14
Acid and alkali	19
Acoustics and sound	21
Adhesive	27
Aerodynamics	29
Agricultural science	33
Agricultural transport and maintenance machinery	37
Agriculture, history of	39
Air bag	45
Air-conditioning and ventilation	46
Aircraft carrier	48
Aircraft design and construction	50
Aircraft engine	56
Airport and airfield	58
Air traffic control	61
Alloy	63
Ambulance and emergency medical treatment	67
Amplifier	72
Anesthetics	74
Animal breeding	77
Animal transport	81
Animation	84
Antenna and transmitter	87
Antiaircraft weapon	90
Antibiotics	91
Antiseptics and sterilization	93
Aquaculture	95
Archaeological techniques	102
Armor	107
Artificial insemination and fertility treatment	109
Artificial intelligence	111
Artillery	115
Automobile	119
Automobile, history of	126
Baking industry	131
Balloon and airship	134
Battery	136
Beverages	138
INDEX	143

VOLUME 2

Bicycle	149
Biological control	151
Bionics and biomedical engineering	153
Biotechnology	161
Blast furnace	167
Blood transfusion	169
Boatbuilding and shipbuilding	171
Body protection	177
Bomb, shell, and grenade	179
Bookbinding	182
Bow and arrow	184
Brake systems	185
Brewing industry	189
Brick making	192
Bridge	193
Building techniques, modern	199
Building techniques, traditional	204
Bus	210
Cable, electrical	212
Canal and inland waterway	213
Cancer treatments	218
Carpet making	220
Casting	221
Catalyst, industrial	224
Cavalry and chariot	226
Cement and concrete	229
Centrifuge	233
Ceramics	235
Chairlifts and gondolas	238
Chaos theory	239
Chemical and biological weapons	241
Chemical engineering	245
Chemical industry, inorganic	248
Chemical industry, organic	254
Cinematography	261
Civil engineering	269
Cleaning agents	272
Cloning	276
Clothing manufacture	278
Coal	282
Codes and ciphers	285
INDEX	287

VOLUME 3

Color	293
Colorants and pigments	295
Communication network	298
Compact disc	301
Composite	303
Computer	306
Computer graphics	316
Construction and earthmoving machinery	319
Control systems and control theory	324
Conveyor	328
Corrosion	329
Cosmetics and perfumes	331
Crane	334
Crop spraying and protection	337
Dairy industry	339
Dam	342
Deep-sea and diving technology	346
Demolition	352
Dentistry	354
Design, industrial	357
Detonator and fuse	362
Diagnostic tests and equipment	363
Digital signals and systems	368
Dock and harbor construction	372
Dredging	374
Dyes and dyeing	376
Ejection seat	379
Electricity and magnetism	380
Electricity transmission and supply	387
Electric motor and generator	391
Electric road vehicle	395
Electrolysis	397
Electromagnetic radiation	399
Electromechanical devices	401
Electronic countermeasures	404
Electronics	406
Electron tube	413
Elevator	416
Endoscope	418
Energy resources	421
Engine	427
INDEX	431

VOLUME 4

Engineering	437
Environmental engineering	440
Ergonomics	444
Escalator and moving walkway	448

Explosive	449	Horticulture	617	Mechanics	795
Facsimile transmission	453	Household appliances	620	Mechatronics	805
Farm storage	454	Hovercraft	624	Medical imaging	807
Fastening and joining	456	Hydraulics and pneumatics	627	Medical monitoring equipment	814
Ferry	460	Hydrodynamics and hydrostatics	631	Medical technology	819
Fertilizer	462	Hydroelectricity	635	Merchant ships	824
Fiber optics	465	Hydrofoil	638	Metals	826
Fibers and yarns	469	Hydroponics	640	Metalworking	834
Firearms	473	Ignition system	642	Meteorological instruments	842
Firefighting and fire protection	477	Imaging technology	644	Microphone and loudspeaker	845
Fishing industry	481	Immunology and immunization	647	Microscopy	848
Flight, history of	487	Incendiary	651	Military aircraft	852
Flight, principles of	493	Information theory	653	Military communications	
Flight simulator	497	Insulation	657	and control	859
Food preservation	498	Integrated circuit	659	INDEX	863
Food technology	502	Intelligence-gathering technology	662		
Footwear manufacture	509	Intensive care unit	666	**VOLUME 7**	
Forensic science	511	Internal combustion engine	668	Military vehicle	869
Forestry	515	Invention and innovation	676	Mining and quarrying	874
Fortification and defense	520	Iron and steel production	680	Missile	880
Foundation	525	Irrigation and land drainage	687	Money and banking technology	885
Fuel cell	529	Keyboard and typewriter	692	Monorail	887
Fuel injection	531	Laboratory equipment	693	Motorcycle	888
Fuels and propellants	533	Land warfare	697	Mountain railroad and funicular	890
Gaming machines	537	Laser and maser	705	Multimedia	892
Gas engine (Stirling engine)	539	Launch site	711	Musical instrument	894
Gases, industrial	541	Launch vehicle	714	Nanotechnology and micromachines	899
Gas industry	545	Leather	718	Navigation	902
Gasoline	548	INDEX	719	Nonferrous metal	908
Gas turbine	550			Nuclear energy	911
Gear	554	**VOLUME 6**		Nuclear fusion	915
Genetic engineering	558	Light and optics	725	Nuclear power	917
Geothermal energy	563	Lighthouse and lightship	733	Nuclear weapons	923
Glass and glassmaking	565	Lighting	736	Obstetrics and gynecology	927
Glider	570	Linear motor	743	Off-road and amphibious vehicles	930
Ground station	572	Livestock farming	745	Oil and natural gas production	933
Gyroscope	574	Lock	749	Oil refining	940
INDEX	575	Lock and safe	751	Oil tanker and bulk carrier	943
		Lubricant	753	Operating room	947
VOLUME 5		Machine tool	755	Ore extraction and processing	949
Hand tool	581	Magnet	759	Organic farming and sustainable	
Hand weapons	585	Magnetic storage media	761	agriculture	953
Harvesting machinery	589	Marine engineering	762	Output and display device	957
Hazardous waste	592	Maritime communication	765	Packaging industry	959
Heart-lung machine	594	Masonry and bricklaying	768	Paint and surface coating	963
Heat exchanger	596	Mass transit system	770	Paper and papermaking	967
Heating systems	597	Materials science	772	Parachute	971
Heat, principles of	601	Measurement	780	Particle accelerator	972
Helicopter	606	Mechanical engineering	784	Pattern recognition	974
Holography	610	Mechanical handling	786	Pesticide and herbicide	976
Horse-drawn transport	614	Mechanical transmission	790	Pharmacology and drug treatment	980

Photocell 988
Photocopier 990
Photography 991
Pipeline 1000
Plant breeding and propagation 1002
Plant hormone 1006
INDEX 1007

VOLUME 8
Plastics 1013
Plow 1021
Pollution and its control 1023
Port and harbor facilities 1027
Pottery 1031
Powerboat 1037
Power station 1039
Precision farming 1043
Prehistoric technology 1044
Pressure measurement 1050
Printing 1052
Production engineering and process
   control 1060
Propeller 1066
Prospecting 1068
Pump and compressor 1071
Race car 1073
Radar 1076
Radiation detection 1078
Radio receiver 1080
Railroad car 1083
Railroad construction and track 1087
Railroad locomotive 1091
Railroad operation and signaling 1095
Railroads, history of 1099
Refrigeration 1105
Resistor, capacitor, and inductor 1107
Retail industry technology 1110
Road building 1112
Road systems and traffic control 1116
Road transport, history of 1122
Robotics 1125
Rocket engine 1129
Rocketry 1131
Rotational motion 1137
Rubber 1140
Rudder 1142
Safety systems 1143
Sailing 1147
INDEX 1151

VOLUME 9
Satellite 1157
Scaffolding and formwork 1165
Seaplane and flying boat 1167
Security equipment 1168
Seismography 1172
Semiconductor and
   semiconductor device 1173
Sewage treatment 1180
Ship and boat 1184
Ship and boat, history of 1188
Siege warfare 1196
Skyscraper 1198
Slaughterhouse 1200
Snow and ice travel 1201
Software and programming 1205
Soil science 1209
Solar power 1211
Solvent, industrial 1213
Sound recording and reproduction 1215
Space flight 1221
Space probes 1224
Space station 1228
Space suit 1230
Space travel and technology 1231
Spectroscopy 1238
Sports equipment 1242
Steam engine 1245
Steam turbine 1251
Steam-powered road vehicles 1252
Steering systems 1255
Stoves and ovens 1258
Strategic defense systems 1260
Streetcar and trolley 1262
Structures 1264
Submarine 1272
Subway system 1275
Surgery 1279
Surveying 1285
Suspension bridge 1288
Suspension system 1290
Tank 1293
INDEX 1295

VOLUME 10
Technology in ancient civilizations 1301
Telecommunications 1307
Telecommunications regulation 1311
Telemedicine 1313
Telephony and telegraphy 1314
Telescope 1319

Television 1322
Television and computer monitor 1328
Textiles and their manufacture 1331
Thermometry 1338
Time measurement 1340
Tire 1345
Torpedo and depth charge 1346
Tracked vehicle 1347
Tractor 1350
Transducer and sensor 1352
Transformer 1355
Transplant surgery 1356
Truck 1360
Tunnel 1364
Turbine 1366
Ultrasonics 1368
Unpiloted vehicles and aircraft 1372
Vacuum cleaner 1373
Valve, mechanical 1375
Veterinary medicine 1379
Videography 1383
Voice recognition and synthesis 1385
V/STOL aircraft 1387
Warship 1389
Washing machine and dishwasher 1396
Waste disposal, recycling,
   and composting 1398
Water power 1401
Water resources technology 1404
Water supply and treatment 1408
Wave motion 1412
Wave power 1418
Weaponry: specialized systems 1420
Weighing machine and balance 1422
Wheel 1423
Wind power 1426
Wireless communication 1430
Wood and woodworking 1434
INDEX 1439

VOLUME 11 (INDEX)
Thematic Contents
Useful Tables
Nobel Prize Winners
Glossary
Further Reading
Time Line
Scientists and Inventions
Thematic Indexes
Comprehensive Index

USEFUL INFORMATION

Use this table to convert the English system (or the imperial system), the system of units common in the United States (e.g., inches, miles, quarts), to the metric system (e.g., meters, kilometers, liters) or to convert the metric system to the English system. You can convert one measurement into another by multiplying. For example, to convert centimeters into inches, multiply the number of centimeters by 0.3937. To convert inches into centimeters, multiply the number of inches by 2.54.

To convert	into	multiply by
Acres	Square feet	43,560
	Square yards	4840
	Square miles	0.00156
	Square meters	4046.856
	Hectares	0.40468
Celsius	Fahrenheit	First multiply by 1.8 then add 32
Centimeters	Inches	0.3937
	Feet	0.0328
Cubic cm	Cubic inches	0.06102
Cubic feet	Cubic inches	1728
	Cubic yards	0.037037
	Gallons	7.48
	Cubic meters	0.028317
	Liters	28.32
Cubic inches	Fluid ounces	0.554113
	Cups	0.069264
	Quarts	0.017316
	Gallons	0.004329
	Liters	0.016387
	Milliliters	16.387064
Cubic meters	Cubic feet	35.3145
	Cubic yards	1.30795
Cubic yards	Cubic feet	27
	Cubic meters	0.76456
Cups, fluid	Quarts	0.25
	Pints	0.5
	Ounces	8
	Milliliters	237
	Tablespoons	16
	Teaspoons	48
Fahrenheit	Celsius	First subtract 32 then divide by 1.8
Feet	Centimeters	30.48
	Meters	0.3048
	Kilometers	0.0003
	Inches	12
	Yards	0.3333
	Miles	0.00019
Gallons	Quarts	4
	Pints	8
	Cups	16
	Ounces	128
	Liters	3.785
	Milliliters	3785
	Cubic inches	231
	Cubic feet	0.1337
	Cubic yards	0.00495
	Cubic meters	0.00379
	British gallons	0.8327
Grams	Ounces	0.03527
	Pounds	0.0022
Hectares	Square meters	10,000
	Acres	2.471
Horsepower	Foot-pounds per minute	33,000
	British thermal units (Btu) per minute	42.42
	British thermal units (Btu) per hour	2546
	Kilowatts	0.7457
	Metric horsepower	1.014
Inches	Feet	0.08333

To convert	into	multiply by
Inches (continued)	Yards	0.02778
	Centimeters	2.54
	Meters	0.0254
Kilograms	Grams	1000
	Ounces	35.274
	Pounds	2.2046
	Short tons	0.0011
	Long tons	0.00098
	Metric tons (tonnes)	0.001
Kilometers	Meters	1000
	Miles	0.62137
	Yards	1093.6
	Feet	3280.8
Kilowatts	British thermal units (Btu) per minute	56.9
	Horsepower	1.341
	Metric horsepower	1.397
Kilowatt-hours	British thermal units (Btu)	3413
Knots	Statute miles per hour	1.1508
Leagues	Miles	3
Liters	Milliliters	1000
	Fluid ounces	33.814
	Quarts	1.05669
	British gallons	0.21998
	Cubic inches	61.02374
	Cubic feet	0.13531
Meters	Inches	39.37
	Feet	3.28083
	Yards	1.09361
	Miles	0.000621
	Kilometers	0.001
	Centimeters	100
	Millimeters	1000
Miles	Inches	63,360
	Feet	5280
	Yards	1760
	Meters	1609.34
	Kilometers	1.60934
	Nautical miles	0.8684
Miles nautical, U.S. and International	Statute miles	1.1508
	Feet	6076.115
	Meters	1852
Miles per minute	Feet per second	88
	Knots	52.104
Milliliters	Fluid ounces	0.0338
	Cubic inches	0.061
	Liters	0.001
Millimeters	Centimeters	0.1
	Meters	0.001
	Inches	0.03937
Ounces, avoirdupois	Pounds	0.0625
	Grams	28.34952
	Kilograms	0.0283495
Ounces, fluid	Pints	0.0625
	Quarts	0.03125
	Cubic inches	1.80469
	Cubic feet	0.00104
	Milliliters	29.57353
	Liters	0.02957
Pints, fluid	Ounces, fluid	16
	Quarts, fluid	0.5

To convert	into	multiply by
Pints, fluid (continued)	Cubic inches	28.8745
	Cubic feet	0.01671
	Milliliters	473.17647
	Liters	0.473176
Pounds	Ounces	16
	Grams	453.59237
	Kilograms	0.45359
	Tons	0.0005
	Tons, long	0.000446
	Metric tons (tonnes)	0.0004536
Quarts, fluid	Ounces, fluid	32
	Pints, fluid	2
	Gallons	0.25
	Cubic inches	57.749
	Cubic feet	0.033421
	Liters	0.946358
	Milliliters	946.358
Square centimeters	Square inches	0.155
Square feet	Square inches	144
	Square meters	0.093
	Square yards	0.111
Square inches	Square centimeters	6.452
	Square feet	0.0069
Square kilometers	Hectares	100
	Square meters	1,000,000
	Square miles	0.3861
Square meters	Square feet	10.758
	Square yards	1.196
Square miles	Acres	640
	Square kilometers	2.59
Square yards	Square feet	9
	Square inches	1296
	Square meters	0.836
Tablespoons	Ounces, fluid	0.5
	Teaspoons	3
	Milliliters	14.7868
Teaspoons	Ounces, fluid	0.16667
	Tablespoons	0.3333
	Milliliters	4.9289
Tons, Long	Pounds	2240
	Kilograms	1016.047
	Short tons	1.12
	Metric tons (tonnes)	1.016
Tons, short	Pounds	2000
	Kilograms	907.185
	Long tons	0.89286
	Metric tonnes	0.907
Tons, Metric (tonnes)	Pounds	2204.62
	Kilograms	1000
	Long tons	0.984206
	Short tons	1.10231
Watts	British thermal units (Btu) per hour	3.415
	Horsepower	0.00134
Yards	Inches	36
	Feet	3
	Miles	0.0005681
	Centimeters	91.44
	Meters	0.9144

ABACUS

A teacher in Beijing, China, uses the classroom abacus in a mathematics lesson.

The abacus can be used to perform simple arithmetical calculations. An experienced abacus user can perform addition, subtraction, multiplication, and division rapidly, even with very large numbers. The abacus can be seen as an early forerunner of modern electronic calculators in use today. Indeed, the first mechanical computers, such as those designed by English mathematician Charles Babbage (1791–1871), worked on similar principles as the abacus (see COMPUTER).

Typical construction
A typical abacus consists of a wooden frame divided into upper and lower halves, called decks. The decks have a series of vertical rods running through them at regular intervals. Some abaci have over 20 rods, others, as few as five. Each rod has a specific number of beads threaded on it in each deck. The decks are divided by a horizontal section called the beam.

Using an abacus
An abacus is usually operated by being placed on a flat service, or the user's lap, and the beads moved with the fingers of one hand. Numbers are represented according to the position of the beads. Looking at the rods from right to left, the first rod represents the ones column of a number, the next rod represents the tens column, the next represents the hundreds column, and so on. The beads in the upper deck each have a value of five. Those in the lower deck each have a value of one. So, for example, a bead in the lower deck of the hundreds column has a value of 100, and a bead in the upper deck of the hundreds column has a value of 500.

Moving a bead toward the beam indicates that it has been used or counted. Once five beads on a rod in the lower deck have been moved toward the beam, they are replaced by moving one bead from the equivalent rod on the upper deck (with a value of five) toward the beam. This is called carrying the value from the lower to the upper deck.

Uses and development
The abacus was probably invented by the Babylonians in ancient Iraq. Its use subsequently spread through Asia to Japan, where a slightly different version has evolved called the soroban. Today, the abacus is considered to be a valuable tool for teaching arithmetic to young children because of the play element. Its use is also taught to blind or partially sighted people, since the beads can be located with ease and manipulated with great skill without looking at them.

Abaci are often used by shopkeepers and staff in modern-day China and Japan, as well as in the areas settled by Chinese and Japanese people in the Western world—usually the large cities of the United States, Canada, and Britain.

Other countries and eras also developed versions of the abacus. An abacus dating from the 10th or 11th centuries C.E. was found in Mexico and may have been used in Mayan times. A different version, in use during the Roman Empire, had evolved by the Middle Ages into a stone tablet with a checkered pattern on it to represent the rods and beam. Pebbles were moved on this instead of beads. Gradually the abacus was replaced by Hindu-Arabic notation, which, with the use of the zero and the system of numbers being represented as columns of figures, allowed rapid calculations to be made on paper.

F. HAMILTON

See also: TECHNOLOGY IN ANCIENT CIVILIZATIONS.

Further reading:
Dilson, J. *The Abacus.* New York: St. Martin's Press, 1994.

CONNECTIONS

● The abacus is an example of **PREHISTORIC TECHNOLOGY**.

ABRASIVE

An abrasive is a hard substance that rubs material away from a softer substance

This picture shows the crystalline structure of silicon carbide. Silicon carbide is the hardest synthetic material after diamond.

Abrasives have long been used to sharpen, cut, smooth, and polish objects. Drawings from ancient Egypt show people polishing jewelry and vases, while emery—a naturally occurring abrasive—is mentioned in the Bible. Sand has been used to polish stone weapons for thousands of years. Diamond, the hardest substance known, was used to cut metal in India as long ago as 700 B.C.E.

From the Middle Ages on, people experimented with fixing abrasive substances onto papers or grinding wheels to meet the growing needs of handcrafts and, eventually, industry. An important breakthrough came in 1891, when U.S. inventor Edward Goodrich Acheson (1856–1931) synthesized silicon carbide (SiC), which he called carborundum. Silicon carbide is a synthetic abrasive with a hardness approaching that of diamond (although it has only a quarter of the hardness of diamond); it is still widely used. Another landmark was the discovery in 1955 of synthetic diamond by scientists at the General Electric Company. Synthetic diamond is as hard as natural diamond.

How abrasives work

When an abrasive comes into contact with a softer substance, it breaks off tiny chips from its surface. This has the general effect of smoothing and polishing the exposed areas of the softer substance. Harder abrasives can also cut through softer substances.

To be effective, an abrasive must be harder than the material it has to grind or cut. It should also be wear resistant; that is, as particles break off its surface during grinding, they should expose a fresh cutting surface. In many applications, abrasives need to be refractory (resistant to high temperatures), since considerable heat can be generated by friction when an abrasive is used.

Depending on the intended use, the abrasive must not be too hard, or damage to the treated object may result. For example, when choosing an abrasive to include in a toothpaste formulation, a material must be chosen that will break down a film of plaque and food debris without damaging the tooth enamel.

A further effect that limits the choice of abrasive is attrition—a chemical reaction specific to certain combinations of abrasives with other materials. Despite its hardness, silicon carbide cannot be used to cut steel because of chemical attrition, a reaction with steel that quickly wears away the cutting blade.

Types of abrasives

Abrasives are generally divided into two classes—natural and synthetic. The natural abrasives include minerals such as sand, quartz, and diamond. With few exceptions (the most obvious being diamond), natural abrasives are softer and more variable in their properties than the synthetic abrasives such as silicon carbide (see MATERIALS SCIENCE). Abrasives are usually ceramics—hard, inert (chemically unreactive), nonmetallic substances with very high melting points. Abrasives are often classified using the Mohs' scale (see the box on page 13).

How abrasives are used

Abrasives are used in a number of forms. An important application of abrasives is the grinding wheel, in which grains of abrasive material are mixed with a bonding resin (see PAINT AND SURFACE COATING). A mixture of solid abrasive and liquid resin is formed into a wheel that is then baked until the resin hardens. A wheel so formed can be used in a machine to sharpen or grind down an object. Sometimes abrasives are used in the form of a coating; the best known example is sandpaper, which consists of tiny grains of silica glued onto a backing paper. Abrasives can also be mixed with other materials, such as cleaning agents, and rubbed onto the surface to be cleaned or polished. Sandblasting involves directing a stream of air or water, mixed with abrasive particles, onto the surface to be treated.

Applications of abrasives

Abrasives have a wide range of uses. The abrasive agent in toothpaste, for example, is finely powdered chalk. Household cleaners contain abrasives such as

CONNECTIONS

● Sandblasting with an abrasive is an efficient way to clean the hulls of **SHIPS AND BOATS.**

● **MACHINE TOOL** components often have abrasive edges or surfaces for cutting and polishing operations.

CORE FACTS

■ Abrasives are used to smooth, polish, and cut softer materials.
■ An abrasive should be hard, tough, and heat resistant.
■ Most abrasives are ceramics.

silica, pumice, or alumina powder mixed with a cleansing agent. The combination of abrasive and cleanser works faster and more effectively than either component alone on bathroom and kitchen surfaces.

In industry, abrasive wheels grind machine components to precise dimensions. For instance, grinding ensures that piston rings and cylinders in automobile engines fit tightly enough to keep flammable gasoline vapors from escaping. Grinding is also important in the manufacture of high-quality lenses and mirrors for space telescopes.

Saws made of abrasive materials such as diamond are essential for cutting through hard materials, like metals, that would otherwise blunt or break conventional saws. Another application of abrasives is in tumbling mills. These are rotating barrels containing abrasive pieces that smooth away sharp edges on machine parts—a job that would otherwise have to be done by hand.

Sandblasting is very important in the cleaning of buildings. This uses a great deal of abrasive, but the abrasive can be collected after the cleaning operation from the ground where it falls. Once it is cleaned, it can be reused. Shot blasting, using small metal balls, is used to clean metal surfaces before they are electroplated or painted. If there is any dirt on the surface, the plating metal or coating may not stick adequately to the object. Also, plating metal and paints bond more effectively to a surface that has been freshly abraded.

A novel application of blasting is the creation of patterns on glass surfaces. The part of the glass that is to remain clear is covered with a paper or cardboard stencil, and the parts to be patterned are left exposed. The blast is then applied to these parts, creating an opaque pattern. This technique is a less hazardous substitute for the etching of glass with hydrofluoric acid (HF)—a very toxic, corrosive chemical that can cause severe skin burns.

S. ALDRIDGE

THE MOHS' SCALE

Mohs' number	Reference mineral	Other materials
1	TALC	
2	GYPSUM	
		fingernail
3	CALCITE	chalk (calcium carbonate)
4	FLUORITE	
5	APATITE	bone, tooth enamel
		pocketknife blade
6	FELDSPAR	
		hardened-steel file
7	QUARTZ	sand, quartz, flint, agate (all forms of silica)
8	TOPAZ	emery (aluminum oxide mixed with iron ore)
9	CORUNDUM	corundum (aluminum oxide)
10	DIAMOND	diamond (natural or synthetic)

In 1812, German mineralogist Friedrich Mohs (1773–1839) devised a scale to rank ten common minerals in order of hardness. Other materials are placed between the hardest mineral that cannot scratch a test sample of the material and the softest that can. Apatite, for example, can be scratched with a pocketknife blade, the blade remaining unaffected. The same blade can be scratched by quartz without the quartz being damaged.

See also: CERAMICS; HAND TOOLS; TECHNOLOGY IN ANCIENT CIVILIZATIONS.

Further reading:
Ball P. *Made to Measure: Materials for the 21st Century.* Princeton, New Jersey: Princeton University Press, 1997.

"DIAMONDS ARE FOREVER"

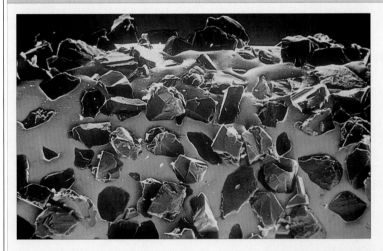

Diamond, the hard crystalline form of carbon, is the hardest substance known. Each diamond is a huge, single carbon molecule with atoms bonded equally throughout. This structure accounts for the hardness of diamond, which is useful in industry for cutting and shaping other very hard substances, such as tungsten carbide. Diamond, bonded onto steel discs, is mainly used for cutting stone and concrete.

Diamonds form when carbon is exposed to extremely high pressure and high temperature, such as are found deep in volcanoes. Synthetic diamonds are also produced using high temperature and pressure, sometimes provided by an explosive charge. Synthetic diamond can now be made in the form of a very thin film for use as a hard surface coating for cutting tools.

Synthetic diamonds are embedded in resin on the tip of a dental drill.

A CLOSER LOOK

ACCIDENTS AND DISASTERS

Accidents can be caused by technology, but technology can also help to save lives in a disaster

The San Francisco earthquake of 1989 left this freeway in ruins. Its collapse killed 42 people.

Disasters and accidents caused by technological mishap, rather than by acts of nature, are part of the price people pay for a technological world. As technology develops, the consequences of errors have grown more lethal and more costly. However, technology can also provide protection against the resulting threats to lives and property.

Even in natural catastrophes, technology can help reduce damage through good design and high-quality engineering, and in cleaning up afterward. The San Francisco earthquake of 1906, for example, devastated a major city, yet killed only about 500 people. The Armenian earthquake of 1988, however, killed nearly 25,000 people, injured about 15,000, and left at least 400,000 homeless, largely because of poor-grade concrete and inadequate reinforcement in high-rise buildings.

Mitigating natural disasters

Most disasters occur naturally. Floods, storms, tornadoes, hurricanes, earthquakes, and volcanic eruptions pose constant threats. On April 18, 1906, San Francisco suffered three violent shocks in a few seconds. Tremors were felt 500 miles (800 km) away, and more than 28,000 buildings were destroyed, yet casualties were surprisingly low. Within hours, fires broke out as gas escaping from fractured mains was ignited by sparks from broken power cables, and winds fanned the blaze. With water mains ruptured by the earthquake, it took three days to put the fires out, the death toll rose, and whole areas of the city that had survived the tremors were burned out.

Yet technology helped the city recover. Automobiles served as makeshift ambulances. Within two days railroad tracks had been replaced and services restored. Electrical supplies were reconnected within two weeks, and in three years one third of the city had been rebuilt. Two years after that, few signs of the disaster remained.

Technology versus disaster

Earthquakes recur in particular regions, specifically those lying on or near major fault lines (the areas where plates of Earth's crust overlap). The San Andreas Fault runs southward through San Francisco

CONNECTIONS

● Flooding of the land through excessive rain affects **WATER SUPPLY AND TREATMENT.**

● Spillages of oil from **OIL TANKERS AND BULK CARRIERS** have an immense impact on **POLLUTION AND ITS CONTROL.**

CORE FACTS

■ Floods, storms, tornadoes, hurricanes, earthquakes, and volcanic eruptions are common natural disasters.

■ Technology can reduce the impact of natural disasters, both by predicting where and when the disaster will happen and in minimizing the damage inflicted on people and the environment when it does.

■ Technology can help identify the factors that have caused a disaster.

■ Some disasters reveal poor equipment design and inadequate laws, which later have to be improved.

and on the inland side of Los Angeles. Further earthquakes are predicted along this fault, and since 1906 San Francisco has been transformed by high-rise buildings. A detailed 1965 survey predicted that another earthquake on the 1906 scale would cause 23,000 deaths and widespread destruction, particularly in the reclaimed Bay area. The earthquake that struck San Francisco in 1989 is the most serious of recent times to occur on this fault line.

In Japan, which lies on a major confluence of continental plates that runs the full length of the eastern Pacific coast, earthquakes are common. Though great efforts have been made to design earthquake-proof buildings, the Japanese, who are world experts in this specialized engineering, were overwhelmed by the intensity and damage of the earthquake that devastated the city of Kobe on January 17, 1995. Damage occurred when glass fragments showered from high-rise buildings that otherwise could withstand earth tremors. Elevated highways, such as those in Japan and the United States, are also extremely vulnerable to destruction by shock waves. Earthquakes occurring during working hours, with people in high-rise office buildings, cause far more deaths than those at night, when most people are asleep in low-rise homes. Sometimes, many lives can be saved by early warning. As yet, however, technology offers no reliable systems for warning of impending earthquakes. At present, the most likely indicator of approaching disasters is a change in the shock waves from small tremors that constantly occur deep within Earth.

As the landmasses along the San Andreas Fault try to move relative to one another, stresses build up to the point where moderate tremors allow some movement and release those stresses. The longer a period without movement, the greater the stress and therefore the probability of a major tremor. Russian scientists have observed that major earthquakes often follow periods of reduced tremor activity. And plate-tectonics theorists have tried to link approaching earthquakes to changes in landmass movements and to variations in sea level and in Earth's magnetic field, all of which are measured precisely.

Human activities can also trigger earthquakes. In 1962, the city of Denver, Colorado, started to experience earth tremors. The onset of these tremors coincided with the pumping of chemical waste into an underground dump to the east of the city. The tremors stopped some time after the pumping ceased. It is thought that the liquid waste lubricated underground faults and promoted the underground earth movements responsible for the tremors.

Planning for disasters

Modern technology can greatly reduce death and destruction from major disasters, provided there are specially trained people and equipment close at hand. Most accidents involve the fire services in several different roles. Where fire itself is a major hazard, as in air crashes, fire engines can deliver a very powerful punch to even the fiercest and wildest of fuel fires (see FIREFIGHTING AND FIRE PROTECTION).

Because three-quarters of air accidents occur within a half mile (less than one kilometer) of an airport, airfield fire services can usually reach accident sites in minutes. Firefighting vehicles can travel at speeds in excess of 70 mph (115 km/h) and discharge up to 10,000 gallons (38,000 l) of foam or water every single minute. Rapid intervention vehicles carry firefighting equipment, lights, stretchers, ladders, and medical supplies; they contain the fire and keep open escape routes (see AMBULANCE AND EMERGENCY MEDICAL EQUIPMENT).

Lava flow from a volcano in Hawaii burned this house to the ground.

This flood has engulfed houses and farms in Tracy, California.

Most airfields open to commercial flights conduct disaster training at regular intervals, with simulated casualties and, in some cases, fires under controlled conditions. The fuselage is set on fire and used for firefighting and casualty recovery drills. Firefighters dealing with road accidents have heavy-duty cutting gear to free trapped passengers; those who are called to collapsed buildings after explosions and earthquakes use thermal-imaging cameras that detect the infrared radiation given off by the heat of a human body and special sensors that are capable of detecting very faint vibrations caused by movements under the rubble. This equipment helps spot signs of life buried in otherwise clueless piles of rubble.

CHALLENGER DISASTER

The worst accident in manned spaceflight took place on January 28, 1986, when the *Challenger* space shuttle left on a mission to launch a satellite and to observe Halley's comet. It blew up at a height of 8 miles (13 km) following an otherwise normal launch, killing all seven astronauts on board. The shuttle was a reliable and well-proven piece of technology, and atmospheric conditions were fair, except for a very cold night before the launch.

The resulting enquiry revealed that engineers had tried to warn that joints between the segments of the casings of the rocket boosters, which were sealed by rubber rings called O-rings, could fail under certain conditions. When film of the launch was analyzed, there were clear signs of a flame escaping from one of the boosters and licking around the fuel tank.

The rubber rings had become brittle in the sharp frost before the launch and failed to seal the joints properly. As the speed increased, the flames grew, and eventually the joints broke apart completely, causing the explosion. Curing the problem was a simple engineering exercise, and the dangerous loophole was plugged, but it had taken seven lives to prove it had existed in the first place.

A CLOSER LOOK

Major disasters like train wrecks, earthquakes, and chemical explosions demand much more extensive drills, which are routinely done by the emergency services. These drills are based on army training operations ("war games"), in which great efforts are made to provide a realistic scenario, with convincingly made-up fake casualties, wrecked vehicles, and damaged buildings in areas where exercises can be set up with minimum disruption. Though accidents are unpredictable, regular disaster drills improve both individual performance and system response to fortunately rare catastrophes.

Maritime disasters: lessons learned

When the great ocean liner *Titanic* sailed on its maiden voyage on April 12, 1912 departing from Southampton, England, to New York, engineers were confident it could not sink. The ship's hull was divided into 15 watertight compartments by transverse bulkheads up to the level of D and E decks. The ship could float with four compartments flooded. However, there was no watertight deck covering the compartment decks, as there were in the Cunard ocean liners *Lusitania* and *Mauretania*.

The Titanic's sister ship, the *Olympic*, had survived being rammed in an accident off Southampton by the cruiser HMS *Hawke*, and the *Titanic* was thought to be equally safe. When the *Titanic* hit an iceberg that tore a gash in its hull a few inches wide, but a full 300 feet (91 m) long, five of the watertight compartments were opened up. As rising water reached the top of each bulkhead, it flooded the next undamaged compartment until the ship sank.

Although the lifeboats on the *Titanic* provided room for only about one-third of the passengers and crew that the ship was legally entitled to carry, this was actually more than the legislation of the time required. After the *Titanic* disaster, ships were required by law to carry enough lifeboats to carry everyone on board to safety.

Since then, RO-RO (roll-on-roll-off) vehicle ferry accidents showed that open bow doors (at the front end of the boat) and bow-to-stern (front to rear) vehicle decks provided new dangers. One such ferry, the *Estonia*, was lost in 1994 in the Baltic Sea in an accident that killed 900 people. But in other maritime disasters, the chief casualty has not been human, but the environment at large.

Supertankers are among the world's largest ships. They are very cumbersome and carry enormous cargoes, which can turn an otherwise uneventful grounding (colliding with shallow ground under the sea surface) into an environmental catastrophe. The oil tanker *Torrey Canyon* ran aground off the southwest coast of England in 1967, spilling 100,000 tons (90,000 tonnes) of oil into the sea. Royal Air Force bombers dropped explosives and napalm on the wreck to burn off remaining oil, and beaches in England and France were sprayed with detergent by thousands of volunteers in an attempt to disperse the oil and reduce the damage to wildlife. Unfortunately, only ten percent of the affected birds were saved and more than 15,000 died. Cleaning methods have improved significantly since the *Torrey Canyon* incident (see OIL TANKER AND BULK CARRIER).

Similarly, when in 1978 the *Amoco Cadiz* broke up after running aground on the French coast, almost a quarter of a million tons (227,000 tonnes) of oil spilled into the sea, overwhelming contingency plans designed to deal with a 30,000-ton (27,000-tonne) spill. Because detergent can damage crops and oyster beds, oil was scraped off the beaches manually,

THE SEVESO DISASTER

Even a minor accident at a chemical plant can release huge quantities of toxic gases in minutes. The Hoffman-La Roche plant in Seveso, Italy, made agricultural herbicides, and in July 1976 an explosion released a deadly cloud of a chemical called tetrachlorodibenzodioxin. In still air, this spread slowly. By the next day, trees, plants, and animals in the area were dying, and children were suffering from painful skin rashes.

At first, local people were unaware of the threat. More than a week passed before the Italian government declared a state of emergency. Troops were brought in to seal off the factory and demolish the center of the town. The authorities announced that the area had been polluted by dioxin, a chemical used to destroy vegetation in the Vietnam War (1957–1975), and people were banned from selling or eating local meat, vegetables, or fruit and from drinking local milk.

More than 10,000 people fled into the surrounding countryside, and many never returned. Five decontamination workers contracted liver disease, even though they had been working for limited periods and had worn full protective clothing. The local birth rate fell dramatically, and traces of the chemical were found in the city of Milan, 13 miles (21 km) away.

WIDER IMPACT

loaded into drums, and buried in leakproof disposal pits. High-pressure hoses blasted away the residue that could not be removed manually.

In 1989 the supertanker *Exxon Valdez* released 40,000 tons (36,000 tonnes) of crude oil into Prince William Sound on the coast of Alaska. By then, regulations required adequate containment and clean-up equipment to deal with oil spills, but the emergency barge for dealing with oil spills had been taken out of service to have storm damage repaired. The clean-up operation took 15 hours to get started instead of

Workers use high-pressure hot water hoses and pump machinery to wash, then vacuum, the oil coatings on rocks after the **Exxon Valdez** *(an oil tanker) struck Bligh reef near the oil terminal at Valdez, Alaska, in 1989.*

PAN AMERICAN AIRLINES FLIGHT 103

An explosion on Pan Am Flight 103 was caused by a terrorist bomb, killing all passengers and 11 people on the ground.

A Pan American Boeing 747 airliner, bound for New York from London on December 21, 1988, broke apart over the small Scottish town of Lockerbie. One engine blew a crater 15 ft (4.5 m) deep, and the wing exploded in a quarter-mile (half-kilometer) fireball. All 259 people aboard the aircraft and 11 people on the ground lost their lives.

The only way to find out what had caused this disaster was to collect all the wreckage and reconstruct the breakup sequence. However, the plane had blown apart 6 miles (9.6 km) up, and fragments were spread over more than 1000 sq miles (2600 km^2) of northern England and Scotland. More than 4 million pieces had to be traced, identified, and reassembled.

The reconstruction showed explosive damage in luggage containers from the baggage compartment toward the front of the airplane. The investigators found a piece of circuit board—part of a radio audiotape cassette player—trapped in the wreckage. There were traces of Semtex explosive, and fibers indicated the cassette player had been hidden inside a suitcase. The bomb had blown a small hole in the fuselage (airplane body), and the metal outerskin of the craft was pulled apart by the force of the passing air. The nose section tore away, and the plane entered a steepening dive, breaking apart as it fell. In little more than 90 seconds, one kilogram of Semtex had destroyed a 300-ton airliner and killed 270 people. Forensic experts deduced that the case must have been placed in luggage loaded from an earlier flight from Frankfurt. Fibers in the case fragments were traced to clothes bought in Malta and flown to Frankfurt on the day of the crash. Subsequently, two Lybians were accused of the bombing. Diplomatic negotiations finally resulted in their release to stand trial in Holland.

A CLOSER LOOK

chemicals in the oil that was spilled, but some oil still remains trapped deep in the rocks and pebbles in the area.

Though research has produced new ways of dealing with oil, from environmentally friendly chemicals to floating booms, the scale of the spill and the promptness of response still determine how effective the cleanup operation will be.

Finding the causes of air accidents

Since the worldwide increase in air transportation, the aerospace industry in the United States and other countries has striven to make airplanes safer. Even though air travel is one of the safest forms of transportation, accidents still happen—many of them due to human mistakes. Some involve the crew, but others, such as an accident that happened at Chicago O'Hare International Airport in May 1979, when a DC-10 rolled over and plunged into the ground after one of its engines fell off the wing during takeoff, were due to the mistakes of maintenance workers.

Sometimes technology can help identify these causal factors. Cockpit voice recorders record flight deck sounds and conversation prior to air accidents. Flight data recorders (FDRs) show what the aircraft was doing at the time leading up to a crash. FDRs are made of heavy steel and lined with fireproof material, so they are strong enough to withstand severe impacts. They show speed, height, course, rate of climb and descent, control settings, position of landing gear, outside air temperature, and the degree to which the airplane was pitching up or down, rolling, or yawing to left or right. Other information on the possible causes of an accident can be revealed by recordings of messages between the flight crew and the air-traffic controllers, or by recordings of the ATC radar displays.

Isolating the cause of a crash from a trail of fragments is still dauntingly difficult. One military aircraft crash was traced to engine failure caused by a tiny particle of grit the size of a grain of salt that became lodged in a fuel valve. The exact cause is even more difficult to identify when an explosion is involved, as was the case with Pan Am flight 103 (see the box at left) and TWA flight 800, which crashed into the Atlantic Ocean on July 17, 1996, when an explosion occurred shortly after takeoff from Kennedy International Airport in New York. A total of 229 passengers and crew members died.

D. OWEN

See also: EXPLOSIVE; MARITIME COMMUNICATION; SEISMOGRAPHY.

Further reading:
Abbott, P. *Natural Disasters*. Dubuque, Iowa: William C. Brown Publishers, 1996.
Arnell, A. *Handbook of Effective Disaster Recovery Planning*. New York: McGraw-Hill, 1990.
Ferrar, C. J. *No Downlink: A Dramatic Narrative About the Challenger Accident and Our Time*. New York: Strauss and Giroux, 1996.

the planned 5. It took three days to bring all the necessary equipment to the spot, and by then violent storms had replaced calm weather. Two weeks later, only some 20 percent of the oil had been recovered, and pollution had spread over 500 sq miles (1295 km^2) of coastal waters. Traces of the oil had been found 70 miles (112 km) away, blown by the wind. In the following 2 years, Exxon spent $3 billion on the cleanup program. Many of the algae, crabs, and barnacles in the area survived the effects of the toxic

ACID AND ALKALI

Acids dissolve in water to give hydrogen ions; alkalis dissolve to give hydroxide ions

By "sweetening" an acidified lake with 8000 tons (7260 tonnes) of agricultural lime (calcium hydroxide), Swedish environmental engineers attempt to counteract the continuing inflow of acid rain in their waterways.

Acids and alkalis are widely distributed in nature. Stinging nettles and some ants, for example, contain formic acid, while lemons and other citrus fruits are a rich source of citric acid. The human stomach contains hydrochloric acid, which aids in digestion. Many rocks, such as limestone, contain basic compounds. Many acids and alkalis are corrosive and can burn the skin and damage the eyes. Most metals will chemically react with acids, and strong alkalis can break down fats and grease. Alkalis belong to a larger group of chemicals called bases—an alkali is simply a base that is soluble in water.

Definitions of acids and alkalis

Toward the end of the 19th century, Swedish chemist Svante August Arrhenius (1859–1927) was exploring the electrical properties of solutions. He observed that when an acid or an alkali is dissolved in water, the solution is able to carry an electrical current. He concluded that the increase in conductivity was caused by the formation of charged particles called ions that could move through the water and thereby carry a current. When a current is passed through a solution of acid, bubbles of hydrogen form at the negative electrode—the electrode attracts positively charged hydrogen ions. From this observation, Arrhenius deduced that acids could be defined as substances that produce positive hydrogen ions when they dissolve in water.

$$HA \rightarrow H^+ + A^-$$
(HA represents a typical acid)

There are many cases in which an acid will react with an alkali to form a salt and water. These are known as neutralization reactions. In Arrhenius' theory, an alkali is a substance that forms the hydroxide ion (OH^-) when it dissolves in water.

$$XOH \rightarrow X^+ + OH^-$$
(XOH represents a typical alkali)

In this way, a neutralization reaction can be considered as a reaction in which hydrogen ions and hydroxide ions combine to form water:

$$OH^- + H^+ \rightarrow H_2O$$

The other product of a reaction between an acid, HA, and an alkali, XOH, is a salt, XA. A limitation of Arrhenius' theory is that it only discusses acid and base solutions in water. There are many examples of acid-base reactions that occur in other solvents. Also, many bases do not contain the hydroxide ion. To accommodate these situations, acids were defined as proton donors—chemicals that provide protons (hydrogen ions). Similarly, bases were defined as proton acceptors. More recently the definition changed again, and modern understanding is based upon the transfer of electrons: an acid is a substance that accepts electrons; a base is a substance that donates electrons.

Manufacture of acids and alkalis

Historically, acids and alkalis were extracted or made from natural sources. Formic acid was obtained by boiling ants in a saucepan or distilling them in a glass

CORE FACTS

- Acids give hydrogen ions in water.
- Alkalis give hydroxide ions in water.
- Alkalis are water-soluble bases.
- Acids and alkalis react together to form water and salts.

CONNECTIONS

- Many **INDUSTRIAL CATALYSTS** are acids or alkalis.

- Both acids and alkalis are causative agents in **CORROSION** processes.

- Sodium bicarbonate, an alkali, is used as a leavening agent in the **BAKING INDUSTRY**.

Sparkling soft drinks are made by dissolving carbon dioxide in water under pressure. The gas reacts with water to form carbonic acid—a weak acid. When the can or bottle is opened, the pressure drops and the some of the carbonic acid decomposes to release carbon dioxide gas, which is the fizz.

laboratory retort. Acetic acid could be prepared by allowing wine to turn sour in air, and lactic acid came from sour milk. Alkalis could be obtained from naturally occurring minerals and wood ashes. Arabic chemists Jabir ibn Hayyān (c.721–c.815 C.E.) and ar-Rāzï (c.865–c.930 C.E.), had their own recipes for making sulfuric, nitric, and hydrochloric acids, and they also studied alkalis. Indeed, the word *alkali* comes from the Arabic *al-qili,* meaning "ashes of (the plant) saltwort"—a source of sodium carbonate.

Sulfuric acid—one of the most important products of the chemical industry—is made by reacting sulfur dioxide with oxygen and dissolving the resulting sulfur trioxide in water. The first large-scale method of sulfuric acid manufacture was the chamber process, invented by British chemist John Roebuck (1718–1794) in 1746. In the chamber process, sulfur dioxide is mixed with air and water in a chamber lined with lead to resist the corrosive fumes. This process yields dilute, rather impure, sulfuric acid and has been superseded by the contact process, where sulfur dioxide is oxidized in the presence of a catalyst (see CATALYST, INDUSTRIAL; CHEMICAL INDUSTRY, INORGANIC). Two other com-

mercially important acids are hydrochloric acid and nitric acid, both of which can be produced by the action of sulfuric acid on ores.

In 1774, British chemist Joseph Priestley (1733–1804) first prepared the alkali ammonia (NH_3) by heating sodium hydroxide with an ammonium salt. Ammonia was produced from nitrate salts until the end of the 19th century, when natural mineral reserves became seriously depleted. In 1908, the growing demand for fertilizers and the need for nitrogen-based explosives led German chemist Fritz Haber (1868–1934) to develop a way of manufacturing ammonia directly from ·its component elements—nitrogen and hydrogen.

Indicators and pH

Acids and alkalis can make certain substances change color (see COLORANTS AND PIGMENTS). Some plants, including bluebells, hydrangeas, and red cabbage, contain pigments that change color according to soil acidity. Hence bluebells turn pink if they grow in ant-infested soil because the formic acid produced by the ants affects the pigment in the flowers.

Indicators change color because they can exist in two forms, each with a different color. The form that predominates depends on the hydrogen ion concentration, which is high when an acid is present and very low when a base is present (neutral water contains small and equal concentrations of hydrogen and hydroxide ions). The acidity of a solution can also be rated on the pH scale, which ranges from 1 to 14. Solutions with pH values below 7 are acidic; those with values above 7 are alkaline; pH 7 is neutral.

The uses of acids and alkalis

Acids and alkalis are chemicals that react with a wide range of organic and inorganic materials, sometimes vigorously. They also promote reactions between other substances—they act as catalysts. Because of these properties, both types of chemicals are widely used in industrial processes, including the manufacture of fertilizers, glass, plastics, and detergents.

There are also several household products that contain acids and alkalis. Vinegar (acetic acid) is used as a preservative in pickles because bacteria cannot grow in an acidic environment. Ammonia is a common ingredient in household cleaners. Very strong household cleaners contain the extremely corrosive alkali sodium hydroxide. (These must be handled with great care.) Antacid tablets usually contain an alkali such as calcium carbonate, magnesium oxide, or magnesium hydroxide. Lime (calcium carbonate) can be added to soil to decrease its acidity, enabling a wider range of plants to grow.

S. ALDRIDGE

See also: CHEMICAL INDUSTRY, ORGANIC; CLEANING AGENTS; METALS; SOLVENT, INDUSTRIAL.

Further reading

Selinger, B. *Chemistry in the Marketplace.* 5th edition. New York: Harcourt, Brace, Jovanovich, 1997.

USES OF COMMON ACIDS AND ALKALIS

Acids	Manufacturing uses
Sulfuric acid	Fertilizers, paints, detergents, textiles; cleaning steel
Nitric acid	Fertilizers, explosives, dyes, drugs; etching metals
Hydrochloric acid	Dyes, textiles, leather
Acetic acid	Food preservation, paints, adhesives, textiles

Alkalis	Manufacturing uses
Ammonia	Fertilizers, household cleaners
Sodium hydroxide	Soap, household cleaners
Sodium carbonate	Glass, water softening agents

ACOUSTICS AND SOUND

Acoustics is the study of sound. Sounds are pressure waves within the range of hearing

The science of acoustics grew out of curiosity about human hearing, the acoustical properties of buildings and other structures, and the design of musical instruments. Acoustic design of early buildings was based on practical knowledge that had been acquired through centuries of trial and error. Musical instruments were also designed by rule of thumb. New designs in either area could have proved to be costly mistakes. Consequently change was very slow. Eventually, research established that sound was the result of pressure waves moving through a medium—often air—and that the behavior of these waves was described by particular laws.

How sound is made

The pressure waves that cause sound are produced when an object vibrates. Such objects include the skin of a drum when it is struck, human vocal cords when someone speaks, a church bell when it is rung, and the vibrating surface of a loudspeaker. As the surface of the object moves outward, an area of compression is created in the air next to it. As the surface moves inward, an area of expansion (rarefaction) forms. As the surface continues to vibrate, these pressure waves spread out and move away from the object. Eventually they may enter the human ear, causing a tiny organ called the eardrum to vibrate. Nerves connected to the eardrum transmit information to the brain, which translate the vibration into the sounds that we hear.

Sound waves can be described by their volume or loudness, which is the amplitude of the sound wave, and by their frequency, which is the speed at which the sound wave oscillates. Most of the sounds that we hear are made up of many different sound

In an amphitheater, the actors' voices can be heard from any point.

waves, with different amplitudes and frequencies. The precise mixture of waves gives a sound its particular characteristics, which is why the sound of a violin seems so different from the sound of an automobile engine.

The speed of sound

Another characteristic of a sound wave is its speed. The sounds that we hear normally travel to our ears through air. Unlike frequency and amplitude, the speed of a sound wave in air at a given temperature and pressure is fixed. Under standard conditions—77°F (25°C) and one atmosphere pressure—sound waves travel through air at 1086 ft/s (331 m/s).

The speed of sound becomes apparent when lightning strikes in the distance and its sound is heard long after the flash. This is because the light from the lightning reaches the observer almost instantaneously, while the sound takes a noticeable amount of time to cover large distances.

CORE FACTS

- Sounds heard by humans are the result of pressure waves in air caused by vibrating objects.
- The loudness of a sound is determined by the amplitude of the sound wave. The pitch (highness or lowness) of a sound is determined by the frequency (speed of oscillation) of the sound wave.
- Hard objects such as walls reflect sound well. Soft objects tend to absorb sound. Interior designers and architects can design and furnish rooms to control their acoustic properties.
- Unwanted sound can be a problem. Large modern buildings are designed to minimize noise transfer between sections. A small amount of continuous background noise is often desirable because it can mask intermittent noises.
- Devices that emit ultrasound (very high frequency sound) can be used for measuring distances, for detecting faults in components, and as cleaning tools.

CONNECTIONS

- **LAUNCH SITES** use water to absorb some of the deafening sound of rocket engines at takeoff.

- Sonar is used in the **FISHING INDUSTRY** for detecting shoals of fish and underwater obstructions.

Whales, such as this humpback, use infrasound to communicate over distances through water.

However, the speed of sound changes with temperature and with the nature of the medium it is traveling through. Sound can travel through gases other than air as well as through liquids and solids. Different materials conduct sound at different speeds. Water conducts sound faster than air.

The speed of sound in air is the basis of the Mach number, which is used to express the speed of airplanes relative to the air around them. Airplanes that fly faster than the speed of sound are said to fly supersonically. An airplane flying at Mach 1 is traveling at the speed of sound. An airplane flying at Mach 2 is traveling at twice the speed of sound. The wavelength of a sound wave is determined by dividing the speed of the sound by its frequency. At a frequency of 100 hertz (cycles per second; abbreviated to Hz) in air, the wavelength is about 11 feet (3.3 m).

Human hearing

Human hearing has two aspects: a loudness range and a frequency range. The loudness range extends from sounds that are only just audible to sounds that are so loud they are painful. The frequency range of the human ear varies from low frequencies that are often more felt than heard to extremely shrill sounds that can just be heard. The human frequency range is from about 15 Hz to 20,000 Hz. The exact range varies from person to person and tends to become narrower with increasing age. One of the reasons hearing changes with age is that loud sounds damage the ears. Given time, the ears can partially recover from the damage caused by loud sounds, but eventually they can no longer recover and noticeable hearing loss occurs. Generally, higher frequencies are the first to go. Ear damage can also lead to a condition known as ringing in the ears (tinnitus). Because the damage accumulates slowly, it is often severe before it is noticed.

The amplitude of sound waves at the threshold of hearing is incredibly small; the average threshold of hearing is less than one millionth of the standard atmospheric pressure. The range of pressure from a soft sound to a painfully loud sound is about a hundred thousand to one. Because of this huge range, it is difficult to express the loudness of sound in conventional pressure units such as pascals (newtons per square meter). A better way to express this huge range is to convert the pressure to a logarithmic value (expressed as decibels: dB). The logarithm of a number is directly proportional to the number of decimal places rather than its size. This is a good method of expressing loudness, since the human ear responds logarithmically to sound pressure. Using this method, a million-to-one range can be compressed to 0–120 dB. Humans can discriminate differences in loudness of about 3 dB.

Many animals can hear well above and below the human frequency range. Frequencies above the human range are known as ultrasonic frequencies, while frequencies below the human range are known as infrasonic frequencies. Dogs can hear ultrasonic frequencies to about 40 kHz; bats can hear to 200 kHz. Elephants use infrasonic sounds that can be heard for miles to communicate with each other. In the ocean, the infrasonic sounds that whales make can sometimes be detected by other whales thousands of miles away.

Sound behavior

Because sound is composed of pressure waves, it behaves like any other wave phenomenon. For instance, in the same way that light is reflected by a mirror, sound can be reflected by distant objects such as cliff faces, producing an echo. The most commonly used device that depends on the wave nature of sound is the sound reflector. The parabolic sound reflectors used in long-range microphones such as those used for recording bird calls focus the sound waves from a large area onto a small microphone to make faint sounds audible (see INTELLIGENCE-GATHERING TECHNOLOGY). Sonar systems also function by virtue of the fact that sound can be bounced off objects (see the box on page 26).

Sound waves grow quieter with distance, since the wave energy spreads out over a larger area. Air will also absorb some of the wave energy, particularly at higher frequencies. Because of this combination of distance and absorption, there is a natural limit to how far voices will carry. The size of theaters was restricted by this limit until the invention of sound amplification. An example of the quieting and absorption of sound in air is the way in which thunder changes with distance. At close range, a lightning strike will make a very loud crack, which contains a large amount of high-frequency sound waves. At a distance, most of the high frequencies are lost, and the familiar low rumble of thunder is heard.

Environmental acoustics

A common type of sound-reflecting surface is a wall. In built-up areas, sounds such as sirens can be reflected so many times by buildings that the siren's location becomes impossible to determine. The fact that curved walls could focus sound was discovered long ago. For instance, an elliptical floor plan results in a whispering gallery, in which the slightest whisper at the center can be heard clearly throughout the whole gallery. The Greeks and Romans designed elliptical amphitheaters for thousands of people without understanding the scientific principles of acoustics. For example, the Colosseum in Rome, completed around 80 C.E., was an amphitheater that could hold up to 50,000 people (see BUILDING TECHNIQUES, TRADITIONAL).

Our perception of spaces is influenced by the sound reflections we hear. This perception is largely unconscious. From the reflections of ambient sound, we can make a good guess as to the dimensions of the space and the character of the reflecting surfaces. Our unconscious evaluation is called room feel. The factors that control the feel of a room are known by architects and interior designers, and rooms can be designed to have specific acoustic properties. For example, a lecture hall requires a different room design than a concert hall does. Surfaces that are hard and heavy, such as concrete, reflect sound waves to the listener. Soft surfaces, such as fabric-covered seats, absorb sound well and reflect very little sound. By adjusting the position of surfaces and the types of surfaces covering the space, the feel of an interior can be adjusted to suit its uses.

The extremes of surface treatment are used in special measuring rooms. A room with highly reflecting surfaces is called a reverberation (echoing) room. A room with surfaces that absorb all sound waves is called an anechoic (no echo) room. Because reverberation rooms and anechoic rooms provide a controlled acoustic environment, acoustics

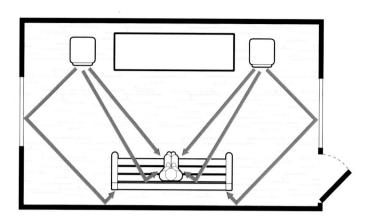

Sound is reflected off hard objects. A room with a wooden floor, no curtains, and little furniture will tend to echo because sound is easily reflected.

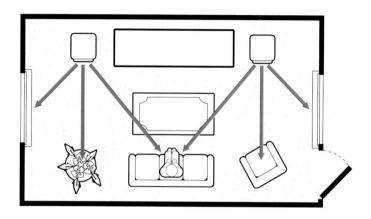

Sound is absorbed by soft objects. A carpeted room with curtains and plenty of fabric-covered furniture is a better environment for listening to a stereo system.

can be measured easily. Most of these rooms are constructed to block out sounds from outside the room, which makes the rooms extremely quiet. In a quiet anechoic room, it is common for people to notice the sound of their own heartbeat.

Spaces that approach either of the extremes of a reverberation room or an anechoic room cause problems for hearing both speech and music. Highly reverberant spaces such as enclosed swimming pools with tiled surfaces have high background noise levels and smear out sounds. This makes speech, in particular, difficult to understand. Highly absorptive spaces have a low background noise level. Speech sounds in these spaces are perceived as strange. In general, humans prefer some moderate level of reflections and background noise in spaces.

Sound waves can also be manipulated by the natural environment. Sound waves in air can be affected by weather conditions. Areas of different air density caused by temperature differences can channel sound, causing sounds that are normally inaudible to be heard and carrying other sounds away. These effects are most noticeable during weather changes. In the ocean, sounds can be confined to channels created by temperature conditions, so that sounds generated hundreds of miles away can be heard.

Sound is produced by vibrations. The small vibrations in the strings of this guitar produce larger and louder vibrations in the wooden front, which amplifies the sound.

Sound and musical instruments

Music is made up of different notes—sounds that tend to have a distinct pitch (characteristic frequency), unlike the sounds of a drum or a gun firing, which are made up of sound waves with a large range of frequencies and consequently have no discernible pitch. A piece of music usually consists of a number of notes of different pitches played together or one after the other. The nature of the music is also affected by the duration and loudness of each note.

Traditional musical instruments fall into two major categories: instruments that use vibrating air directly as the sound source and instruments that use an indirect source. The pipe organ is an example of a musical instrument that relies on the direct use of vibrating air columns: sound is generated by pressure waves bouncing back and forth inside the pipe.

Making an instrument respond at a given frequency is known as tuning an instrument. Tuning an instrument results in resonance when a pattern of vibration known as a standing wave occurs. The resonant frequency of the vibrating air column in an organ pipe depends on the length and shape of the pipe. In the same way, the resonant frequency of air vibrating in a narrow-necked bottle when a person blows across the top depends upon the size of the space inside the bottle. Because each pipe in an organ is a specific length, each one produces a note with a specific pitch.

A guitar is an example of an instrument that uses a vibrating string as the indirect source of sound. The guitar string is the resonating element, and the sound is coupled to the air through the wooden front,

which vibrates sympathetically with the string. Each musical instrument is carefully shaped to reinforce the desired resonances and suppress unwanted ones. The shapes of traditional instruments have been derived from years of experimentation. The exact combination of resonances produced gives each instrument its characteristic sound. When the frequencies of resonances are integer multiples of one another, they are said to be harmonically related. The lowest frequency is called the fundamental frequency or tone, and the others are known as harmonics or overtones. The frequency that is twice the fundamental is called the first harmonic, the frequency that is three times the fundamental is the second harmonic, and so on (see MUSICAL INSTRUMENT).

Noise reduction

Unwanted noise is a by-product of the mechanical age. Sources such as road traffic generate noise. To help control traffic noise, features such as walls, banks, and double-glazed windows are used to deflect or absorb noise. Vegetation on banks also helps to absorb traffic noise. Although these means of noise reduction are effective, traffic noise reduction is still one of the most difficult acoustic problems.

Designing buildings to minimize noise transfer between sections and to provide a desirable level of background noise is another important area of noise reduction. Some level of background noise is desirable to mask noises that cannot be avoided in spaces such as offices. On the other hand, loud noises from necessary mechanical devices such as elevators and ventilation fans need to be isolated from quieter spaces. Mufflers used on internal combustion engines are another common form of noise control (see INTERNAL COMBUSTION ENGINE).

There are three components to every noise problem: the source, transmission path, and receiver. Changing the source is usually the most effective way to solve a noise problem, such as banning cars from roads in residential areas, but can be difficult to achieve. A more common method is to change the transmission path. For example, noise is transmitted inside buildings by internal vibrations through paths such as walls, windows, and doors. Special designs can be used to reduce internal transmission. However, changes made after the building is constructed are expensive. The perception of a noise problem by the receiver can be changed by deliberately introducing a controlled source of background or masking noise. Sometimes a building's air-conditioning system is designed to make more noise than necessary to provide masking noise (see AIR CONDITIONING AND VENTILATION). Distance is one of the best noise control measures, and this is one reason airports and factories should be located far from areas of human habitation.

Signal processing

The invention of sound amplification allowed much more flexibility in the use of sound and is crucial to modern uses of sound. Early attempts to amplify sound include the megaphone and several amplifiers powered by air. But no early attempt had anywhere near the combination of flexibility, convenience, and low cost that electronic amplification provided. The use of electronic amplification has revolutionized the practical use of sound.

Electronic amplification works by converting the input sound into an electronic signal, boosting the amplitude of this signal, and then converting the signal back into a sound wave. The output sound wave has the same frequency pattern as the input sound, but it is louder because it has a larger amplitude. Public-address systems would not be possible without electronic amplification, and the size of theater auditoriums have greatly increased as a consequence of this advance.

Computers have also had a great effect on sound reproduction technology. One of the most interesting is the modification of existing sounds so that the sound characteristics of different spaces can be simulated. For instance, microprocessors in an amplifier can be used to reproduce the feel of a concert hall in a small living room (see AMPLIFIER; COMPUTER).

Practical uses of sound

Sound waves can be used for locating objects and measuring distances. In some types of automatic cameras, small ultrasonic distance-measuring devices are used to focus precisely, so photographers do not need to use a tape measure or guesswork. These devices emit a short burst of sound from a transducer, and the round-trip time required for the burst to reflect off the surface of the object is determined. Since the speed of sound is known, the distance to the surface can be calculated (see PHOTOGRAPHY).

The rapid pressure changes caused by ultrasound can produce tiny bubbles in liquids. This is a process known as cavitation, which is put to use in ultrasonic cleaning systems. These use high-power sound waves to produce cavitation in a liquid such as kerosene. When the bubbles collapse they produce shock waves, which can be used to dislodge dirt on objects that could be damaged by conventional cleaning, such as electronics components.

Ultrasonic devices can also be used to detect structural faults. These systems work on a similar principle as sonar by analyzing reflected sound waves within the component for characteristic changes caused by faults such as cracks. Such devices are useful for rapidly assessing the condition of railroad tracks, for example.

Deliberate noisemaking to attract attention has been used for centuries. Church bells were used as a way of attracting attention over a wide area. Another, more recent, example is the use of sirens. Originally sirens were mechanical and consisted of a rotating disk with holes along its periphery. Behind the disk was a jet of air or steam. As the disk rotated, the holes chopped up the jet at rapid and regular intervals, producing the characteristic siren sound. Other devices for attracting attention by making loud noises are the whistle and the horn. Today most warning

This technician is using an ultrasonic testing device to examine a large gear wheel for faults.

devices are electronic. High-intensity sound has also been used as a form of crowd control (see WEAPONRY: SPECIALIZED SYSTEMS).

Sound measurements

Sound can be measured by instruments that typically consist of a microphone, an electronic amplifier, and an indicating device of some kind. The basic noise measurement is the total loudness of the noise across all the frequencies in the range of hearing. Most measuring devices also include an electronic circuit that mimics the human ear's varying sensitivity to different frequencies of noise by multiplying the noise level at each frequency by a different factor.

ACTIVE NOISE REDUCTION

One growing application of sound is noise cancellation, also known as active noise reduction. This system reduces the level of unwanted noise by applying further sound. It is based on the principle that when a given sound wave is merged with another sound wave that is a reversed exact replica of it, the two waves will cancel each other out and no sound will be heard. Although this theory has long been known, the ability to do this at a practical level is recent and is based on the availability of low-cost computing power.

The first applications of noise cancellation were in high-noise environments such as aircraft where voice communication is necessary. The application of noise cancellation makes speech possible even with high background noise. One recent consumer application is a portable noise cancellation device for use on commercial airliners. This device does not cancel out all the noise but reduces the level of the regular noise from the engines so that music can be heard in its earphones at a reasonable level. Major active noise reduction efforts are under way for use inside automobiles, where the traditional sound reduction techniques are bulky and heavy. Active noise reduction is still expensive and currently has limited performance. However, as computer power increases and becomes cheaper, noise cancellation is likely to become more commonplace.

A CLOSER LOOK

SONAR AND UNDERWATER LISTENING DEVICES

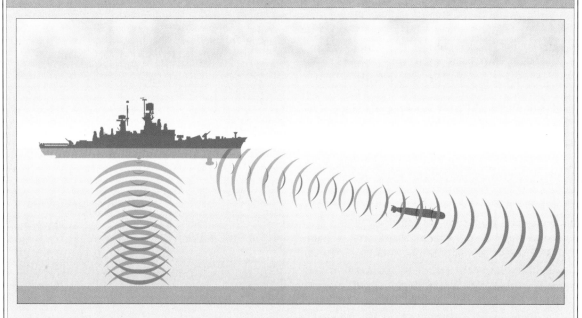

SONAR (*sound na*vigation *r*anging) is a system that uses sound waves to locate the position of distant objects and is commonly used underwater. Sonar was developed during World War II (1939–1945) for locating enemy submarines. A burst of extremely loud sound was generated by an underwater loudspeaker. Some of the sound would be reflected or echoed from the submarine, and the reflected sound could be picked up by a microphone. The time interval between the initial sound and the returning echo gave the distance to the submarine. Submarines a long way off gave a very faint echo, and the detection distance was limited by how faint an echo could be heard above the background noise of the sea.

Sonar is still in widespread use for submarine location. Today sound-generating buoys dropped by air are used for the sound source while other buoys are used for listening. During the cold war, listening arrays of many underwater microphones (hydrophones) spread over large areas of the ocean floor were installed. A submarine passing over the listening array could be detected by its propeller noise, water rush noise, and the noise of its internal machinery. Sound signatures for types of submarines and even individual submarines were developed. Data banks of these signatures were assimilated and the arrays could often identify individual submarines that passed over them.

Some animals such as bats and dolphins use a natural form of sonar for building up an image of their surroundings. This is called echolocation.

A CLOSER LOOK

More complex measuring devices now measure the loudness within a series of narrower bands. There are two different systems that enable sound to be divided up into frequency bands before measuring the loudness of each band. The older type of system is called the octave band system, which breaks the frequency measurement range into bands of variable width. These bands are related by powers of two, such that each band covers twice the frequency range of the lower band. Octave band measurements cover the range of human hearing in just 11 bands. The bands can be further subdivided into even smaller units such as one-third or one-twelfth octave bands.

Newer sound-measuring instruments use a method of band division known as the fast Fourier transform (FFT) to break the frequency range into much smaller bands than the octave band system. Each frequency band has a constant width, and hundreds of bands are used over the range of human hearing. This allows FFT instruments to measure different noise sources that produce sound at very similar frequencies.

R. DENNETT

See also: MICROPHONE AND LOUDSPEAKER; SOUND RECORDING AND REPRODUCTION; WAVE MOTION.

Further reading:

Advances in Acoustics Technology. Edited by J. Hernandez. Chichester, New York: E. & F.N. Spon, 1993.
Barren, M. *Auditorium Acoustics and Architectural Design.* Chichester, New York: E. & F.N. Spon, 1993.
Encyclopedia of Acoustics. Edited by M. Crocker. New York: John Wiley & Sons, 1997.
Frisk, G. *Ocean and Seabed Acoustics: A Theory of Wave Propagation.* Englewood Cliffs, New Jersey: Prentice-Hall, 1994.

ADHESIVE

Adhesives are substances that are used to bind objects together through surface attachment

Before a true understanding of synthetic organic chemistry had been achieved, adhesives were derived from a number of natural sources. Papyrus—a kind of paper used by the ancient Egyptians, Greeks, and Romans—was made of plant fibers stuck together with flour paste. Egg white was used to stick gold leaf (foil) onto illuminated medieval manuscripts. Carpenters and furniture makers used glues made from animal horns, blood, cheese, and fish to bond together pieces of wood. Large-scale production of adhesive from boiled animal bone dates from the 18th century.

In the 20th century, stronger and more reliable adhesives were developed to meet the challenges of new applications, such as those used in aviation, military equipment, and space travel. At the same time, advances in chemistry made new materials, such as polyurethane and epoxy resins, available for use in new adhesives.

How adhesives work

Adhesives work by a combination of physical (mechanical) and chemical interactions. A good adhesive spreads over a surface and enters its pores and crevices. As it hardens, it forms plugs of solid adhesive that key into these crevices and take hold, just as chewing gum sticks in the grooves of the sole of a shoe. At the same time, the reactive groups on the molecules in the adhesive may form attractions to molecules in the surface of the material that is being bonded. If the adhesive is sandwiched between two surfaces, this bonding process occurs on both surfaces; when the adhesive solidifies, the surfaces are bonded together. A good adhesive bond is resistant to shear forces, which pull parallel to the surfaces, and also to compressive (squashing) forces. Peeling forces are harder to resist, since they are focused on one edge of the bond.

The choice of adhesive is important and depends on the nature of the surfaces to be joined. An adhesive that joins paper to wood will not necessarily be able to join two pieces of metal together. Fortunately, there is such a wide range of adhesives available today that it is usually possible to select one to do the job at hand—from sticking a stamp on an envelope to attaching wings to an aircraft.

A curator at the British Museum in London assembles fragments of the Portland vase, which was shattered in an act of vandalism in 1845. To achieve near invisible joins, the curator uses a resin adhesive that is both stable (that is, it will not react chemically with substances in the vase) and an exact match in color.

Two rough surfaces are easy to join, since they have many pores into which the adhesive can creep and form physical bonds. Smooth surfaces are more difficult to bond, since they possess fewer keying points. As a result, the adhesive needs to form a strong chemical attraction to the smooth surface to bond effectively. Fibrous surfaces, such as wood or paper, are easily bonded, since they have absorbent surfaces that allow the long, chainlike adhesive molecules to penetrate them. The adhesive then holds the bonded surfaces together by entangling its own molecules with those of the bonded surfaces. Contact adhesives, which are usually dissolved in an organic solvent, work in a similar way to form strong bonds between plastic surfaces. The solvent molecules diffuse into the surface of the plastic, causing the it to swell and increasing the space between the plastic molecules. The chainlike adhesive molecules can then penetrate the surface and entangle with the plastic molecules.

Types of adhesives

Most adhesives, whether natural or synthetic, are polymers (giant molecules that are made of small repeating units; see PLASTICS). Natural adhesives are

CORE FACTS

- An adhesive makes strong bonds with a surface, so it can join two surfaces together.
- Most adhesives are polymers. They can be natural or synthetic in origin.
- Thermoplastic adhesives soften when they are heated. They can be used as hot-melt adhesives.
- Thermosetting adhesives harden when they are heated.

CONNECTIONS

● Many adhesives are chemically related to **PLASTICS**.

● Many types of adhesives contain **INDUSTRIAL SOLVENTS**, which make them easier to apply.

● Adhesives are widely used in modern **BOOKBINDING**.

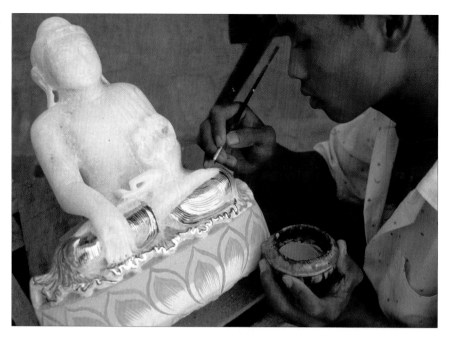

An artist paints an adhesive onto a stone-carved Buddha in preparation for gilding.

SOLVENT-FREE ADHESIVES

Conventional adhesives contain solvents to reduce their viscosity. This is important because a low-viscosity (runny) adhesive can penetrate the pores of the surface to be bonded better than a high-viscosity adhesive. As the solvent evaporates, the adhesive layer becomes tacky and then solidifies, making a strong bond.

The disadvantages of solvents are that many are harmful to health and the environment, they are often flammable, and they tend to have strong odors. For these reasons, efforts are currently being directed to develop reduced-solvent and solvent-free adhesives.

One approach is to replace the solvents with water. Indeed, some epoxy- and polyurethane-based adhesives are now water-based. However, the use of water is limited, since it is not a good solvent for the polymers used to make adhesives. As a result, water-based adhesives are emulsions (suspensions of one liquid in another, like milk) rather than solutions. Emulsions are more difficult to prepare than solutions and often require special additives to prevent them from clotting.

Solvents are not used in hot-melt adhesives, which require a heated applicator to make the solvent-free adhesive runny at the point of application. However, the application of hot-melt adhesives requires special equipment, and care must be taken to avoid burns.

An adhesive's viscosity increases with the length of the polymer chains it contains. However, the chain entanglement required for good adhesion depends on the adhesive polymer having long chains. The ideal is an adhesive that is runny enough to apply but that also provides a good bond and contains little or no solvent. This can be done by mixing together low-viscosity, short-chain components that react together to form long chains at the site of the bond.

In a two-pack system, usually based on epoxy resin, two liquids with little or no solvent are mixed together in measured proportions just before they are applied. Immediately, the adhesive starts to thicken as the two components react and form longer chains. The reaction continues after the surfaces are joined and the bond becomes even stronger.

In another type of system, typically based on acrylics, a mixture of monomers—the building blocks of the polymer—are made to react by exposure to ultraviolet light or to a beam of electrons. Polymerization takes places in just a few seconds. These new adhesives are already being used in the electronics and automobile industries, as well as in medicine.

A CLOSER LOOK

still used today despite their tendency to swell in damp conditions and encourage the growth of fungi. Suitable natural materials include starches, from flour, potatoes, corn, rice, or other cereal grains; gums, from the sap of trees and other plants; collagen, from animal tissues; albumen from blood; and casein, from milk. Natural adhesives are cheaper than synthetic materials.

Where performance is more important than economy, a synthetic adhesive is likely to be chosen. The synthetic adhesives are of two kinds: thermoplastics and thermosets (see PLASTICS). Thermoplastics soften when they are heated; they include a wide range of polymer types, such as acrylics, nitrocellulose, and polyvinyl acetate. Thermoplastic adhesives form a reasonably strong, durable bond but will deform over time and at high temperatures. Thermosetting adhesives become harder when they are heated. Examples include the epoxy, polyurethane, and phenol-formaldehyde resins. Elastomer-based adhesives are based on natural or synthetic rubber and can be either thermoplastic or thermosetting. They are cheap, resilient, and versatile.

Other adhesives, such as those used for adhesive tapes, require pressure activation—the surfaces must be pressed together briefly for adhesive bonding to take place. Pressure-activated adhesives are also used for removable message notes, which stick when pressed onto a surface but can easily be removed.

The uses of adhesives

Natural adhesives are still used for joining wood and paper, in and sandpaper, and for bookbinding (see BOOKBINDING). Gum arabic, from the sap of acacia trees, is the adhesive on some envelopes and stamps; it becomes effective when moist. Starch-based glues are used in wallpaper paste.

Synthetic adhesives are more widely used. Thermosets are used in the aerospace industry, and rubber-based contact adhesives are used to join furniture together. Adhesives such as the epoxy and acrylic resins are used as general-purpose adhesives, where wear-and-tear resistance is essential in industry, in construction, and outdoors. Elastomer adhesives have good stretching properties are are useful where flexible bonds are desirable.

S. ALDRIDGE

See also: CHEMICAL INDUSTRY, ORGANIC; FASTENING AND JOINING; MATERIALS SCIENCE; PAINT AND SURFACE COATING; PLASTICS; WOOD AND WOODWORKING.

Further reading:
Adams, R., Comyn, J., and Wake, W. *Structural Adhesive Joints in Engineering.* 2nd edition. New York: Chapman & Hall, 1997.
Adhesive Bonding. Edited by L. H. Lee. New York: Plenum Press, 1991.
Ball, P. *Made to Measure: New Materials for the 21st Century.* Princeton, New Jersey: Princeton University Press, 1997.

AERODYNAMICS

Aerodynamics is the study of the forces acting on objects as they move through the air or another gas

Aerodynamics is concerned with any system where air or another gas is moving past an object. This may be happening because the object is moving through the air, as in the case of an aircraft in flight or an automobile driving along a road, or because moving air is passing a stationary object, as in the case of wind blowing past a building. The relative movement of the object and the air around it creates aerodynamic forces on different parts of the object. If the object is moving through the air, these forces will affect its motion. If the object is a stationary structure, aerodynamic forces can cause structural stress or strain.

CORE FACTS

- Aerodynamic properties are important for stationary structures such as bridges and buildings as well as for moving objects such as aircraft, automobiles, rockets, and bicycles.
- The airflow at the back and behind a moving object tends to become turbulent. Reducing the amount of turbulence by altering the object's shape decreases the drag that the object experiences, allowing it to travel at high speed more effectively.
- Designers and engineers examine the aerodynamic properties of an object by placing it or a scaled-down model of it in a wind tunnel.
- Automobiles can be shaped so that the air around them pushes them down, improving tire traction.

Types of airflow

When air flows around an object, four distinct areas of airflow are created. These are the free stream, the laminar flow region, the turbulent flow region, and the wake flow (see the diagram on page 30).

The free stream is the area in front of the object or far enough away from it for the air not to be disturbed by the object. Closest to the object is the boundary layer. The air closest to the object is attracted to the object's surface and moves at practically the same speed as the object (or at near-zero speed for a stationary object). The layers of air farther out from the object's surface move at speeds progressively closer to the free stream speed. Near the front of the object—the end that is moving "forward" through the air—the boundary layer is smooth and follows the shape of the object's surface, but eventually it begins to break up into eddies and swirls. These two areas of the boundary layer are called the laminar flow region and the turbulent flow region. The wake flow is an area of turbulent air created behind the object. This flows more slowly than the free stream. It swirls and moves in circular patterns (vortices) that can continue long after the object has passed.

Flight

It is often said that the most important aspect of an aircraft wing is its airfoil shape, with a curved top and a flat underside. This is not entirely correct. In fact, the wing's angle of attack is of more importance in

CONNECTIONS

- The aerodynamic properties of **PARACHUTES** are such that parachutes can only move very slowly through the air.

- The aerodynamic design of **LAUNCH VEHICLES** and other vehicles designed for **SPACE FLIGHT** has no effect once the spacecraft have left Earth's atmosphere.

TYPES OF AIRFLOW AROUND AN OBJECT

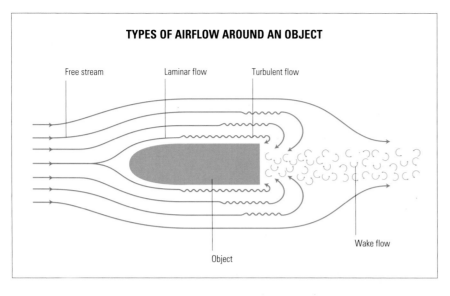

Free stream   Laminar flow   Turbulent flow

Object

Wake flow

THE SPEED OF SOUND

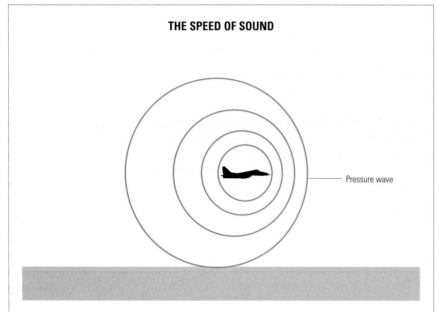

Pressure wave

An aircraft flying slower than the speed of sound creates pressure waves from its surfaces. These travel out in all directions at the speed of sound.

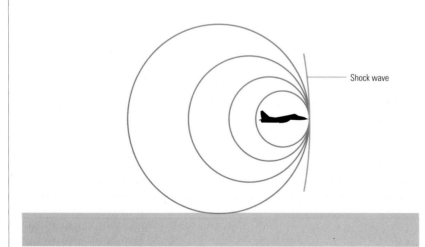

Shock wave

Pressure waves from an aircraft flying at the speed of sound can no longer move ahead of the craft. Instead they build up to form a shock wave.

providing lift. Imagine an aerobatics display in which an airplane flies upside down. An airplane that has wings that are more curved on the top surface than the lower surface is able to fly upside down quite easily, even though the shape of the wings is then inverted. This is because the angle of the wing also has an effect on lift. If the wing is inclined at an angle with its trailing edge lower than its leading edge, air above the wing surface is forced up and over the wing in a curve. As it does so it is accelerated, and this causes its pressure to drop, creating an area of low pressure over the wing. Because the air below the wing is at a higher pressure than that which is above it, the net force on the wing from the air around it pushes it up. In fact, aircraft specially designed for aerobatics usually have a wing with an airfoil that is symmetrical; the curvature is the same on the top as it is on the bottom (see FLIGHT, PRINCIPLES OF).

Supersonic flight

The introduction of the jet engine around 1940 allowed aircraft manufacturers to design airplanes that were faster than any that had gone before (see AIRCRAFT ENGINE). But it also brought new problems as, for the first time, airplanes approached the speed of sound. The passage of an aircraft through air creates pressure waves as the aircraft displaces the air around it. These pressure waves spread out from the aircraft at the speed of sound in subsonic flight. However, when the speed of the aircraft relative to the surrounding air reaches the speed of sound, the aircraft catches up with the pressure waves in front of it. Because they cannot travel faster than the speed of sound, the pressure waves build up into a shock wave, which is heard as a sonic boom.

The first aircraft to approach supersonic speeds encountered serious problems with control, since large pressure changes could occur without warning. These changes could cause the wings and control surfaces to flutter and the whole aircraft to pitch suddenly, which would often overstress the airframe and lead to its destruction. Many pilots lost their lives in supersonic flight research.

Designers soon learned to cope with the problems of supersonic flight. The most visible change in the shape of high-speed airplanes was the swept wing. Swept wings with knifelike leading edges and narrow, thin profiles have a smaller cross-sectional area than conventional wings and produce less drag.

Supersonic aircraft designs use a principle known as the area rule: the fuselage of a supersonic craft narrows to compensate for the cross-sectional area of the wings and engines. This avoids abrupt changes in the overall cross-sectional area of the craft from nose to tail and minimizes the disturbance caused by its passage through air, thereby reducing drag.

Buildings

For thousands of years, people have been making houses and other buildings that take into account the effects of the airflow around them. Long before a formal scientific understanding of aerodynamics existed, the ancient Egyptians were building houses with a structure on the roof called a *mulguf*. This is a type of ventilator that scoops cooling air into the house and at the same time removes hot, stale air. The design of the *mulguf*, like many similar systems around the world, came about as a result of years of experimentation. Today, many architects study traditional buildings to learn how elements of their construction might be used to control airflow in modern designs (see BUILDING TECHNIQUES, MODERN; BUILDING TECHNIQUES, TRADITIONAL).

The Tacoma Narrows Bridge

In 1940, a spectacular failure taught civil engineers valuable lessons that changed the way suspension bridges are built. In July of that year, a new bridge was opened that spanned the narrows between Tacoma and Gig Harbor, Washington. At over a mile long, it was one of the longest bridges in the world at the time (see BRIDGE).

However, local people soon noticed that all was not as it should have been. When the wind blew up the narrows, the bridge began to swing and flex, moving vertically so much that it became known as Galloping Gertie. By November of that year the twisting motion had gotten so great that finally, on November 7, a gale-force wind caused the bridge to tear itself to pieces. Fortunately, the only casualty was a pet dog left in a car that had been abandoned in the middle of the bridge.

How could a bridge weighing thousands of tons be destroyed by the wind? The answer lay in the aerodynamic shape of the deck, which is the part of the bridge structure that carries the roadway. The underside of the deck was reinforced with box girders of such a shape that, when the wind blew at right angles to the bridge, they produced aerodynamic lift, causing the deck to rise many feet into the air. This changed the forces on the deck so that it twisted, and aerodynamic forces drove it back down again. Four months of this punishment was enough to cause serious structural damage, and the 40 mph (64 km/h) winds on the bridge's final day were the last straw. Following this disaster, civil engineers became more aware of the possible problems of airflow around structures, and bridges were designed so that lift could not be produced.

Wind tunnels

A wind tunnel is a chamber in which air is forced over a scale-model prototype of an aircraft or a fixed structure to facilitate a study of its aerodynamics.

In 1901 the Wright brothers—the inventors of the first powered aircraft—used an old starch box to make their first wind tunnel. With this, they were able to test their theories on airfoil design; this led directly to the success of their airplane.

The basic design of the modern wind tunnel is quite simple: an engine or electric motor turns blades that move air through the tunnel and over a test specimen, such as a section of an airfoil or a model of an aircraft. The aim is to simulate the air-

This photograph from 1940 records the final moments of the ill-fated Tacoma Narrows Bridge in Washington.

flow that the test specimen will undergo when in use, and then to measure the forces on the specimen or its movement and analyze the airflow.

However, it is difficult to make wind tunnels that perfectly replicate airflow. One of the problems is that the rotating blades cause the air to spin, giving misleading results. In most tunnels, vanes are placed in the airflow to counteract the spin, and the test specimen is placed well downstream so that the air can stabilize before reaching it. Smoke is often injected into the airstream so that airflow over the test specimen can be seen and photographed.

Although wind tunnels are mainly associated with aeronautics, they have many uses in other areas of research. Architects use wind tunnels to study the effect of wind on proposed buildings. Because the wind at ground level is very turbulent, architectural wind tunnels have an uneven floor surface upstream of the test model to mimic real conditions. Models of surrounding structures are also placed in the tunnel because of their significant impact on the airflow.

No modern race car is built until the design is tested in a wind tunnel. To test the design in as realistic a way as possible, the model's wheels turn on a continuous roll of material, like a treadmill, that is

THE RACE CAR

Since the earliest race cars appeared over a hundred years ago, designers have been aware of the effect of aerodynamics on performance. For the first half of the century, improving performance involved streamlining the cars so that they would disturb the air as little as possible, thus creating less drag. By the 1960s, radical new ideas were tried that led to aerodynamics becoming one of the most important aspects of race car design.

As early as the 1950s, Mercedes had fitted their race cars with an air brake—a surface at the front of the car that could be raised to slow the car down before corners.

In the mid-1960s, U.S. designer Jim Hall became the first person to mount an inverted wing on a sports car. Hall realized that if an airplane wing can generate lift as it moves through the air, then an inverted wing (with its more cambered surface toward the ground) would generate negative lift (down force). Hall's car was a success, and among the many designers to be impressed by it was British designer Colin Chapman, head of race car manufacturer Lotus. Chapman went on to develop the idea much further. He started by mounting wings on high struts that kept them clear of the turbulent air close to the car. Mounting the wings on the body would only have pushed the car down onto its springs. Instead, the struts were connected directly to the wheels, so that the body of the car could move normally on its suspension while the tires were pushed onto the ground by the down force, giving more grip.

A series of crashes caused by wing failure led to a ban on these devices as well. However, soon Chapman had a better idea that would lead to the famous ground effect cars of the 1970s, such as the Lotus 79. Pods (streamlined housings) on the sides of these cars were shaped so that air entering at the front expanded as it moved toward the back. The outer wall of the pod had a sliding skirt attached to it that rubbed along the ground, sealing the airflow under the car and maintaining the area of low pressure. This design produced enormous amounts of down force to suck the car onto the track and was soon copied by other constructors. Today, despite continual rule changes aimed at slowing down race cars by reducing down force, a Formula One car still produces two and a half times its weight in downforce when traveling at high speed (see RACE CAR).

The shape of race cars helps to minimize drag and improve handling.

A CLOSER LOOK

used to represent the road under the car. This is called a rolling-road wind tunnel. Many automobile manufacturers use full-size tunnels in which complete finished cars can be tested (see AUTOMOBILE).

Wind tunnels have found another use in recent years—as a way of improving performance in sports. British cyclist Chris Boardman, winner of a gold medal at the 1992 Olympic Games, first spent many hours in the wind tunnel of Lotus Cars in England, perfecting his riding position. Streams of smoke were moved across his body as he sat on his experimental carbon-fiber bike. Wind tunnels have also been successfully used by skiers, bobsleigh teams, javelin throwers, and skaters (see SPORTS EQUIPMENT).

More recently, computers have been used to simulate airflow around objects. This technology may eventually replace the wind tunnel.

C. UTTLEY

See also: ACOUSTICS AND SOUND; AIRCRAFT DESIGN AND CONSTRUCTION; BALLOON AND AIRSHIP; CHAOS THEORY; DESIGN, INDUSTRIAL; GLIDER; HELICOPTER; HOVERCRAFT; HYDRAULICS AND PNEUMATICS; HYDRODYNAMICS AND HYDROSTATICS; LAUNCH VEHICLE; MISSILE; PRESSURE MEASUREMENT; PROPELLER; ROCKETRY; RUDDER; WIND POWER.

Further reading:

Anderson, J. *Fundamentals of Aerodynamics.* New York: McGraw-Hill, 1991.
Houghton, E., and Carpenter, P. *Aerodynamics for Engineers.* London: Edward Arnold, 1993.
Hubin, W. *The Science of Flight: Pilot-Oriented Aerodynamics.* Ames, Iowa: Iowa State University Press, 1992.
Katz, J. *Low-speed Aerodynamics: From Wing Theory to Panel Methods.* New York: McGraw-Hill, 1991.

AGRICULTURAL SCIENCE

Agricultural science is the experimental method that allows the discovery of new farming methods and inventions

Contour plowing helps to decrease water runoff and soil erosion, thus maintaining a good quality of soil.

As long as farming has existed, farmers have wondered about, and tried, new farming methods. For many centuries, however, this work was unsystematic, depending on accidental discoveries and observations. Only with the rise of scientific experimentation, from about the 16th century on, have revolutionary improvements in agriculture occurred (see AGRICULTURE, HISTORY OF).

What is experimental research?

The experimental method compares carefully controlled events in which only one property differs in each event. For example, suppose that somebody wants to learn about the type of fertilizer that is best for growing tomatoes. A field trial should be done in which plots of tomatoes are raised under as nearly uniform conditions as possible but with a different fertilizer in each plot (see FERTILIZER). Whole plots are compared rather than individual tomato plants, because too many chance occurrences could affect any one plant. Anomalous conditions will probably even out and be about the same between whole plots.

The difficulty in conducting any experimental research is to keep all the conditions the same. The soil might be unpredictably different between plots: there may, for example, be more water in one plot compared to another, or there may be different pests and diseases (see IRRIGATION AND LAND DRAINAGE; PESTICIDE AND HERBICIDE).

Conditions are more easily kept constant by performing the experiment in a laboratory. However, it is often difficult and expensive to find laboratory space for large numbers of plants, and agricultural scientists usually like to duplicate the local agricultural conditions as closely as possible so that their findings will be useful to local farmers. Most universities and many private businesses have experimental farms on which field trials are staged.

At the end of the trials, a conclusion may be drawn as to which fertilizer works best with the particular type of tomato in the particular conditions that were tested. However, the agricultural researcher can never be absolutely sure about the results of such experimentation. Other conditions may have been involved that the researcher did not know about. It takes great patience, time, and care to

CORE FACTS

- Experimental research in agriculture requires patience, time, and careful analysis but often pays off with accurate new knowledge about crops.
- Much has been learned about the environmental requirements of plants and animals, and new ways to meet them have been invented.
- New methods of combatting diseases and pests of plants and animals are constantly being discovered.
- Plant and animal reproduction is under the artificial control of humans as never before.

CONNECTIONS

- **FERTILIZER** applied to the soil provides nutrients, such as nitrates, sulfates, and phosphates, that are essential for plant growth.

- Research in **GENETIC ENGINEERING** is producing new strains of plants.

These orange predatory mites (Phytoseiulus persimilis) attack spider mites (Tetranychus urticae), a pest of bean plants. The predatory mites are commercially bred for the biological control of the pest mites.

analyze the results of experimental research. Careful, logical work of this kind—asking specific questions and solving problems—has led to the amazing scientific discoveries of today. As Louis Pasteur said, "In the fields of observation, chance favors only the mind that is prepared."

As with all scientific research, statistics are employed in agricultural research to evaluate the results of experiments. For example, when evaluating the effectiveness of different types of tomato

fertilizers, a number of plots must be planted with tomato plants. Each plot is treated with a different test fertilizer and the average productivity of the plants in each plot is recorded. Typically each fertilizer will be applied to several plots, scattered throughout the test field, and some plots will be left untreated. The productivity results then undergo a statistical analysis to separate the true effects of the fertilizers from effects due to other factors.

As in other scientific areas, the scientific methods used in agricultural research follow a general pattern. First, there is observation of unusual phenomena or patterns. Then a hypothesis is developed. This is a prediction based on theory, an educated guess that derives from various assumptions that can later be tested using experimental procedure. After testing, the results are analyzed, then a new hypothesis is formed. This hypothesis may then be open to subsequent testing.

Plant nutrition and soil needs

Each crop has fairly specific requirements for temperature, water, light, and minerals. These have been identified, and efficient methods have been found to meet these needs. We now know that the temperature of the soil, rather than of the air, is most crucial for plants, and thus cold conditions can be combatted by mulching—spreading a covering such as compost on the ground to reduce evaporation of water and, in winter, to reduce heat loss to the surroundings.

Fields that lie on sloping sites can be plowed in a series of flat terraces, each at a different height to its neighbors. This technique, called contour plowing, is recognized to decrease water runoff and soil erosion (see PLOW). Occasionally certain bacteria or algae are added to soils. They affect the size of soil grains and the spaces between them, and thus change the capacity of the soil to hold water. Some green algae are also used because they secrete polysaccharides that help bind soil particles together.

Photoperiodism—the functional response of the plant to the length of the day—may trigger several plant processes, including flowering and the growth of many plant parts. Farmers now raise plants under artificial light sources that can be programmed to mimic summer day lengths and get the crops ready for winter markets.

Research into the effects of different fertilizers is advanced and the mineral needs of different plants can be met. All plants need nitrogen, phosphorus, and potassium in large quantities; sulfur, calcium, and magnesium in smaller amounts; and tiny traces of other minerals. Nitrogen-fixing bacteria in the root nodules of certain plants can also be added to the soil to change nitrogen from the atmosphere into ammonia, a chemical that plants can easily absorb (see SOIL SCIENCE).

Plant physiology and pathology

A particularly exciting research area is the study of plant hormones—the compounds mainly responsible for directing the various processes in different parts

AGRICULTURAL ENGINEERING

Agricultural engineers design a remarkable variety of items, such as tools and machinery, drainage projects, systems for packaging and transporting, and barns with automated feeding and waste-disposal systems. For example, laser-controlled land graders create unusually level land, which helps to optimize the absorption of rainwater and minimize the loss of soil in heavy rain.

Agricultural engineers are developing sensors that feed information on plant and animal health, soil moisture, climatic conditions, and water quality in aquaculture into computers, which then calculate the amount of feed, water, heat, or fertilizer that needs to be delivered (see AQUACULTURE). These factors are crucial in determining the suitability of water environments for the breeding of fish. Agricultural engineers usually work for companies that manufacture farm equipment, feeds, or chemicals. They must be trained in the fields of engineering, biology, and agricultural science.

A CLOSER LOOK

of a plant, many of which accelerate or delay growth in various ways (see PLANT HORMONE). These hormones, sometimes known as auxins, promote such physical changes as root initiation, cell elongation, xylem (the water-carrying vessels) differentiation, and tropism (a reflex turning of a plant toward or away from an external stimulus such as sunlight).

Some hormones are now sprayed directly on plants to prevent or delay fruit drop before the harvest time, to stop plants from reaching their full heights, or to increase vegetative growth. Another new approach is the cloning of plants, so that a desirable genetic property, such as resistance to viruses, can be replicated over and over. Cloning plants from cells in culture in the laboratory (tissue culture) has also been used to create successful hybrids between species of plants that normally cannot cross. Scientists are also exploring techniques of introducing DNA (deoxyribonucleic acid) into plant cells to engineer new genetic varieties. Research in these areas is expanding rapidly (see BIOTECHNOLOGY; CLONING; GENETIC ENGINEERING).

Fungicides and pesticides

Effective fungicides (see the box on page 36) and insecticides now exist that help to combat the two biggest killers of plants—fungi and insects. Organic insecticides made in laboratories, such as DDT, are especially deadly, harming insect growth and life systems. Unfortunately, insecticides are sometimes poisonous to humans and other animals. DDT and several other organic insecticides are now banned in the United States. This is partly because they are endocrine disrupters, affecting hormones and so, in turn, animal development. Organophosphates are currently the largest, most versatile class of insecticides, although their use has been linked to the development of certain ailments in humans, including central nervous system disorders. They are effective at eradicating insects, such as aphids and mites, which feed on plant juices. Chemical absorption occurs either by spraying the leaves or applying solutions impregnated with chemicals to the soil, so that intake occurs directly through the roots.

Safer methods to kill insects have been discovered by entomologists (insect biologists), including the use of radiation, light-reflecting materials, and sounds to drive off insects or attract them to traps. Secretions from insects called pheromones—substances that attract the sexes to each other—are also used to draw insects to traps. Some plants secrete substances that kill insects, such as nicotine, which kills aphids, and pyrethrins from flower petals—most notably chrysanthemum petals—that kill flies.

Entomologists have also developed bacterial sprays that cause infections in insects. Biological control is another method of insect population control. In this process, natural enemies such as parasites, predators (ladybugs, for example), or disease organisms are introduced into the pest's environment to reduce its population. If a predator is already present it may be encouraged to multiply. An effective

example of biological control was the eradication of the citrophilus mealybug in California by the introduction of two types of parasitic species of chalcid flies from Australia (see BIOLOGICAL CONTROL).

These researchers are planting different genetic strains of barley to test the growth of each strain.

ANIMAL BEHAVIOR

Research into animal behavior has revealed that distressed animals may be calmed by enclosing them in stalls that press into their sides. This discovery has been used to make the last minutes before slaughter less stressful for cattle (see SLAUGHTERHOUSE). A variation on this method is to enclose a frightened wild horse (except for its head) in a small shed in which hay continually flows down around it. After 30 minutes, the horse is usually calm enough to undergo some training (see LIVESTOCK FARMING).

Methods of training animals owe much to the important observation of the behavioral psychologists who suggest that rewarding an animal is more effective than punishing it. In many problem animal behaviors, there are nutritional, genetic, or learned causes involved. For instance, abusive pecking (cannibalism) among hens can be learned, but it also may be due to genetically determined responses to the environment and feed or to disease.

A CLOSER LOOK

CHEMICALS THAT KILL FUNGI

One of the main threats to plants is fungi. Also known as antimycotics, fungicides are any toxic substances used to kill or inhibit the growth of fungi. Most fungicides are applied to crops as sprays or dusts. Seed fungicides are applied to protect seeds before germination, while systemic fungicides are applied to plants. They become distributed throughout the tissue and help eliminate current disease or protect against possible disease.

One of the earliest fungicides was Bordeaux mixture, a liquid made of hydrated lime, copper sulfate, and water; this is still used to treat orchard trees. Other substances in use include cadmium chloride to control turfgrass diseases, creosote to stop dry rot in wood, and mercury (II) chloride to protect bulbs from fungi. Synthetic organic compounds are also used as versatile fungicides.

A CLOSER LOOK

GEORGE WASHINGTON CARVER

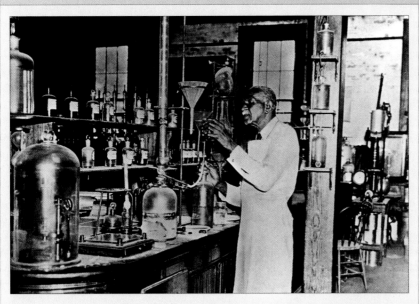

U.S. chemist George Washington Carver worked in his laboratory on research into commercial uses for crops that could successfully grow in the Southern states.

U.S. agricultural chemist George Washington Carver (c. 1864–1943) was born into slavery near Diamond, Missouri. He managed to get a high school education while working as a farm hand, and by the age of 30 he had graduated in agricultural science at the Iowa State College. Carver spent two more years studying botany at Iowa before becoming director of agricultural research at Tuskegee Institute in Alabama.

At the end of the 19th century, agriculture in the Southern and Southwestern United States was entirely dependent on cotton, a crop that depletes the levels of nitrogen present in the soil. Carver knew that other crops—peanuts, soybeans, and sweet potatoes—were suited to the local soil and could maintain soil quality by replacing the nitrogen that was consumed by the cotton. However, he realized that farmers would be unwilling to grow crops they could not sell. To address this, Carver started a program to develop products that could be obtained from the nitrogen-fixing crops. He developed hundreds of new products, including cheese and cosmetics derived from peanuts, and flour, vinegar, and glue from sweet potatoes. The development of these products made it possible for farmers to protect their soil by growing the alternative crops in addition to cotton.

PEOPLE

Bacterial sprays are another form of biological control. Weeds and plant parasites, such as mistletoe, can be killed by herbicides that target the plant parasite and leave the cultivated crop unharmed.

Animal physiology and nutrition

Exact feeding requirements have been calculated for different breeds of domestic animals. These depend on such factors as weight and growth, among others. Animals need a healthy balance of fats, carbohydrates, protein, vitamins, and minerals. Animal feed containing brain and spinal-cord tissue is now banned in the United States to prevent the spread of bovine spongiform encephalopathy (BSE, known as mad cow disease), a disease of the nervous system that is fatal to cows and causes a life-threatening brain disease (new-variant Creutzfeldt-Jakob disease) in humans (see LIVESTOCK FARMING). Farmers must also be aware of the chemical substances that are involved in blocking the absorption of other substances. For example, too much molybdenum in the diet may result in a deficiency of copper. In addition to advances in the understanding of animal nutrition, the 20th century has seen significant advances in the diagnosis and cure of many animal diseases (see VETERINARY MEDICINE).

Advances in animal and plant breeding

Scientists are improving and expanding technologies of artificial insemination (fertilizing eggs in lab cultures) and cloning, which has made animal reproduction and the breeding of new strains of plants more efficient. New strains of plants have also been created by fusing protoplasts (plant cells without cell walls) from two species that cannot be crossed by the usual natural sexual reproduction or by grafting one plant on to another plant (see PLANT BREEDING AND PROPAGATION).

M. COBERLY

See also: ANIMAL BREEDING; ARABLE FARMING; ARTIFICIAL INSEMINATION AND FERTILITY TREATMENT; CLONING; CROP SPRAYING AND PROTECTION; GENETIC ENGINEERING; HORTICULTURE; ORGANIC FARMING AND SUSTAINABLE AGRICULTURE; PRECISION FARMING.

Further reading:
Encyclopedia of Agricultural Science. Edited by C. Arntzen and E. Ritter. San Diego: Academic Press, 1994.
Canine, C. *Dream Reaper: The Story of an Old-Fashioned Inventor in the High-Tech, High Stakes World of Modern Agriculture.* New York: Random House, 1995.
Hurt, R. *The History of Agricultural Science and Technology: An International Annotated Bibliography.* New York: Garland Publishing Company, 1994.
Manci, W. *Farming and the Environment.* Milwaukee: Gareth Stevens Publishers, 1993.
Practical Handbook of Agricultural Science. Edited by A. Hanson. Boca Raton, Florida: CRC Press, 1990.

AGRICULTURAL TRANSPORT AND MAINTENANCE MACHINERY

Farming vehicles and machinery are used for transportation and maintenance needs

The development of larger, more productive farms means that materials such as harvested animal feed, crops, and fertilizers need to be moved around the farm in bulk. Maintenance tasks need to be performed quickly and efficiently to avoid loss of productivity, and these developments have led to a need for specialized machinery.

Agricultural transport

Most agricultural commodities are moved in general-purpose vehicles. Historically, the traditional wooden farm wagon—sturdy, low-sided, and roofless for easy loading—would be pulled by horses or oxen (see HORSE-DRAWN TRANSPORT). This versatile vehicle has been the mainstay for agricultural transport throughout history. Variations on the design include two- and four-wheeled types and wagons with an open back for dumping.

When farm productivity increased, agricultural wagons had to adapt. In the 18th and 19th centuries, for example, framework sides were added to either side of the wagon to extend its carrying capacity during the hay harvest.

From the 1930s on, motorized vehicles began to replace horse-drawn transport on farms. Today, the general-purpose wagon, pulled by a tractor, is an essential piece of machinery on every farm (see TRACTOR). Trucks or vans are also used, but tractor-drawn trailers are preferred due to their versatility and suitability for rough terrain.

Most modern trailers are constructed of metal, sometimes with wooden flooring or sides, and can have a load capacity of up to 22 tons (20 tonnes). Many trailers are equipped with hydraulic dumping systems and tailgate-lifting mechanisms (see HYDRAULICS AND PNEUMATICS). Various conversion kits can be added to a standard trailer to adapt it to carry specific loads. There are also some specialized trailers that carry only certain materials, such as grain trailers with motorized unloading augers (rotating screw-type devices for digging and moving solids, such as soil, grain, or fertilizer). Tanker trailers, also known as nurse wagons, are used to carry liquid loads, such as irrigation water or liquid fertilizers, to the site where they will be applied.

This excavator is being used to clear debris from a drainage ditch.

Various loading vehicles are used to load and unload trailers and trucks or to move heavy materials around farm buildings. These loaders can be hydraulically powered arms that attach to a general-purpose tractor, or specialized vehicles—usually rough-terrain forklifts with telescopic booms.

Tractors or off-road automobiles are used for everyday personal transport around a farm, but smaller, lighter vehicles are increasingly used, especially on farms in hilly terrain. These vehicles, known as all-terrain vehicles (ATVs), are modified motorcycles with three or four large, rugged tires. They provide access to the most inaccessible areas, and they are light enough to be driven on ground too wet for a tractor. They are suitable for accessing ranging livestock, such as sheep in upland areas, and can pull a small trailer or lightweight equipment, such as fertilizer spreaders.

Maintenance machinery

The general upkeep of a farm is an important part of agriculture, and nearly all farms have machinery and equipment for maintenance tasks. Economic factors dictate that expensive equipment be as versatile

---

CORE FACTS

- Most agricultural transport is done by general-purpose vehicles, most often tractor-drawn trailers.
- Common farm maintenance tasks include fence repair and ditch digging. Tractor-mounted machinery performs most maintenance tasks.
- Livestock may often be transported to market, to the slaughterhouse, or between distant pastures in mechanized vehicles.

CONNECTIONS

- Some types of **CONSTRUCTION AND EARTHMOVING MACHINERY** are used for agricultural maintenance tasks.

- Many types of agricultural machines are powered by **TRACTORS**.

TRANSPORTING LIVESTOCK

Animals are usually herded when they need to be moved around a farm, but on rare occasions they may need to be transported in vehicles, when they are taken to the market or slaughterhouse or to distant pastures—such as from an upland to a lowland area.

Vehicle transport is always stressful for animals, and most vehicles are modified to improve travel conditions. Horse trailers have a stall for each horse (usually two or four per trailer), with feeding racks and window slits for air and light. The rear door is hinged at the base so that it folds down to form a ramp for easy entry and exit. Smaller livestock, such as goats and sheep, are generally transported in larger trucks that hold many animals. These trucks may also be divided into stalls and are often arranged in two stories to accommodate more animals. Some vehicles have slatted wooden floors so that dung can fall through into a collecting space underneath.

These sheep are being unloaded from trailers.

A CLOSER LOOK

as possible. Therefore, most farmers prefer to use machinery that can be hooked up to a tractor or adapted to existing equipment. Most tractor-mounted machinery is powered either by its own hydraulic system or is driven from the tractor power takeoff shaft, which is a rotating shaft connected to the engine of the tractor that transmits power to the trailing equipment. Some equipment is driven from the tractor's hydraulic pump.

There are many important farm maintenance tasks. Some tasks, such as clearing snow from farm roads in cold climates, require the use of a snow-plow blade fitted to the front of the tractor. Other tasks, such as clearing storm-blown trees, are achieved with hand tools.

Digging and clearing ditches is another essential farm maintenance job, especially if the ditches are part of an irrigation or field-drainage system (see IRRIGATION AND LAND DRAINAGE). An industrial excavator is most often used to dig large ditches (see CONSTRUCTION AND EARTHMOVING MACHINERY), but smaller jobs may be completed by a bucket attached to an articulated hydraulic arm and hooked up to a standard farm tractor. A selection of bucket sizes is available. Narrow buckets are used to dig trenches and to lay drainage pipes. Alternatively, buckets several feet wide are used to clear ditches.

In many parts of the world, hedges were used to mark boundaries or to prevent livestock from straying. Traditionally, hedges were cut by hand. Today, however, hedge trimming is more often done with tractor-mounted mechanical cutters. Most mechanical cutters are of the flail type, with numerous metal teeth attached by pivoting bolts to a rotor. The rotor spins at speeds of up to 3000 revolutions per minute. This gives the teeth a powerful, although rough, cut-

ting effect. The flail head, which is typically 3–4 ft (just over 1 m) wide, attaches to the end of a jointed hydraulic arm, so a wide range of cutting positions can be achieved.

On the majority of livestock farms, fences are used to mark boundaries. Some fences are electrified to repel livestock. Most fences are built and repaired by hand, although tractor-powered augers are sometimes used to dig deep holes for large fence posts. Wire fences are erected under tension so that they remain taut; this may be achieved using either a hand winch or motorized equipment.

Mechanical cutters may be used on the sides of banks, ditches, and shoulders. Cutters with blades instead of flail teeth are also used. These give a much cleaner cut and a neater result but will only handle thinner branches.

T. ALLMAN

See also: AGRICULTURE, HISTORY OF; ARABLE FARMING; FARM STORAGE; HAND TOOL; HORSE-DRAWN TRANSPORT; OFF-ROAD AND AMPHIBIOUS VEHICLES; TRACTOR.

Further reading:
Culpin, C. *Farm Machinery.* 12th edition. Boston, Massachusetts: Blackwell Scientific Publications, 1992.
Hunt, D. *Farm Power and Machinery Management.* Ames, Iowa: Iowa State University Press, 1995.
Hurt, R. *Agricultural Technology in the Twentieth Century.* Manhattan, Kansas: Sunflower University Press, 1991.
Johnson, D. et al. *Mechanical Technology in Agriculture.* Daneville, Illinois: Interstate Publishers, 1998.

AGRICULTURE, HISTORY OF

Agriculture has revolutionized human society, and it is now undergoing a new technological revolution

Agriculture is the world's most important industry. Not only does it supply humans with almost all their food, it also supplies materials for two other basic human needs: clothing and shelter. Agriculture produces raw materials that are used in many industrial products, such as paints and medicines, and provides employment for about half the world's workforce.

Early agriculture

Before the end of the last ice age, about 13,000 years ago, our ancestors lived by hunting, fishing, and gathering wild vegetables and fruits, traveling from place to place to find their food. Around 10,000 years ago or earlier, however, people living in the Middle East, the Indus Valley in the Himalayas, the Nile Delta in Egypt, and the Fertile Crescent in the Near East started to control their food supplies. This was achieved by planting, cultivating, and harvesting field crops; herding or corralling animals (keeping them in enclosures); and selecting and breeding for the best strains of plants and animals. The exact dates and places of this early agriculture are not known, because most traces of it have disappeared or have not yet been discovered. At first glance, it seems odd that hunters and gatherers should have taken on the farming life, which often requires harder work and longer hours than hunting and gathering. However, many archaeologists suspect that it happened in the following way.

As the ice age ended, the warm, moist climate caused plants and animals to flourish. In some places, humans were able to settle in permanent villages where food supplies, within walking distance, were abundant year-round. Fields of cereal crops, which grow in thick, widespread stands, were probably the hub of these human settlements. Consequently, grains became the first major staple crops: wheat and barley in the Near East, Egypt, and later India and Europe; pearl millet, African rice, and sorghum in central Africa; foxtail millet and later corn in Central America; quinoa (a pigweed) in South America; lamb's-quarters (another quinoa species) and sunflowers in eastern North America; rice in India and along the Chang River, China; and Chinese millet

The traditional method of winnowing grain is by tossing it in the wind.

along the Huang River, China. Farmers in these regions realized that they could grow crops successfully if they used river water for irrigation, and by about 3000 B.C.E. Egyptian farmers had developed the world's first large-scale irrigation systems. At the same time, they invented an oxen-drawn plow (see the picture on page 40). Earlier farmers had pulled their plows by hand, but plows pulled by oxen were much more efficient (see the box on page 41).

Occasional food shortages must have occurred, especially in areas that continued to grow warmer and drier. As people adapted to a settled life, however, they did not want to return to nomadic wandering to find food. They had accumulated breakable, heavy, or unmovable possessions that would have been left unguarded while they roamed. Therefore, they took steps to protect crops and animals against disaster. They created food plantations near their villages and grew a variety of crops, so that if one crop failed they would have other crops to supply food. They began to sow seeds from the best plants, breaking the soil beforehand and cultivating and weeding afterward, to produce better yields. They tamed, fed, corralled, or herded animals to

CORE FACTS

- Archaeologists are uncertain about the dates and locations of the earliest agriculture.
- Various plants and animals were domesticated in different parts of the world, but the methods and tools used were similar.
- In the 19th and 20th centuries, agricultural technology accelerated dramatically due to scientific discovery and the pace of scientific invention.

CONNECTIONS

- **ARABLE FARMING** is the use of land suitable to grow crops for human and animal consumption or other purposes.

- **GENETIC ENGINEERING** techniques have contributed to greater crop yields.

Egyptian art depicts a farmer plowing a field with an ox-drawn plow in Thebes, Egypt.

prevent them from straying. They bred selectively for the best animals, keeping the females to produce more young and killing and eating all but the best males to breed.

The first animals domesticated and kept for food were those that lived in herds—such as cattle, sheep, goats, llamas, alpacas, and water buffaloes—or family-group animals such as pigs that were naturally submissive and easy to control. Placid, hardy animals that could be raised on a wide variety of fodder

and in confinement—such as cattle, pigs, guinea pigs, and chickens—were also preferred. Honeybees were also domesticated early. They are easy to capture in containers when they swarm, and they pollinate fruits and vegetables as well as provide honey. In time, domesticated animals became different from their wild cousins. Humans selected and bred them from the less aggressive individuals that produced the most food.

Plants also changed (see PLANT BREEDING AND PROPAGATION). Almost half of the world's crops are believed to have originated in India and China, because the wild species from which they were cultivated still grow there. These crops include soybeans, lettuces, onions, peas, many fruits, sugarcane, flax, tea, spices, and rice. The early Chinese farmers grew water plants along with rice, and they probably domesticated other plants. Early farmers in India grew wheat and barley, various millets, rice, dates, sesame, peas, cotton, and lentils. In Central America, peppers, avocados, and amaranths were grown before corn was domesticated. Grains were cultivated that produced higher yields of seeds that were larger, clustered together, and harder to dislodge. These properties made the grains easier to harvest. Unlike wild plants, which have easily dislodged seeds that scatter widely and reproduce more rapidly, domesticated plants are grown from specially collected and planted seeds. Beans, chili peppers, zapotes, cacao, tomatoes, and cotton accompanied corn agriculture. Little is known about early South American agriculture. The potato and other roots were probably the first domesticated plants. Beans and cotton were grown before corn, and irrigation was introduced—probably learned from the north.

AGRICULTURAL HAND TOOLS

The first hand tools were made of wood with stone, and more rarely bone, cutting blades. The same basic tools appeared in successive generations. Axes and saws were used to clear trees and brush from forest or jungle land. Mattocks (pick-formed digging tools), spades, shovels, and digging sticks were used to break the soil and to harvest root crops.

In most parts of Europe and Asia, dirt clods were further broken down with hoes or by dragging a heavy wooden harrow over them. Seeds were often broadcast (scattered) and then trampled or plowed in. Rice, corn, and other grains, however, were planted in holes made with digging sticks. Hoes were used after planting to aerate the soil and to remove weeds, which compete with crops for moisture and nutrients.

Forks or rakes, sickles, scythes, and billhooks (curved pruning blades) were used to harvest grain, while other crops were picked by hand, sometimes using knives. Grain kernels were threshed (loosened from their husks) by being beaten with a stick or flail (hand-held sticks with short, free-swinging sticks attached). The kernels were then winnowed (or separated from the husks) by being tossed into the wind from baskets; the seeds would fall back into the baskets while the lighter husks (chaff) blew away (see HAND TOOL).

A CLOSER LOOK

Throughout history, agricultural crops have been passed from culture to culture and farming techniques have been learned from successful farmers. Wheat and barley seem to have spread from the Near East into Egypt, Africa, and Europe. Irrigation techniques may have been learned from early Indian farmers and passed to China. However, scientists cannot be sure that irrigation was not independently discovered in different locations.

Agriculture brought about dramatic changes in human life. Land and animals were owned individually or by families, not shared with a larger group as nomads will share their large harvests of meat and plants. Living in one place, families could store large amounts of food and accumulate goods. With time, considerable differences in wealth developed. Putting more labor into agriculture will produce more food from the same land, so farmers tended to have large families and put them to work, and the numbers of farmers grew. By contrast, putting more labor into hunting and gathering will quickly reach a point of diminishing returns and depleted resources, so hunters and gatherers tended to restrict their offspring to the numbers their territories would support. The burgeoning populations of farmers gave them an advantage in warfare. Food surpluses made it possible for some farmers to specialize as managers, artists or craftspeople, traders, soldiers, priests, or rulers. Many people believe that modern civilization developed from these agricultural beginnings. However, hunting and gathering of wild foods is still important today in some farming economies.

Agriculture in the Roman Empire

After the Roman conquest of the Middle East in the first century B.C.E., the Romans spread throughout their empire the advanced farming techniques they had seen used in the Middle East. The Romans quickly adopted the ox-drawn plow and irrigation techniques, both of which had been used in the Middle East since the second millenium B.C.E., and also introduced methods of their own. For example, they began the practice of leaving half of every field fallow (unplanted) each year, which allowed the soil to recover its natural fertility for a crop the following growing season. The Romans also developed various systems of crop rotation. In one system they used legumes, or pulses, as a rotation crop. Legumes enrich the soil with nitrogen, one of the chief nutrients that all crops need to grow. By building terraces, Roman farmers were able to grow such fruits as grapes and olives along the steep shoreline of the Mediterranean Sea. In various parts of the empire, Roman engineers built long irrigation channels, waterwheels, and water-lifting devices and designed huge containers to store grain.

The selective breeding of plants and livestock began in Europe during Roman times. For example, migrant farmers who settled in the part of Europe that is now the Netherlands produced the first specialized breed of dairy cattle, the Holstein, in the first century C.E.

DRAFT ANIMALS

A farmer uses an ox to plow a flooded rice field in Sumatra, Indonesia.

A revolutionary increase in power occurred when oxen, donkeys, and onagers (an Asian cousin of the donkey) were trained to pull plows and wheeled wagons. Wheeled wagons were more efficient carriers of crops and other items than mats or rafts dragged on the ground. Draft animals were used to thresh grain by treading on it in the Near East and surrounding regions, and they could grind the grain by pulling stone mills. Horses, with bits and bridles, were adopted in the Near East from nomadic herders. Horses were especially valuable in warfare because of their speed, but oxen were cheaper to raise and remained the draft animal of choice for many centuries. In Europe during the Middle Ages, the horse collar (probably invented in China) replaced harness bands that had pressed on the windpipes of horses. This made horses equal to oxen in power, with more speed, and they soon replaced oxen as the main draft animal. From an early period, elephants were probably draft animals in India. Wheeled vehicles and draft animals probably came late to East Asia, and they apparently were not used in farming in the Americas before European draft animals were imported. The indigenous animals in East Asia and the Americas apparently did not lend themselves to draft work.

A CLOSER LOOK

The Middle Ages

The civil wars that resulted from the barbarian invasion of the Roman Empire in the fourth century C.E. changed the shape of farming in Europe. Farms became organized into large estates called manors, which were controlled by rich lords and worked by peasants. Agricultural technology changed very little from this time up until the British agricultural revolution during the 1700s. Plows, wheeled carts, and stone mills for grinding grain were the most complicated farming machines for many centuries.

However, some improvements were realized. For example, the development of iron smelting and hammering provided iron and even steel blades for various tools, including plows. European farmers also invented a three-field system of crop rotation during the Middle Ages that replaced the Roman two-field system. One field would be left fallow, and

An artist's impression shows a steam plow being tested at Grimethorpe, England, in 1850.

in each of the two remaining fields, farmers would grow a different crop. In this way two-thirds of the land was farmed each year instead of half of it.

Another important development in the ninth century was the introduction of a horse collar. This was used to hitch a horse to a plow, increasing the speed at which farmland could be plowed compared to those drawn by oxen (see the box on page 41).

The development of complex farm machinery was a slow process. Around 1000 C.E., the Chinese had water-driven machines for pumping irrigation water, threshing, and milling grain. Windmills were used extensively in Europe by the late Middle Ages.

European farmers continued to improve plants and livestock by selective breeding during the Middle Ages, and many special-purpose livestock breeds were developed. A breed of dairy cow called the Guernsey was developed around 960 C.E. from selected French cows. Guernsey cows produce a particularly rich milk that is ideal for making butter.

Voyages of discovery

The European voyages of discovery that began in the 1400s had a worldwide impact on agriculture. Crops and livestock developed in isolated regions suddenly became popular in many regions of the world. Corn spread widely from Mexico. European explorers carried new crops throughout the world, including sugarcane, pineapple, rubber, tomatoes, sweet potatoes, potatoes, and peanuts.

Native Americans had developed advanced systems of agriculture by the time the first European settlers arrived. These experienced farmers grew cocoa beans, maize, peanuts, peppers, rubber trees, gourds, sweet potatoes, tobacco, and tomatoes. European settlers learned much from their techniques. They also brought their seeds, livestock, farming tools, and methods to the regions they explored and settled.

European explorers also established plantations in parts of Asia, but the farmers were reluctant to adopt European farming methods. Instead, they continued to use and improve the methods that had developed in their countries over thousands of years. For example, the wetland crops of India and southern China, including rice, were grown in fields called paddies that were enclosed by earthen dikes and deliberately flooded. In hilly country, flat land for paddies was created by building terraces (see IRRIGATION AND LAND DRAINAGE). In tree-covered areas, such as parts of Southeast Asia, slash-and-burn agriculture was practiced: areas would be cleared for cultivation by hacking down the vegetation and burning the residue. After a few crops the nutrients in the soil would be depleted and the land would be abandoned. Land that has been used for slash-and-burn cultivation takes years, sometimes decades, to recover.

The agricultural revolution

During the early 1700s, a great change in farming, called the agricultural revolution, began in Britain. The revolution resulted from a series of discoveries and inventions that made farming more productive than ever. By the mid 1800s, the agricultural revolution had spread throughout much of Europe and North America. One of the revolutions chief effects was the rapid growth of towns and cities in Europe and the United States during the 1800s. Since fewer people were needed to produce food, farm families moved by the thousands from rural areas to towns and cities. The agricultural revolution occured mainly by four developments: improved crop-growing methods, advances in livestock breeding, the development of fertilizers, and the invention of new farm equipment.

Improved crop-growing methods. Early in the 1700s, retired English politician Charles Townshend (1674–1738) was experimenting with crop rotation.

He found that turnips could be used as a fourth crop in a four-field rotation system. The other crops consisted of two grains, especially varieties of wheat, and a legume such as alfalfa or clover. Each crop either added nutrients to the soil or absorbed different kinds and amounts of nutrients. Farmers therefore did not have to leave any land fallow.

Townshend's experiments went largely unnoticed until English nobleman Thomas Coke (1752–1842) produced vastly increased yields of crops using Townshend's system. Coke encouraged other farmers to adopt the method, and it soon became widely used in England. The system enabled farmers to grow crops year-round, making their land much more productive. Both Townshend and Coke lived in the county of Norfolk, England, and the four-field system came to be called the Norfolk system.

Before the development of the Norfolk system, farmers could not grow enough crops to feed livestock through the winter months, and most animals had to be slaughtered in the fall. However, the increase in productivity resulting from the Norfolk system meant that livestock could be fed all year; as a result, farmers could produce fresh meat all year.

Advances in livestock breeding. In the late 1700s, English farmer Robert Bakewell (1725–1795) showed how livestock could be improved by intensively breeding animals for desirable traits. Bakewell improved breeds of cattle, horses, and sheep, becoming best known for developing a breed of sheep that could be raised for meat as well as for wool. Earlier sheep breeds fattened slowly and were too expensive to raise for meat (most sheep were raised for wool only). Bakewell's breed, however, fattened quickly and could be raised for slaughter at low cost. Mutton became so cheap that it was soon the most popular meat in England (see ANIMAL BREEDING).

The development of fertilizers. Since the beginning of agriculture, farmers have used various substances to enrich the soil. For example, fields have been fertilized by adding human and animal waste, ash, garbage, and later slag (the calcium-rich waste from steel manufacture). Although these substances undoubtedly worked, little was known about why or how they did. By the late 18th century, however, scientists began to identify what chemicals crops need to stay healthy. For example, they found that legumes are useful rotation crops because they incorporate nitrogen from the air into the soil. Scientists also identified other elements that the crops needed, such as calcium, phosphorus, and potassium. It soon became evident that combinations of these chemicals could be added to depleted soils to insure that crops had a supply of all the nutrients they required (see FERTILIZER).

The invention of new farming equipment. In contrast to the slow change in previous centuries, technology accelerated in the 19th and 20th centuries. The first important inventor of the agricultural revolution was English farmer Jethro Tull (1674–1741). Tull invented the first seed drill, a machine that could dig small trenches in the soil and deposit seeds in them. Threshing machines, reapers, and more efficient plows spread through Britain and its colonies, Europe, and the United States, turning uncultivated, unoccupied lands in the United States, Australia, and New Zealand into rich farmland using fewer workers. The tough prairie soils of North America could not be plowed effectively until U.S. blacksmith John Deere (1804–1886) invented a steel plow in the 1830s. As wheat farms spread widely in the American West, they were threatened by the free-ranging cattle herded by ranchers. Traditional European fences of hedge bushes, stone, or rails

Farmers gather a potato crop using a mechanical harvester in Salon-de-Provence, France.

A harvester stands surrounded by cranberries at a processing plant in Wisconsin. The fruits will be pressed and processed into cranberry juice.

would have been expensive and time-consuming to put up on the prairie. However, the invention of barbed wire in 1874 provided a cheap fence material that could be used to enclose vast areas quickly.

The most important innovation for agriculture in the 19th century was probably the steam engine, first invented in the 18th century (see STEAM ENGINE). By the 1860s, steam plows had been widely adopted in industrial countries, and machines such as threshers, hay-loaders, and milking machines were all steam-powered. At the same time, steamships and railroads were constructed in many countries, making the sale of agricultural goods to market possible for the first time. The 19th century also saw a great interest in research and education. The potato blight in Ireland and the grapevine fungus in southern Europe underlined the need for continued research. The United States, Britain, France, and Germany established farms for experimentation on plant and animal nutrition and set up schools and professorships of agriculture. In 1862, the U.S. Congress established land grant colleges in certain states to teach agricultural and mechanical arts.

20th-century agriculture

In the first half of the 20th century, tractors run by internal combustion engines became available in Germany, Britain, and the United States (see INTERNAL COMBUSTION ENGINE). As rubber tires, four-wheel drive, and finally diesel power were invented, tractors became more efficient and labor less time-consuming. The invention of power-takeoff systems meant that tractors could be attached to other equipment to supply mechanical power for a variety of uses (see AGRICULTURAL TRANSPORT AND MAINTENANCE MACHINERY). Self-propelled, single-purpose machines also came into use, such as the grain combine harvester, which cuts grain and separates out the kernels, and the corn picker, which husks and shells corn kernels. Trucks were used to transport produce to market, and aircraft became a highly efficient way of spraying crops with fertilizers.

After World War II (1939–1945), machinery continued to cut down the number of farm laborers, and the proportion of farmers in the population continued to fall. New methods of farming, such as the highly intensive practices of aquaculture and hydroponics, were developed (see AQUACULTURE; HYDROPONICS). Arsenic-based chemical insecticides, invented in the first half of the 20th century, gave way to more effective, synthetic organic insecticides such as DDT, a number of which were banned because of toxicity. Safer ways to combat insects began to be developed. Crops continued to be transplanted to new environments. Soybeans from Asia and sorghum (or milo) from Africa, originally raised as human foods, were grown in the United States for mainly oil and animal fodder, respectively. Rapidly expanding research in plant and animal physiology and genetics, including cloning and genetic engineering, revolutionized plant and animal breeding. In developing countries, mechanized equipment, insecticides, fungicides, and synthetic fertilizers were used more and more. New varieties of rice and other crops and large-scale farms, dams, and irrigation systems all helped to increase farm yields in desperately overpopulated lands (see AGRICULTURAL SCIENCE).

M. COBERLY

See also: ARABLE FARMING; CLONING; CROP SPRAYING AND PROTECTION; GENETIC ENGINEERING; HORTICULTURE; ORGANIC FARMING AND SUSTAINABLE AGRICULTURE; PESTICIDE AND HERBICIDE; PLANT BREEDING AND PROPAGATION; PLANT HORMONE; PRECISION FARMING; SOIL SCIENCE.

Further reading:
The History of Agriculture and the Environment. Edited by D. Bowers. Washington D.C.: Agricultural History Society, 1993.
Hurt, D. *American Agriculture: A Brief History*. Ames, Iowa: Iowa State University Press, 1994.
Smith, B. *The Emergence of Agriculture*. New York: Scientific American Library, 1995.

AIR BAG

Air bags are safety devices that protect a car's occupants from impact with its interior by inflating during a collision

Air bags are now standard equipment in most new vehicles. They are designed to inflate within milliseconds when their sensors detect an impact of sufficient force and deflate again immediately, cushioning the effects of the collision.

Most air bags are intended to deal with frontal collisions. They are released from the steering wheel and above the glove compartment to protect the driver and front seat passenger, who are the most vulnerable in this sort of accident. Some automobiles are now being manufactured with additional air bags placed on the sides of the passenger compartment to react to broadside impacts.

Air bags are often called supplemental restraint systems, because they are designed to work along with seat belts rather than replace them. Without a seat belt, passengers are not only in more danger from almost any type of accident, but they may also be injured by the air bag itself.

When the air bag's sensor is triggered, it detonates a pellet of gunpowder, causing a chemical called sodium azide (NaN_3) to decompose. The rapid decomposition of sodium azide generates harmless nitrogen gas that fills the air bag, which until then is stored folded inside its compartment. The cushion of the air bag prevents the occupant from coming into direct contact with the interior of the vehicle. Slots in the air bag allow the gas to escape and the bag quickly deflates, but not before it has lessened the force of the collision on the occupant. After its release, the air bag must be professionally repacked.

The impact sensor of the air bag is carefully designed to recognize the rapid deceleration that occurs in a collision at speeds greater than about 25 mph (40 km/h). It is designed to avoid reacting to such situations as a minor bump in a parking lot or the jolt caused by hitting a pothole. A secondary sensor (the safing sensor) acts as a check so that a faulty impact sensor will not cause the air bag to inflate.

Between 1990 and 1998, air bags saved more than 3000 lives in the United States. However, during the same period, the deaths of 111 people, mostly women and children, were blamed on them. Traditionally, the crash dummies used in safety tests on automobiles resembled adult males in size and weight. Some of the fatalities occurred when shorter passengers were hit in the neck and face by the rapidly inflating air bags. Many women drivers face the additional risk of having to sit closer to the air bag compartment in the steering wheel than most men in order to reach the pedals. The air bag tragedies caused an outcry, and many car owners had their automobile air bags deactivated or removed.

The advantages of air bags could be retained while reducing the potential risk posed to automobile occupants by educating the public on the proper use of air bags. Passengers and drivers should sit as far back from the air bag compartments as possible, and they should always wear seat belts. Unbelted passengers have accounted for many of the fatalities caused by air bags; without the seat belts, they were thrown closer to the air bags during the collision. Similarly, children under 12 and children in child safety seats should ride in the back seat, not in the front where they would be close to the air bag.

New air bags are also being tested that would activate with less force or have more than one reaction mode, depending on the force of the crash or the weight of the passenger. Perhaps the most lasting improvement to come out of the air bag debate is the realization that crash dummies representing adult males do not adequately represent the entire population. "Families" of crash dummies are now being planned. They will test new air bag technology in greater detail and, hopefully, make the highways safer for everyone who uses them.

S. CALVO

See also: SAFETY SYSTEMS.

Further reading:

Bowman, B. M. *Computer Simulation of an Airbag-restrained Passenger in Impact Simulator and Crash Barrier Tests: Development of an Improved Procedure for Using a HYGE Sled.* Ann Arbor: University of Michigan, Transportation Research Institute, 1993. *Safety Belts, Airbags, and Child Restraints: Research to Address Emerging Policy Questions.* Washington DC: Transportation Research Board, National Research Council, 1998.

Demonstration of an air bag inflating on collision during a safety test with crash dummies.

CONNECTIONS

● Improvements to the **AUTOMOBILE** over the years have reduced the risk of death in automobile accidents.

● Air bags are triggered to inflate on collision by **TRANSDUCERS AND SENSORS**.

AIR-CONDITIONING AND VENTILATION

Air-conditioning and ventilation regulate the temperature, humidity, and purity of air in enclosed spaces

A single air-conditioning unit, such as the one shown, can provide air for a large office building. The large, square ducts carry the treated air around the building through shafts and spaces between floors.

CONNECTIONS

● Air-conditioning systems can be integrated with **HEATING SYSTEMS.**

● Deep **MINING** uses forced ventilation to supply air to underground workers.

The history of air-conditioning

The earliest techniques for cooling air used a principle that is still employed today: the evaporation of a liquid requires an amount of heat—the latent heat of evaporation of the liquid (see HEAT, PRINCIPLES OF; REFRIGERATION). In the dry climates of ancient Egypt, Greece, and Rome, wet mats or blankets were hung over doors so that the wind would be cooled and humidified by evaporating water as it entered the houses. Later—around 1500—Italian artist, scientist, and inventor Leonardo da Vinci (1452–1519) built a mechanical fan that was powered by waterwheel. He used the fan to build the first recorded forced-air evaporative cooler. A modern evaporative cooler is the cooling tower, in which water is cooled by partial evaporation.

Industry has played a major role in the development of air-conditioning and ventilation technology. The need to get fresh air to miners working under ground prompted the development of the rotary fan in Britain in 1553. In the 1700s, textile manufacturers improved production by controlling humidity and temperature using a combination of heat, boiling water, and ventilation. In 1897, Joseph McCreery of Toledo, Ohio, patented a water-spray humidifier that is still used in modern air conditioners. Certain industrial processes require uniform humidity to avoid changes in the properties of the materials being processed, such as shrinkage or swelling. The most recent advances in air conditioning have been stimulated by the need for meticulously sterile and dust-free environments for the manufacture of pharmaceuticals and sensitive electronic components.

Air-conditioning processes

The precise air-conditioning requirements for a building depend mainly on the size of the building, the climate, and the nature of the activities held there. However, there are elements that are common to almost all air-conditioning systems.

Purification. Air that is drawn in from the surroundings may contain dust and fumes. Similarly, air that is to be recirculated within the building may become dirty while inside the building. Filters are used to remove this dirt. The simplest filters are pads of a woven material that capture dirt from the air as it passes through them. Good filters trap all but the smallest of particles and are adequate in most cases.

O̲ur first records of modern civilizations show that humans took shelter from the elements and used fire to warm their surroundings. As their dwellings became more enclosed, vents were used to exhaust the smoke from fires. In tropical climates, people designed their houses to provide shade from the sun and to take advantage of cooling breezes.

Heating and cooling ambient air to a comfortable temperature are basic air-conditioning processes. However, human comfort is also affected by the humidity (moisture) of the air. Excessively humid air, especially at higher temperatures, leads to discomfort and excess perspiration, while excessively dry air can cause irritation and soreness of the eyes and throat. A further problem exists on industrial premises, where equipment and processes can introduce dust, odors, and noxious fumes.

Air-conditioning encompasses the processes of both heating and cooling air, adjusting its humidity, removing harmful foul-smelling or similarly unpleasant substances, and moving it around a building. Ventilation is the removal of stale, dirty air from an indoor environment while supplying clean, fresh air from outside.

CORE FACTS

■ Air-conditioning is used to provide a comfortable environment for a building's occupants.
■ Ventilation in buildings is essential to human health.
■ Water and refrigeration fluids are used to remove heat from indoor air.

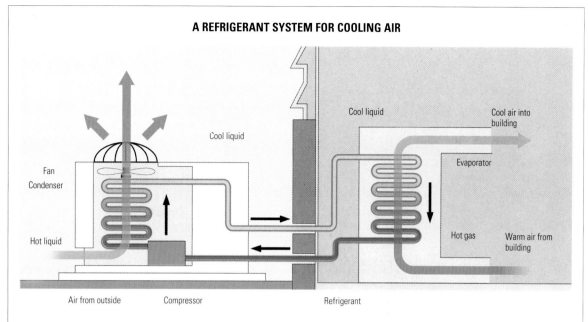

A REFRIGERANT SYSTEM FOR COOLING AIR

Cool liquid

Cool air into building

Fan
Condenser

Cool liquid

Evaporator

Hot liquid

Hot gas

Warm air from building

Air from outside   Compressor   Refrigerant

When refrigerant vapor is compressed and liquefied, it gives up heat to the outside air. The liquefied refrigerant then passes to the internal part of the circuit, where it evaporates and takes in heat from the building.

Where a higher standard of cleanliness is needed, such as in a clean room for electronics assembly, an electrostatic precipitator may be used, in which the stream of intake air passes through a comblike metal grid that is positively charged at high voltage. Particles that have escaped the normal filters pick up a positive charge from this comb and are attracted to a negatively charged surface, to which they stick.

Cooling. Once the air has been filtered, it may need to be cooled before passing into the building. In dry climates, where water evaporates easily, air can be cooled and humidified by passing through a moist fiber mat. In more sophisticated systems, the air is passed through a heat exchanger, in which piped water takes in the heat from the air (see HEAT EXCHANGER). The warm water from the outlet of the heat exchanger is pumped to a cooling tower, where it is cooled by fan-driven evaporative cooling, then returned to the heat exchanger. However, cooling towers are only effective in relatively dry climates. Little evaporation (and therefore cooling) takes place when the outside air is already very humid. Also, cooling towers can be breeding grounds for harmful microbes and must be maintained regularly.

Air-conditioners with refrigeration units have the advantage that they are effective in humid climates, since they do not rely on the evaporation of water for their cooling effect. Refrigeration also removes excess moisture, which condenses as water on the cooling pipes. The cycle begins outside, where an electric compressor increases the pressure on the refrigerant gas and causes its temperature to rise. When compressed, the gas gives off heat to the surroundings and condenses as a liquid, releasing more heat. The cool fluid then moves to an evaporator inside the building where it passes through a nozzle. The pressure is released and the fluid evaporates, taking in heat and condensing moisture from the air.

Heating. In cooler climates, the intake air may be heated before it is circulated around a building. Since the heating process consumes energy, air-conditioning systems often recirculate a large proportion of air. Outgoing air may be passed through a heat exchanger to warm the intake air and save energy.

Humidity adjustment. The water content of the air may change as a consequence of the cooling process used. Sometimes, though, an additional adjustment may be necessary. Water sprays, steam generators, or moist mats can be used to increase the humidity of the air. Air can be dried in an additional chiller, which condenses airborne humidity.

Energy efficiency versus air quality

While older buildings were sometimes drafty and difficult to heat, concerns about energy efficiency have lead to well-insulated buildings with little air leakage. In recent years, it has become apparent that this situation is not ideal. Materials in the everyday environment—furniture, carpet, and paint, for example—release gaseous compounds, as does the operation of electrical machinery. Some of these compounds are known to be harmful, and it is widely believed that they contribute to sick building syndrome, whereby the occupants of a building suffer from tiredness, headaches, and infections, among other problems. To avoid the accumulation of gaseous toxins, air-conditioning systems now include planned ventilation, so that the air in the building is constantly replenished with fresh air from outside.

P. WEIS-TAYLOR

See also: HEATING SYSTEMS.

Further reading:
Bobenhausen, W. *Simplified Design of HVAC Systems.* New York: John Wiley & Sons, 1994.

AIRCRAFT CARRIER

Aircraft carriers are very large naval vessels equipped to launch planes and helicopters

Commissioned in 1977, the U.S.S. Dwight D. Eisenhower is a U.S. Navy Nimitz-class nuclear aircraft carrier. At 1092 ft (333 m) long, 252 ft (77 m) wide, and weighing 95,000 tons (93,500 tonnes), it can carry 75 aircraft and a crew of 6287 personnel. It is armed with U.S. Sparrow standard air defense missiles.

CONNECTIONS

● Recently, aircraft carriers have been built to launch **V/STOL AIRCRAFT** as well as types of **MISSILES** used to hit aircraft or other ships.

● An aircraft carrier run by **NUCLEAR POWER** can go for months or even years without needing to be refueled.

The modern aircraft carrier is a floating city equipped with aircraft that can launch bombs and missiles at enemy installations from a distance. About 4500 people live and work on these vast ships for months at a time, and they require all the services that a comparably populated town would need. Such lengthy periods at sea are necessary because aircraft carriers must be kept at the ready so that a nation can deploy a formidable level of military power to almost any location in the world.

The first aircraft carriers

The cruisers U.S.S. *Birmingham* and U.S.S. *Pennsylvania* were the first aircraft carriers. On November 14, 1910, a pilot named Eugene Ely undertook the feat of flying a Curtiss biplane off a specially built wooden deck covering the bow of the U.S.S. *Birmingham*. The biplane was loaded aboard ship, anchored in Hampton Roads, Virginia, and positioned at the end of the 83-ft (25-m) ramp. Though it was reported that the plane's wheels touched the water after it disappeared over the bow, the pilot got it back up into the air. Ely followed with another triumph on January 18, 1911, when he flew another Curtiss plane across San Francisco Bay in California, landing on a similar wooden deck on the U.S.S. *Pennsylvania*. Although lengthened to 119 ft (36 m), the deck was short enough for an arresting gear. This consisted of 22 parallel ropes laid across the deck, their ends tied to sandbags. The airplane had three grappling hooks beneath its tail. As it

landed, it snagged the ropes, dragged the sandbags, and rapidly slowed down. Ely's feat was made more difficult by the platform being only 4 ft (1.2 m) wider than the plane's wingspan, but he was able to land almost in dead center. He had only 100 ft (30.4 m) in which to brake the plane.

Despite such valiant efforts, naval aviation took years to advance. For the most part, it was limited to reconnaissance (scouting) planes launched from modified cruisers. Many ships were equipped with hangars for storing aircraft. They also had cranes so they could launch aircraft, have them land on the water by the ship, and then pick them up for reuse.

British advances

Britain led the world in carrier aviation. During World War I (1914–1918), the Royal Navy modified the hull of an existing merchant ship to become the first true aircraft carrier: H.M.S. *Argus*, which had no

CORE FACTS

■ Bombers and missiles can be launched from aircraft stationed aboard carriers to attack a distant enemy.

■ Modern aircraft carriers, such as those in the U.S. Nimitz class, are among the world's largest ships.

■ Specially designed decks on carriers enable planes to land and take off without colliding.

■ Aircraft carriers remain at sea for long periods and thus need a wide range of onboard support services.

observation and command tower or any other structure protruding above the deck. However, the war ended before the ship could be put into service. Later, they modified another ship, H.M.S. *Eagle*, to be the first carrier with an offset bridge (a bridge moved to one side to create space for aircraft maneuvers). H.M.S. *Hermes* was the first ship to be launched specifically as a carrier in 1919.

Britain continued to pioneer carrier aviation until after World War II (1939–1945). Developments included the angled deck, which prevented planes coming in to land from being aimed almost directly at those waiting to take off; and the offset deck, which prevented planes that missed the grappling hook and ran off from being hit by the ship. Another innovation was the steam catapult. This was like a gigantic rubber band pulled back by steam pressure that could launch aircraft in the short distance available on carriers built after 1951. The catapults were powerful enough to replace the hydraulic catapults operated by water pressure in use on other ships.

Transforming naval warfare

The effects of aircraft carriers on battleships could be devastating, since battleships could be reached and attacked by bombers launched from carriers hundreds of miles away—having already been detected by carrier reconnaissance aircraft. Advances in carrier and military aircraft design opened a new chapter in the history of naval warfare (see MILITARY AIRCRAFT). Where once ships had sailed almost alongside one another, firing massive broadsides, aircraft carriers enabled ships to dispatch planes to attack an unseen enemy. World War II proved to be the testing ground for this technology, as it was for so many other kinds of technologies.

The war in the Pacific Ocean exposed the potential, as well as the weaknesses, of aircraft carriers. It was from these vessels that Japanese planes were able, on December 7, 1941, to attack and destroy Pearl Harbor in Hawaii, undetected until the moment they struck. In the period between the two world wars, Japan had built more aircraft carriers than any other country. Conversely, aircraft carriers enabled the United States and its allies to attack Japanese forces and to support the battles fought to reclaim lost territories.

Aircraft carriers began to be constructed to fulfill their expanding role in modern navies. Wooden decks were replaced with steel, armor was increased in vulnerable areas, and new materials and technologies were introduced. Engines were made more powerful and efficient, because carriers needed to be able to operate far away from friendly ports. There was also a strong need to sail the ships at a speed that would supply the initial momentum to help the new, heavier planes get off the decks. The ability to remain at sea for long periods was eventually attained by using nuclear power. While a nuclear-powered ship is not necessarily faster than conventionally powered vessels, in peacetime it can cruise for 20 years without being refueled.

H.M.S. Hermes, *a British Royal Navy aircraft carrier built in 1919, was sunk by Japanese aircraft in the Indian Ocean off Ceylon on April 9, 1942. H.M.S. Hermes was 598 ft (182 m) long, weighed around 10,950 tons (9930 tonnes), and held 664 crew and up to 10 aircraft.*

Modern supercarriers

With their increased capability for extended cruises came the need for carriers to store provisions for longer periods. This led to the construction of larger ships and the provision of support services for crews. The end result was the modern supercarrier.

Examples currently in service with the U.S. Navy are the *George Washington*, launched in 1989, and the *Harry S. Truman*, commissioned in 1998. These great vessels carry a combined payload of planes and support aircraft and are capable of carrying more firepower to a given spot than was ever possible for ships in World War II.

Carrying large numbers of military planes, fuel for each of them, and ordnance (weapons) requires the ships to have greater firefighting capability than a medium-sized city. Carriers are especially susceptible to fire; the U.S.S. *Forrestal* suffered a major fire in 1967 that came close to sinking the ship. As a result, a number of changes were made in the type and amount of firefighting equipment placed on U.S. carriers (see FIREFIGHTING AND FIRE PROTECTION).

There are now various types of smaller carriers, featuring ski-ramp decks and other innovations designed for vertical short takeoff and landing (V/STOL) aircraft (see V/STOL AIRCRAFT). As technology changes military aircraft and the weapons they carry, the aircraft carrier will also change, with new types coming into use. The carrier-plane combination will no doubt continue to be a powerful and important part of military aviation, particularly in remote areas of the world that do not politically support the use of ground-based launches.

C. POWERS

See also: HELICOPTER; MILITARY AIRCRAFT; WARSHIP.

Further reading:

Davis, J. K. *Aircraft Carriers and the Role of Naval Power in the 21st Century.* Cambridge, Massachusetts: Institute for Foreign Policy Analysis, 1993.

AIRCRAFT DESIGN AND CONSTRUCTION

A wide variety of aircraft is designed and constructed for private, civil, and military air transport

The main fuselage and wing section of a Boeing 747 jumbo jet is under construction in a hangar at a Boeing factory in the United States.

CONNECTIONS

● Stealth aircraft are made of **COMPOSITE** materials to make the aircraft invisible to **RADAR**.

● In fly-by-wire technology, the link between the pilot's controls and a **COMPUTER** has revolutionized **MILITARY AIRCRAFT**.

● **FLIGHT SIMULATORS** are used to test aircraft for handling and safety.

Every airplane is a compromise in its design. Top speed, for example, might be sacrificed for high-altitude performance, or long range for maneuverability. The overall design and shape of an aircraft is determined by its intended use.

As designers rely more heavily on computers to help them with the design process, it is not surprising that many modern airplanes that are built for the same purpose bear an uncanny resemblance to each other. Even an expert can find it difficult to distinguish between a Boeing 777 and an Airbus A330, for example. However, there is still room for individualistic aircraft that expand the boundaries of aeronautical design.

DESIGNING AN AIRCRAFT

The design of a high-tech modern aircraft can involve hundreds of designers and engineers who may work on it for many years before it is ready for flight (see DESIGN, INDUSTRIAL). The rows of drawing boards that once filled design offices have been replaced by a few personal computers.

It is now possible to have a computer-generated virtual airplane on which to try out design changes. Engineers can explore the interior of the yet-to-be-built aircraft to see how its components fit together and make changes to it without having to manufacture any real objects. They can even virtually fly the aircraft by inputting atmospheric data onto the computer. Once the design is ready, construction can begin, and the computers can then send manufacturing instructions to the machine tools that will make the actual components of the aircraft.

CONSTRUCTING AN AIRCRAFT

Most aircraft are assembled on a production line. However, many aircraft components are made by subcontractors, which, in turn, ship their components to the final assembly plant. In Europe, Airbus Industries uses specially constructed airplanes called Belugas to ferry parts as large as complete airplane wings to sites throughout the continent.

The basic structure

There are many ways to build an airplane, but the most popular is the stressed-skin construction technique, in which a metal skin is stretched over a metal framework to give a combination of strength and lightness. The basic construction of an aircraft, according to its main structural components, is as follows (see STRUCTURES).

The main body. Most early airplanes were built from a wooden frame covered with linen that was doped (treated with a substance that gave it more

CORE FACTS

■ Fighter aircraft have relatively short wings to permit the very rapid rate of roll necessary for air combat.

■ The stressed-skin technique has been the most popular method of aircraft construction since the 1930s.

■ Today, any emergency situation will be brought to the pilot's attention by onboard computers.

■ Boeing and Airbus are building "super jumbos" that will be able to carry a thousand passengers on two levels by the early 21st century.

flexibility) to produce its aerodynamic shape (see AERODYNAMICS). However, the linen gave very little strength to the airplane. Later, the wooden structure was replaced with steel or aluminum tubing, but it still had a fabric covering. In the stressed-skin technique, the whole structure, including the outer skin, contributes to the strength of the airplane.

Made of metal alloys in most airplanes, the skin is traditionally attached to the ribs and spar with rivets (one-headed metal bolts that, when set in place, are hammered to form a second head) to produce the outer surface of the wing.

Although experiments with this method of construction began in the earliest days of aviation, it wasn't until the 1930s, in the United States, that it was developed on a large scale. The success of airplanes such as the Douglas DC-2 and the Boeing Model 247 encouraged designers throughout the world to use this technique, and it soon supplanted almost every other method of construction (see FLIGHT, HISTORY OF).

The wings. In a typical airplane, the wings are built around a strong girderlike object called a spar (see the diagram on page 52). The spar usually reaches from wing tip to wing tip, passing under, through, or over the fuselage (the aircraft's central body, which holds the crew, passengers, and cargo). Often, more than one spar is used and, in some designs, the leading edge of the wing (the curved, front edge of the wing) is formed by a spar that is D-shaped when viewed from the side.

Attached to the spar is a series of structures called ribs (see the diagram on page 52). These are usually positioned at right angles to the spar. Ribs give the wing its airfoil shape (a design that reacts to the force of air to lift the wing) and provide a structure on which to attach the metal alloy skin. A wing structure of this type has many advantages. It combines strength with lightness and has enough space inside to contain the fuel tanks of the aircraft. Engines can be attached to the spars, and compartments can be placed between ribs for stowing the landing gear.

The fuselage. On most airplanes, the fuselage is constructed using a similar stressed-skin technique. A series of ring-shaped structures, called frames, are placed transversely at regular intervals along the length of the fuselage. These are connected by longitudinal objects, called longerons, that run the whole length of the aircraft. The exterior skin of the fuselage is then attached to the ribs and to the longerons, usually with rivets.

In some places, bulkheads (upright partitions) take the place of frames. These are used to form the ends of compartments and are often used for attaching equipment. The bulkhead at the front of an airliner's cockpit (the pilot's compartment), for example, forms the end of the pressurized cabin and is also used to mount the aircraft's radar dish.

Alternative construction techniques

Although the process explained above is an example of the most common type of aircraft construction, there is an increasingly large number of alternative construction techniques.

For example, the Lockheed Martin F-22 Raptor—an air fighter—has a wing with no less than 18 spars, some made from titanium and others from carbon fiber. The wing skin is made of carbon fiber composite material.

Another example of an alternative construction technique is the Beechcraft 2000A Starship—an executive jet. The aircraft is made from an exotic combination of boron, carbon, Kevlar (a synthetic fiber), and fiberglass, and it became the first pressurized, composite-built airplane to receive a certificate of airworthiness (see COMPOSITE).

The Beechcraft Starship 2000A, with its elegant, streamlined design, was a product of experimentation with composite materials.

THE MAIN COMPONENTS OF AN AIRPLANE

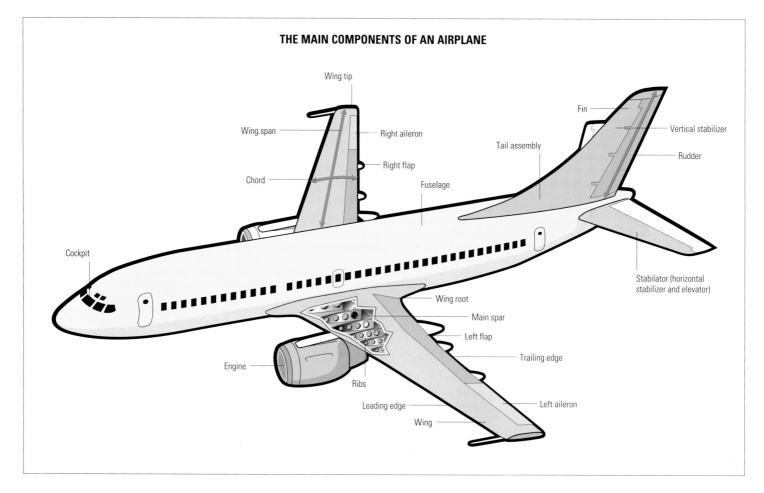

Wing tip

Wing span

Right aileron

Chord

Right flap

Fin

Tail assembly

Vertical stabilizer

Rudder

Fuselage

Cockpit

Stabilator (horizontal stabilizer and elevator)

Wing root

Main spar

Left flap

Trailing edge

Engine

Ribs

Leading edge

Left aileron

Wing

Testing the aircraft

The components of an aircraft are first tested by being placed in hydraulic rigs that mimic the stresses experienced by an aircraft in flight. Tests begin long before the real aircraft takes to the air, and the tested components are subjected to repeated simulated flights that include conditions far worse than any that would normally be encountered. In this way, if a fault occurs in the aircraft structure, it will happen on the ground first, enabling various design or construction changes to be made to the aircraft before it is put into service.

Every new airplane is subjected to a rigorous test and development program by a team of test pilots. As the test crew will have been able to "fly" a computer-simulated version of the new aircraft long before the actual first flight, it is unusual today for test pilots to be caught with unexpected handling problems in the real aircraft.

TYPES OF AIRCRAFT

There are many types of aircraft in use today, but two of the most typical are airliners and fighter aircraft. A knowledge of their basic features is useful in understanding how the majority of aircraft function.

The airliner

A typical airliner has a wing that is swept back from the fuselage at about 30 degrees. To give good economy for cruising speeds of around 560 mph (900 km/h) and altitudes in the region of 35,000 ft (11,000 m), the wing is designed to have a high aspect ratio. The wing aspect ratio is a comparison of the length of the wing to the wing chord (the distance from the leading edge to the trailing edge—see the diagram above). A high aspect ratio means that the wing's span (length) is fairly long compared to its chord. Flaps, slats, and other aerodynamic devices are used to increase lift for takeoff and landing. The airliner's horizontal tail is attached to the fuselage and, along with the tail fin, is swept at an angle similar to that of the wing.

The airliner's fuselage is essentially a cylinder for most of its length. This has two advantages. Firstly, modules of seats or cargo containers with the same dimensions can be interchanged with ease to enable rapid changes of seating and freight configurations. The other is that the aircraft's basic design can be changed by adding or removing sections of fuselage. This technique of "stretching" enables manufacturers to offer various aircraft designs that closely match the requirements of the airlines.

The airliner is fitted with high-bypass-ratio turbofan engines for high thrust and good economy (see AIRCRAFT ENGINE). This type of engine also has the advantage of low noise levels on takeoff. The engine mountings are designed so that the engines can be easily serviced, maintained or changed for new engines. The engines are fitted with thrust reversers: movable metal cowlings that direct the engine's thrust forward to slow the aircraft on landing. The engine position also allows different types of engines to be fitted, without the need for extensive changes to the airframe (the aircraft's structure).

Fighter aircraft

A typical state-of-the-art, air-to-air combat fighter airplane has a wing with a low aspect ratio. Indeed, the chord at the wing root (the part of the wing nearest the fuselage) is often greater than the distance from fuselage to wing tip. These stubby wings allow for the very rapid rate of roll that is essential for air combat. The wing is swept back relative to the fuselage at an angle of about 45 degrees for flight at up to 1500 mph (2400 km/h).

The vertical stabilizer, which comprises the fin and rudder, is mounted at the tail of the aircraft and controls the angle of the airplane's centerline to the direction of flight. The horizontal stabilizer in a fighter aircraft can be mounted either at the tail or near the cockpit, in which case the configuration is known as a canard.

The horizontal stabilizer controls the pitch and roll of the aircraft. Pitch—the angle of the nose-tail axis relative to the horizontal—is altered by moving the fins on the left and right of the aircraft either up or down at the same time. By moving the two fins in opposite directions, the aircraft can be made to roll (dip one wing or the other). These controls, called elevons, leave the main wing structure free to carry high-lift devices and weapons.

The engines are low-bypass-ratio turbofans, fitted with afterburners (devices used in the exhaust flow of the engine that inject fuel into the hot exhaust gases and burn it to provide extra thrust). Afterburners help to give the aircraft increased power for takeoffs and steep climbs, as well as high-speed flight conditions. The engines are mounted inside the fuselage to keep their mass as close to the center of the aircraft as possible and thereby improve the aircraft's agility. The jet exhaust of some of the latest fighter aircraft can be directed using variable-geometry (movable) nozzles that make them extremely maneuverable.

The underside of the aircraft is fitted with "hard points"—connection points to which extra fuel tanks, missiles, and a whole range of other military equipment can be attached. An in-flight refueling probe enables the aircraft to extend its range by taking fuel from tanker aircraft.

Other types of aircraft

As well as the airliner and fighter aircraft mentioned above, the following are some of the main types of aircraft in use today, each one a result of almost a hundred years of development, and each one perfectly suited to its task.

Short take-off and landing (STOL) aircraft. Short take-off and landing aircraft have engines that are powered by turboprops. This means that the turbine in the jet engine turns a propeller to produce the necessary thrust. They are designed to operate from small regional airstrips and inner-city airports (see PROPELLER; GAS TURBINE; TURBINE).

Military transport aircraft. Giant military transport aircraft, usually used for carrying heavy loads, are turbofan-powered, meaning that they use a compressor fan that is connected to and driven by a turbine that supplies air for combustion. They have high mounted wings to keep their engines clear of the ground, and multi-wheeled landing gear to spread their weight over soft ground.

Business jets. Business jets are like miniature airliners. They tend to have a low fuselage for ease of boarding and the engines are normally mounted on a high rear tail.

Aerobatic airplanes. Special aircraft for aerobatics displays have fantastically strong wing and fuselage structure that can withstand loads greater than 16 times the weight of the aircraft—in any direction. Aerobatic aircraft also often have specially shaped wings to allow them to fly upside down more easily.

Vertical take-off and landing (VTOL) aircraft. Vertical take-off and landing aircraft are fighter planes that can hover in one spot on the thrust of a powerful turbofan engine. They can then accelerate to over 700 mph (1100km/h).

Stealth aircraft. Stealth aircraft use special materials, shapes, and engines to make themselves invisible to radar and infrared detectors.

Amphibious airplanes. Amphibious aircraft have boat-shaped hulls that are capable of taking off and landing as easily from water as from land (see SEAPLANE AND FLYING BOAT).

AIRCRAFT CONTROL SYSTEMS

In early aircraft, the control column (also called the joystick) and rudder bar (a foot-operated rudder control) were physically connected to the flying control surfaces of the airplane by wires or rods. So, for example, a sideways movement of the joystick would cause wires to move over a series of pulleys. The ends of the wires, attached directly to the control surfaces in each wing, would move, causing the airplane to bank.

This McDonnell Douglas AV-8B version Harrier II jump jet is a vertical/short take-off and landing (V/STOL) aircraft. This means it can take off, hover, and land like a helicopter, aided by the flexibility of its jet exhaust nozzles, which are directed horizontally to the rear while in regular flight but vertically downward when landing and taking off in order to create lift. Flown by the U.S. Marine Corps, it is called a jump jet because, when it has a heavy load, it takes a short run to help it to "jump" into the air.

AIRCRAFT MATERIALS

One of the most common materials used in aircraft construction today was in use 70 years ago—aluminum alloy. This is due to aluminum's combination of strength and light weight. In the 1930s, it was mainly used for all-metal stressed-skin construction. Now, advanced aluminum alloys are used in many aircraft parts, including wing spars, ribs, and skins.

Even lighter than aluminum, magnesium alloys form the huge cylindrical casting that is the main structural part of large turbofan engines. Magnesium is also used in seat frames and control panels.

Plastic is often used for aircraft components—interior fittings and insulation, as well as large structural parts. Many modern gliders and microlights are almost exclusively plastic. Various forms of plastic have been used in airplanes for years. Acrylic resin (known by its trade name of Perspex) is used in cockpit and cabin windows. Scratches can be smoothed out of its surface using fine diamond polishing disks (see PLASTICS). The latest aircraft construction materials are composites (see COMPOSITE). One of the oldest materials used in aircraft construction was glass-reinforced plastic (GRP). Still used today, it was first used for radar antennas (see RADAR).

Like GRP in the way that the fibers are set in resin, carbon fiber and aramid fibers (known by the trade name Kevlar) allow designers to tailor the material to a specific job. Two and a half times stronger than steel, carbon fibers can cope with the particular stresses expected on particular components (see FIBERS AND YARNS).

Kevlar is often used in aircraft construction because of its aramid fibers—some of the strongest fibers of any material yet developed.

A CLOSER LOOK

Later, servomotors (hydraulic motors used to drive various types of mechanical systems) were developed for larger aircraft to assist the pilot in moving the airplane's control surfaces—still with a physical link between them and the pilot. Servomotors are similar to the hydraulic motors used in power steering in automobiles. However, the incredibly high speeds at which many aircraft travel today exert such extreme forces on the rudder and ailerons that it has become necessary to develop even more efficient control systems.

A virtual-reality computer design of a joint strike fighter (JSF), developed by Lockheed Martin.

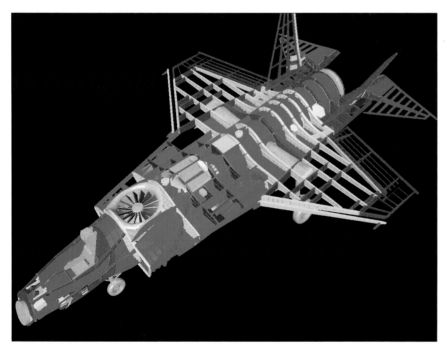

Fly-by-wire technology

The biggest advance in the history of aircraft control systems has been the introduction of fly-by-wire technology. It allows airliners to fly in greater safety, and military aircraft to carry out maneuvers that would once have seemed impossible.

In fly-by-wire systems, there is no mechanical link between the pilot and the control surfaces. Instead, the pilot's controls feed electrical information to a computer. The computer interprets the information and sends instructions to move the appropriate control surface. This system has many advantages. The wires that carry the computer's instructions are not nearly as heavy as the mechanical and hydraulic systems they have replaced. They also take up far less room and require very little maintenance. The computer is linked to sensors that allow it to continually monitor the aircraft's flying condition. If the pilot were to pull back on the stick and close the throttle, thereby putting the aircraft into a stalled condition, the computer would sense the imminent danger and allow the controls to move only within safe limits. Since the fly-by-wire system is better at sensing these limits than any human pilot, it is possible to get maximum performance from the aircraft without fear of reaching dangerous flight conditions.

Fly-by-wire has led to new design possibilities for military aircraft. The most maneuverable aircraft are those that are the most unstable, but they are also the most difficult to fly.

The Sopwith Camel, the World War I (1914–1918) classic aircraft fighter, was highly unstable. This enabled it to change direction very

The Sopwith Camel 2 F.1. fighter plane was designed by Sir Thomas Octave Murdoch (1888–1989) at Sopwith Aviation Company Ltd. Because of its high maneuverability, the Sopwith Camel was used with great success in air battles during World War I; but its inherent instability also caused the deaths of many of its pilots.

quickly, so as to outmaneuver its opponents in a dogfight. But this same characteristic led to the deaths of many Camel pilots—they would lose the battle to control these aircraft. In the ensuing years, makers of fighter planes have been forced to balance maneuverability against stability in a series of compromises.

Fly-by-wire allows inherently unstable airplanes with high levels of maneuverability to be flown with ease. The computer system constantly monitors the airplane's flight condition and makes corrections far more quickly than any human pilot could possibly do. At the same time, the airplane can be made to feel stable and easy to handle for the pilot.

Modern control systems

Thirty years ago, aircraft had individual dials monitoring every aspect of the operation, and switches to control every function. The confusing group of dials and switches cluttered the flight deck (the forward compartment where the pilot sits).

Today's airliner flight deck looks far more streamlined and less complicated. Multifunction display screens provide the information that pilots need at any one time. Other information can be called up on the screen when it is required. Any emergency situation will be brought to the pilot's attention by the onboard computers. These systems, known as glass cockpits because of the display screens, give clear information and lessen the chances of confusion and mistakes by the crew. They have the added advantage of being lighter than previous cockpits.

Military cockpits take these ideas a stage further. A head-up display (HUD) projects information onto a screen in front of the pilot so that it can be seen without the distraction of looking down into the cockpit. The display is arranged so that the pilot can read the information while still focusing on the horizon. Further information is projected onto the inside of the pilot's helmet visor. Called a helmet-mounted symbology system (HMSS), it is always in sight, even when the pilot's head is moving.

The latest development is the voice throttle and stick (VTAS). This system allows the pilot to control basic functions of the airplane by voice command, even allowing for the voice distortion that can be caused by high g (gravity) loads and stress levels that can be expected in combat.

C. UTTLEY

See also: AIRCRAFT CARRIER; AIRPORT AND AIRFIELD; AIR TRAFFIC CONTROL; CONTROL SYSTEMS AND CONTROL THEORY; EJECTION SEAT; FLIGHT, PRINCIPLES OF.

Further reading:

Drezner, J. *Maintaining Future Military Aircraft Design Capability.* Santa Monica, California: Rand, 1992.
Fishbein, S. B. *Flight Management Subsystems.* Westport, Connecticut: Praeger, 1995.

THE FUTURE OF AIRCRAFT

The world's airports are stretched to the limit. With landings every two minutes and restrictions on night operations, there is simply no room for any extra flights. This is one of the main reasons that the world's largest manufacturers of commercial aircraft, Boeing and Airbus, are building "super jumbos" that will carry a thousand passengers. Taking advantage of the latest materials to reduce structural weight, and using the most powerful engines ever made, they will enter airline service early in the 21st century. To keep the aircraft's length within practical limits, these airliners will carry passengers on two levels. They will also be designed with future development in mind, so that subsequent versions can be stretched to meet increasing demand.

In the future, many military aircraft will go into action with no pilot on board. Called UCAVs (unmanned combat aerial vehicles), they will be controlled either from the ground or by built-in computers. Without the weight and space requirement of a pilot and all the associated life-support systems, they will be smaller and more agile. They will also be able to perform maneuvers that create extremely high g (gravity) forces that no human could withstand without injury.

LOOKING TO THE FUTURE

AIRCRAFT ENGINE

Aircraft use internal combustion or jet engines to provide propulsion through the air

The British Spitfire fighter aircraft was manufactured en masse for the Royal Air Force during World War II. These aircraft were powered by the Merlin engine, developed in the late 1920s and early 1930s by British engineering company Rolls-Royce.

CONNECTIONS

● The size of an aircraft **ENGINE** can affect the shape of the aircraft.

● Ultralight aircraft are a type of **GLIDER** that run on small, low-powered **INTERNAL COMBUSTION ENGINES**.

All early aircraft were powered by internal combustion piston engines. These share many of the design characteristics of the standard gasoline engine found in automobiles, consisting of a piston moving up and down by the expansion of burning gases inside a cylinder. Usually a number of pistons inside separate cylinders are used to drive a single rotating crankshaft inside a crankcase. The crankshaft is traditionally used to rotate the aircraft's propellers. The jet engine, introduced around 1940, offered greater power and was much lighter than any piston engine. Piston engines are still used in some small aircraft, but gas turbine engines have now replaced them in all larger aircraft.

The first aircraft engines

The first person to build a successfully powered aircraft was French aeronautical engineer Henri Giffard (1825–1882). In 1852, he flew a hydrogen-filled airship 17 miles (27 km) from Paris to Trappes, France. Power for this flight was provided by a small steam engine driving a large propeller at 110 revolutions per minute. This was sufficient to carry the craft at a speed of 6 mph (10 km/h). The engine was slung well away from the bag filled with hydrogen: Giffard was well aware of the potential danger of bringing a hot engine too close to highly explosive gas (see BALLOON AND AIRSHIP).

Many people have suggested that the success of U.S. aeronautical engineers and brothers Orville (1871–1948) and Wilbur Wright (1867–1912) was largely due to the engine that powered their *Flyer* aircraft—the first successful airplane. However, only a good combination of aircraft and engine design could realize this success. The brothers were forced into designing and building their own engine because no suitable alternatives were available. Their four-cylinder, liquid-cooled, internal combustion engine was built for lightness and simplicity of operation, since once in the air, there would be no time to regulate engine controls. Aluminum alloy was used in its construction (see INTERNAL COMBUSTION ENGINE).

By the time of World War I (1914–1918), there were two main aircraft engine designs. One was the in-line, liquid-cooled engine that began with the Wright brothers and would reach its peak in popularity thirty years later. In-line engines have their cylinders arranged in a line either above or below the crankcase. A variation is the V-type configuration, which had its cylinders arranged in two banks to form a V shape. The alternative to these engines was the rotary engine.

The rotary engine

One of the great problems with early aircraft engines was in keeping them cool. Engines need to operate at a specific temperature or their internal components may be damaged. To cool engines, a liquid is passed through and around the cylinders. However, the problem with using liquid-cooling systems is that they increase the weight of the engine, and with aircraft design, weight should always be minimized. The rotary engine solved this by having the whole engine revolve with the propeller. The cylinders of the rotary engine were arranged radially around the crankcase. The crankshaft was attached to the airplane, while the rest of the engine including the cylinders was allowed to spin. The propeller was attached to the rotating crankcase, rather than to the stationary crankshaft. This meant that even on the ground, cooling air could flow around the cylinders. The rotary engine was also light and reliable, making it the dominant design of World War I.

Despite its success, there were inherent problems with the rotary engine design, and it was eventually replaced by the radial engine. The spinning design of the rotary engine produced strong gyroscopic forces that affected the handling of any airplane it was fitted to (see GYROSCOPE).

CORE FACTS

■ All early aircraft were powered by internal combustion piston engines that drove propellers.

■ In-line engines were liquid-cooled engines that had a number of cylinders arranged in a line down the crankcase.

■ Rotary engines were designed to have their cylinders arranged radially around the crankcase. Air-cooling was assisted by having the whole engine rotate around a stationary crankshaft.

■ Jet engines have now replaced piston engines in all large aircraft.

Radial, in-line, and V-type engines

After World War I, engine development continued to be split between liquid and air-cooled engine designs, although the air-cooled radial engine had taken the place of the rotary engine. The radial engine shared the basic layout of the rotary engine, with the cylinders arranged radially around the crankcase. However, in the radial engine, the crankcase and cylinders remain stationary and the propeller is turned by the rotating crankshaft. Although the cylinders of the radial engine do not spin, their arrangement around the crankcase allows more cooling air to pass over them than if they were lined up behind one another, as they are in V-type and in-line engines.

Radial, in-line, and V-type engines each had their advantages. The radial engine was generally lighter and more reliable, while the in-line and V-type engines offered aerodynamic advantages due to their smaller frontal area. The success of V-type engines such as the Curtiss D12 in the 1920s spurred Rolls-Royce to develop a line of V-12, liquid-cooled engines that would ultimately lead to the Merlin engine that powered such famous aircraft as the Spitfire and Mustang. By the 1930s, the V-type Rolls-Royce *R* engine developed an astonishing 2350 horsepower (1750 kW).

Jet engines

The end of World War II (1939–1945) saw the arrival of a new type of engine that would radically alter the design of airplanes and allow previously unheard of improvements in performance. This was the jet engine. Unlike previous piston engines, jet engines do not need to power a propeller. Instead they use a gas turbine to produce a high-speed jet of gas that provides thrust as it is ejected from the rear of the engine. A jet engine works by taking in air at an inlet, compressing it, heating it with burning fuel, and then releasing it at high speed through a discharge nozzle. Jet engines are simpler, lighter, more powerful, and more reliable than piston engines because they only have rotating components.

German aviation designer Hans von Ohain (1911–) and British inventor and aviator Frank Whittle (1907–) each developed successful jet engine designs. But in both countries, it was the established aero-engine manufacturers who took over the development of this new technology. After the war, engine manufacturer Rolls-Royce helped to start the jet engine industry, first in the United States and later in the Soviet Union. Their early jet engines were inspired by Whittle's design.

The relatively low power and slow response of early jet engines led some designers to consider the rocket engine as an alternative, particularly for fighter aircraft. (Rocket engines burn fuel using an oxidant from an onboard tank; jets use air.) A few mixed-power aircraft, with rocket and jet engines, were built and tested. But advances in jet engine design soon rendered them unnecessary and rockets were used only to boost takeoff performance.

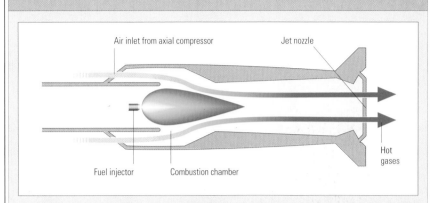
Types of jet engines

Rapid developments were made to jet engines that increased their performance by using some of the power of the expanding combustion mixture to propel air backward and drive the aircraft forward. In turboprop engines, the turbine that harnesses the power of the burning gases at the exit of the combustion chamber drives both the compressor for the intake air and a propeller. In this case, around 90 percent of the forward thrust is provided by the propeller. Turboprops are more efficient than simple jets at airspeeds under 400 mph (640 km/h).

Turbofans used huge fans in place of the propeller at the front of the engine. The fans—visible at the front of commercial aircraft turbofans—provide a stream of low-pressure air, most of which bypasses the combustion chamber and mixes with the hot gases at the rear of the engine. The latest turbofan engines for airlines are a hundred times more powerful than the first jet engines.

Helicopter gas turbine engines were introduced in the 1940s and 1950s. They are related to turboprops, but use the power provided by the turbine to drive the rotor of the helicopter, rather than the turboprop propeller.

C. UTTLEY

See also: AIRCRAFT DESIGN AND CONSTRUCTION; FLIGHT, HISTORY OF; FLIGHT, PRINCIPLES OF; FUELS AND PROPELLANTS; SEAPLANE AND FLYING BOAT.

Further reading:
Kerrebrock, J. *Aircraft Engines and Gas Turbines*. Cambridge, Massachusetts: MIT Press, 1992.

AIRPORT AND AIRFIELD

Airports are the busiest and most important centers of transportation throughout the world

This diagram of an airport shows the ring-shaped passenger terminals that can be seen in newly designed airports such as the Los Angeles and Houston international airports. Passengers park in the middle of the ring, enter the terminal at the gate marked for their flight, and walk only a short distance to the airplane. The clear zones (colored blue) at the ends of the runways give space for the planes to rise or descend during takeoff and landing.

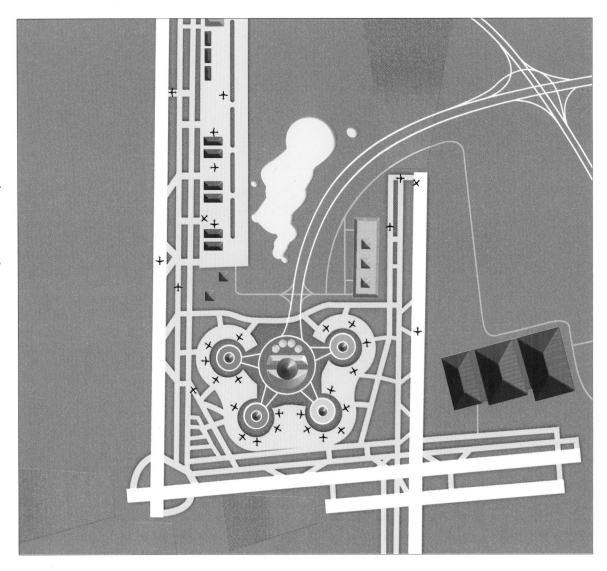

CONNECTIONS

● Most major international airports have sophisticated **SECURITY EQUIPMENT** to detect the illegal presence of **FIREARMS** and **EXPLOSIVES**.

● **ESCALATORS AND MOVING WALKWAYS** are vital in airports to speed up the movement of passengers and heavy luggage.

Modern airports involve a considerable range of technology concentrated in one place, and require careful design and planning. Today, the volume of transportation by air rivals that of any other mode. For long-distance movement of business and leisure passengers, air travel far exceeds that of travel by land and sea. According to the International Civil Aviation Organization, some 40,000 civilian airports are now in operation worldwide. The terminal facilities that safely and efficiently allow the movement of this quantity of people and freight have to be far larger than those of any other kind of transportation system. They need space to accommodate long runways and the associated aircraft taxiways (the runways that lead into the main takeoff runways), vast passenger terminal buildings, extensive parking lots, cargo storage facilities, and buildings for aircraft service and maintenance. They also need garage space for numerous administrative vehicles such as aircraft tugs, catering and supply trucks, sanitation vehicles, passenger buses, aircraft fuel tankers, fire engines, and boarding stairway vehicles.

Historical development

In the early days of civil aviation, any reasonably level grass field was suitable for the landing and taking off of the airplanes of the time. Some of the earliest passenger aircraft were modified from the large bombers of World War I (1914–1918).

The first airports were characterized by their tin-roofed administrative buildings and a wind-sock pole. The wind sock gave a visible indication of wind strength and direction (landing and takeoff direction is determined by the direction of the wind). With the development of radio communication between air

CORE FACTS

■ Airports need a vast amount of space to accommodate passenger terminals, airplane hangars, runways, parking facilities, shops, and other services.

■ Airport runways must be at least 200 ft (60 m) wide and at least 14,000 ft (4,300 m) long so that they can safely handle all sizes of aircraft.

and ground personnel, towers were built to support radio antennas and provide ground personnel with a better view of approaching aircraft.

The first transatlantic flight by Charles Lindbergh (1902–1974) in 1927 was important in making the public aware of the real possibility of rapid, long-distance transport by air and was a major factor in establishing the airplane as a viable means of transportation. Transcontinental routes were set up in the early 1930s, and by the end of that decade, coast-to-coast air travel, with many stops for refueling and meals, had become routine. As aircraft increased in size and weight, and as the demands for reliability in schedules increased, permanent weatherproof paved runways became essential. By the end of the 1930s, paved runways were commonplace in the United States; they were slower to develop in Europe.

During World War II (1939–1945), U.S. military airfields were set up in many parts of the world, and after the war many of these were converted to civil airports. As air travel continued to grow and successive generations of new and ever larger airplanes were designed and built, a corresponding development in airport facilities became necessary.

Airport design and layout

The location of airports always involves a compromise between several factors. Easy access to main towns suggests that they should be located close to populated areas. However, noise and ecological considerations suggest otherwise, and there is increasing opposition from residents when new airports are being planned near their homes. Flat ground is necessary but is not always available in otherwise suitable locations. Airports should be close to main highways but, ideally, at least 10 miles (16 km) from mountains or other major obstructions for safety reasons. Prevailing winds (winds that blow persistently in a particular direction) must also be considered, since they may rule out certain runway orientations and make otherwise ideal sites unsuitable.

Airports vary in design and layout depending on their size and on the number and orientation of the runways. Although the aim is to make the layout as simple as possible, many factors have to be considered. For example, aircraft land and take off into the wind, so parallel runways are preferred, since they can allow simultaneous landing or takeoff by several aircraft (see FLIGHT, PRINCIPLES OF). Changing wind conditions, however, often require that runways be oriented in more than one direction. Another factor in the design of the airport is the weight of the aircraft. Fully loaded, wide-bodied jumbo jets are very heavy and require large, strong runways. These runways are constructed from slabs of concrete sometimes more than 2 ft thick, some 200 ft (60 m) wide, and at least 14,000 ft (4300 m) long. In addition, housing such large aircraft in maintenance hangars requires very large buildings.

Every airport must have an up-to-date air traffic control tower that is equipped with radio transmitters and receivers, air-traffic-control equipment and personnel, and computer systems. Without these, the enormously complex task of keeping track of and maintaining safe distances between arriving and departing aircraft, and issuing instructions for landing and takeoff, would be impossible.

Passenger terminal design

Passenger terminals must have good access to parking lots and highways, as well as direct connections to rail and other commuter transportation systems. They must be carefully designed to allow optimum flow of passengers from the parking lot to the various airline ticket counters and reception desks. In addition, they must provide temporary seating accommodation for large numbers of passengers waiting for delayed flights. A typical international airport terminal also has extensive baggage-moving and retrieval facilities, baggage cart areas, customs facilities, restaurants, shopping malls, banks, and other services.

The larger the airport, the greater the proportion of the cost that must be devoted to the terminal. This may amount to 70 percent of the total cost. With the development of ever larger aircraft and greatly increased numbers of passengers, many older and smaller terminals have become inadequate and have had to be replaced or extended. One important factor determining their design is the need to provide immediate access to a large number of aircraft. Larger airports adopt a linear design, which has numbered gates at which passengers can board aircraft either directly through short tunnels or by a short walk across the apron (tarmac surface). This design, however, requires a very long building with long walking distances for passengers trying to reach their correct gate. Many airports have moving walkways to speed up movement of passengers and heavy luggage (see ESCALATOR AND MOVING WALKWAY). More compact airport designs use buses to carry passengers to the aircraft and some terminals are shaped like the spokes of a wheel, with gates on both sides of each spoke.

Cargo is being loaded from cargo pallets onto an American Airlines Boeing 707 jet at John F. Kennedy Airport in New York. The plane has been modified from an airliner to a cargo plane by removing passenger seats, blacking out windows, and adding a large cargo door.

O'HARE INTERNATIONAL AIRPORT, CHICAGO

An elegant modern concourse at Chicago's O'Hare International Airport

O'Hare International Airport is the busiest airport in the world, and one of the best designed. At least 180,000 travelers pass through O'Hare every day. In 1997, it handled over 70 million passengers. Fifty passenger, commuter, and cargo airlines use the airport. To handle this amount of traffic, O'Hare has four terminal buildings and total facilities covering almost 7700 acres (3120 hectares) of land. There are 162 aircraft gates. The international terminal (Terminal Five), opened in 1993, is a 100-acre (40-hectare) facility three times the size of the previous terminal. There are 68 U.S. Customs booths to process 4000 entering passengers an hour. It has a fully automated baggage-handling system and a signage system that greets passengers in any of 17 languages.

A CLOSER LOOK

In spite of these varied and sometimes conflicting requirements, much imagination and creative design has been put into the aesthetics of airport terminals, and some award-winning artistic designs have resulted, such as the TWA (Trans World Airlines) terminal at John F. Kennedy Airport in New York. This terminal symbolizes flight, with its two winglike roof sections.

Airport security

Air transportation terrorism includes the hijacking of aircraft and explosions (or the threat of explosions) on aircraft. Due to this terrorism, security systems at major international airports continue to improve. Countries such as Israel have long been in the forefront of security technology. An essential facility at all airports today is security inspection, which includes X-ray screening to detect metal (for firearms) and explosives. High-resolution television monitors show up even tiny metal items, and detection devices can zoom in on baggage contents. Airlines vary in the amount and intensity of their questioning of passengers on flight check-in, and body searches and baggage searches are not uncom-

mon at many international airports, such as those in the United States and at London's Heathrow and Gatwick Airports.

Cargo facilities

Because air shipment is much more expensive than surface freight for the same route, air freight tends to be reserved for high-value items or urgent shipments. Consequently, the volume is small—even the largest airports will usually handle no more than about a million tons (907,000 tonnes) per year—but the economic value of this freight is enormous. Much of it must be moved immediately, and some is perishable, so delays are unacceptable. Nearly all bulk cargo is carried in standard containers, and all large airports are equipped with container-handling machinery (see MECHANICAL HANDLING). Door-to-door courier services that specialize in overnight express deliveries, for which high rates are charged, also carry an increasing volume of individual packages. This cargo is handled separately from the general freight and is cleared as rapidly as possible.

Navigational aids and lighting

Safety in the congested airspace above and around an airport is the responsibility of the air traffic controllers (see AIR TRAFFIC CONTROL). Safety during landing depends on pilot skill and experience, supplemented by visual clues from painted markings in the runway, and the instrument landing system (ILS). This is based on a narrow radio signal beam directed along the center line of the runway and at an upward angle of three degrees to the horizontal. An approaching aircraft picks up this beam up to 15 miles (24 km) away from the runway and is informed, on cockpit instruments, of any deviation to either side of the correct line of approach and of any inaccuracy in the slope of its descent.

Besides ILS, the pilot has direct visual information from approach lighting systems. These have two components: a line of high-brightness white lights down the center of the runway that marks the correct line of approach, and a colored lighting system that shows the correct angle of descent. If the aircraft is at or above the correct angle of descent, the lights show white; if below, they show red. In addition to these directional systems, the runway edges are indicated by lights. The usable end of the runway is marked by a line of red lights. Taxiway edges are shown by blue lights, their centers by green lights.

R. YOUNGSON

See also: AIRCRAFT DESIGN AND CONSTRUCTION; AIRCRAFT ENGINE; MICROPHONE AND LOUDSPEAKER.

Further reading:

Blow, C. J. *Airport Terminals*. Boston, Massachusetts; Oxford, England: Butterworth-Heinemann, 1996.
Doganis, R. *The Airport Business*. London; New York: Routledge, 1992.
Wells, A. T. *Commuter Airlines*. Malabar, Florida: Krieger, 1996.

AIR TRAFFIC CONTROL

Air traffic control is the personnel and equipment that guide aircraft through their journeys, from takeoff to landing

Air travel to any destination in the world is safer, on average, than driving a car to the local grocery store, thanks to the worldwide air traffic control system. Air traffic over each country is managed by a system of rules, people, and equipment, following the air safety standards of the International Civil Aviation Organization of the United Nations. Using these safety standards, the job of air traffic controllers is to keep aircraft from colliding with each other, with obstacles, or with the ground for safe takeoffs, flights, approaches, and landings.

Airspace

Just as roadways have become more and more crowded over time, routes for air travel have also become much busier, while space is becoming more limited. The use of airspace is governed by flight rules that require aircraft to keep minimum distances from each other. These rules define the carrying capacity of airspace much the way traffic lanes divide and limit the number of cars on a road. The air traffic controllers' job is to keep aircraft safe within the airspace around their position.

Air traffic control equipment

As air traffic has increased since passenger airlines began operating in the 1920s, the equipment available to air traffic controllers and pilots to avoid collisions and bad weather has become more and more sophisticated. To keep all aircraft positions coordinated, air traffic controllers use microwave instruments, computers, radio communication, and radar. During takeoff and landing, the aircraft is in constant communication with the air traffic control tower, which uses increasingly complex electronic equipment around the airport. This is why airline passengers are requested not to use personal stereos, mobile phones, or laptop computers at these crucial locations, since the cumulative signals from these devices interfere with vital communications.

In addition to these airport navigational aids, airliners—and, increasingly, other aircraft—carry some form of traffic alert and collision avoidance system (TCAS). The TCAS technology communicates the position of the plane and alerts the pilot to the presence of nearby aircraft. In the near future, global

positioning systems using satellites orbiting Earth will further improve the ability of pilots to know exactly where they are.

How it all works

Every stage of an aircraft's journey is recorded by the air traffic control system, from the initial flight plan to the aircraft's arrival at its final destination.

Planning the flight. First, the pilot or airline must file a flight plan with the authorities that provide air traffic control services in the areas that will be crossed. A flight plan includes aircraft and pilot identification, radio call information, airspeed, cruising altitude, origin and destination airports, planned departure and arrival time, planned route, amount of fuel, types of instruments, and the number of people on board. The flight plan is kept on file to inform the air traffic controllers of all aircraft movements.

Takeoff. When it is time to take off, the pilot comes under the direction of the airport. Most busy airports have air traffic control towers where specially trained personnel use various navigation aids to direct aircraft. From their glassed-in vantage points atop these towers, air traffic controllers direct aircraft, based on weather and traffic conditions. They communicate with pilots by radio and use airport surveillance radar to watch all aircraft within about 50 miles (80 km) of the airport. Watching air traffic on their workstation screens, they assign the safest route for pilots to follow on leaving the airport.

CORE FACTS

- International air traffic control standards govern aircraft takeoff, flight, and landing procedures.
- Airport surveillance radar shows air traffic controllers the position of aircraft within 50 miles of the airport.
- In the United States, air-route traffic control centers monitor aircraft flying between airports under instrument flight rules.

CONNECTIONS

- **ACCIDENTS AND DISASTERS** in the air are prevented by the worldwide air traffic control system's use of **RADAR, COMPUTERS,** and **RADIO RECEIVERS.**

- Radio **NAVIGATION** systems send signals to pilots during the flight, informing them of their aircraft's location and direction.

Inside the glassed-in control tower at O'Hare International Airport in Chicago, air traffic controllers check their computer workstations for aircraft locations and other important information needed to guide aircraft to safe takeoffs and landings.

During periods of poor visibility or heavy traffic, air traffic controllers use only instruments to locate incoming aircraft and guide departing aircraft safely away. Their workstation display, called a plan view, shows a map of the airport with radar information superimposed above it. Quick actions are required to avoid problems when new aircraft appear on the screens or when unexpected weather develops.

In flight. After takeoff, a system of flight rules governs the way an aircraft must fly. When the pilot's visibility is not obstructed by clouds, visual flight rules apply. These are specific rules for the distance that must be maintained above, below, and horizontally from other aircraft and obstacles. The pilot looks for and talks via radio to nearby aircraft and maneuvers to avoid collisions. If minimum visibility is unavailable, the pilot uses instrument flight rules.

To fly under instrument flight rules, pilots must have specific training and carry special instruments on the aircraft. Once aircraft leave the airport's control area, a system of radio navigation stations sends pilots signals that tell them the location and direction of the plane from each station. Pilots flying in or above clouds use a map of routes between these radio navigation stations. Over water, long-range navigational (LORAN) systems send radio signals from maritime stations to help planes navigate. The LORAN system uses radio signals from two or more pairs of ground stations to establish aircraft position at any one time. In the United States, pilots flying under instrument flight rules are monitored by air-route traffic control centers. Using up to seven long-range radar detectors, 20 communication sites, and 150 air traffic controllers, a center might oversee 100,000 sq miles (259,000 km^2).

Landing. Landing safely would be difficult without air traffic control at airports. Poor visibility and busy runways can be overcome by using the electronic instrument landing system (ILS), adopted by the International Civil Aviation Organization in 1949. In this system, a device in the aircraft detects a sloping radio beam from transmitters along the runway. The beam shows pilots the approach path, regardless of weather. The microwave landing system (MLS) is similar to ILS but uses higher frequencies, which are less sensitive to interference. MLS has replaced the ILS at the busiest airports. The original landing guidance system—runway and aircraft lighting—is still used worldwide.

P. WEIS-TAYLOR

STACKING

"Stacking" is a vital tool used by air traffic controllers worldwide—one that is responsible for preventing aircraft from colliding with each other on landing at some of the world's busiest airports, such as London's Heathrow, New York's John F. Kennedy, and Chicago's O'Hare international airports.

Changing factors, such as weather conditions and wind speed, make it impossible for the exact distance and time of an aircraft's flight to be known beforehand. Therefore, despite attempts to regulate flight arrivals so as not to coincide with each other on the same runway, many aircraft approach the airport airspace at the same time. Because pilots are often unable to see other aircraft and are traveling at different speeds, it is the air traffic controllers' job to keep them at a safe distance from each other. To do this, they direct the aircraft into a stack, one above the other, with 1000 ft (300 m) between them, circling in an oval pattern. As the aircraft lowest in the stack heads toward the runway, each plane above is told to descend to the next level until each, in turn, is at the bottom of the stack and ready to land.

A CLOSER LOOK

See also: AIRPORT AND AIRFIELD.

Further reading:
Turner, J. E. *Air Traffic Controller.* New York: Prentice Hall, 1994.

ALLOY

An alloy is a metallic substance that is composed of two or more elements

The properties of a pure metal can be modified, and often improved, by combining the pure metal with other elements. The materials that result from such combinations are also metallic and are known as alloys. In the majority of cases, the added elements are also metals, but this is not always the case. Steel, for example, is an alloy of iron that includes carbon.

If two metals are mixed, the resulting alloy often has properties superior to those of the component elements. For example, both pure copper and pure silver are very soft. However, the alloy sterling silver (composed of 92.5 percent silver and 7.5 percent copper), is harder than either of the component metals and is used in tableware, jewelry, and coins.

There are thousands of alloys with different chemical compositions. They are divided into two groups: ferrous alloys and nonferrous alloys. Ferrous alloys are those that contain iron, while nonferrous alloys do not. Steel and cast iron are two important examples of ferrous alloys (see IRON AND STEEL PRODUCTION). Important examples of nonferrous alloys include those based on copper, aluminum, magnesium, and titanium.

The history of the use of alloys

Bronze is the oldest alloy; it is likely that it was first produced in the Middle East around 3000 B.C.E. Since it is stronger than either copper or tin (its components), it became widely used in weapons and tools, leading to an era known as the Bronze Age. Brass, an alloy of copper with zinc, was first made in Egypt around 30 B.C.E. and was soon taken up by the Romans, who used it for currency.

Although steel, the most widely used alloy today, was known in India and in China at least 2000 years ago, it was not until the 19th century that its large-scale production became commonplace.

Other alloys had to wait for their component elements to become available. Aluminum is difficult to extract, requiring the use of electrical power (see ELECTROLYSIS), and did not become widely available until the early 20th century. Consequently, alloys of aluminum were not available until that time.

Dental amalgam, used to fill decayed teeth, is an alloy of silver, tin, copper, zinc, and mercury.

In 1950, the results of a U.S. Air Force study showed that the good strength-to-weight ratio of titanium alloys could play a vital role in the construction of aircraft engines. This led to the development of the titanium industry.

How alloys are made

Most alloys can be manufactured by melting a mixture of the component metals, then allowing the resulting mixture to cool and solidify. However, this technique does not work well if the melting and boiling points of the components are incompatible. Brass, for instance, is made of copper, which has a melting point of 1982°F (1083°C), and zinc, which has a melting point of 788°F (420°C) and a boiling point of 1665°F (907°C). If a mixture of the two metals is heated, the zinc starts to boil long before the copper has even melted. To make brass, therefore, copper is first melted, solid zinc is added to it, and the mixture is then cooled. An excess of zinc has to be added, because some boils off before it can dissolve in the molten copper.

Some alloys cannot be made from their liquid components because the components of the liquid mixture would separate before solidifying. In such cases, the alloy must be made by physically mixing the powdered components of the alloy, then heating and squeezing the mixture to allow the atoms of the components to intermingle without melting (see the diagram on page 64).

CORE FACTS

- Alloys are metallic materials that are obtained by mixing a metal with one or more other elements, which may or may not be metals themselves.
- Properties of alloys can be very different from those of the component metals.
- Structures and properties of alloys depend on their composition.
- Steel is the most widely used alloy.
- Heat treatment can improve the properties of alloys.

CONNECTIONS

● Certain types of alloys are useful for **AIRCRAFT ENGINES** and **GAS TURBINES** because of their heat resistance.

● Other alloys are used to build **RACE CARS** and other types of **AUTOMOBILES** because of their combination of strength and lightness.

ALLOYS COMPARED TO PURE METALS—STRENGTH FROM DIVERSITY

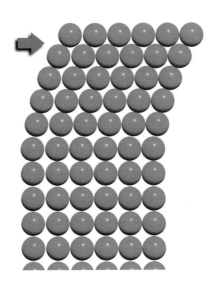

Pure metals are relatively soft, since their crystal structures are easily deformed.

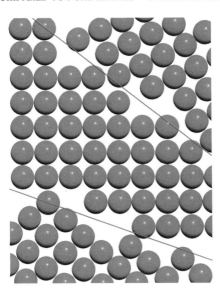

Dislocations (indicated by the lines) are sources of brittleness in metals.

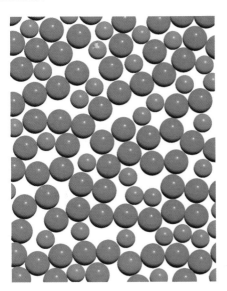

The different sizes of atoms in alloys reduce softness and brittleness.

Physical structure of alloys

The properties of any material come from its internal structure—that is, the way its atoms are arranged. The internal structure of an alloy, then, depends on the types of components that the alloy contains, its composition, how rapidly it was cooled from the liquid state, and the nature of any heat treatment.

In the liquid state, most metals are completely miscible—they mix with one another in any proportion. Some metals are also miscible with each other in the solid state and are said to form a solid solution. In the case of a solid solution, the metal that is present in the larger quantity is considered to be the solvent, and the solute is the metal that is present in the smaller quantity. This terminology mirrors the terms used for a liquid solution, such as salt (the solute) in water (the solvent). Alloys form two types of solid solutions: substitutional and interstitial. Two or more metals can form intermetallic compounds, and metals with low solubility in each other can form multiphase alloys.

Substitutional solid solutions. When the solute and solvent atoms are of a similar size, the solute atoms can fit into the spaces normally occupied by atoms of the solvent metal without too great a distortion of structure. This is called a substitutional solid solution—the solute atoms directly substitute solvent atoms. Nickel and copper form a substitutional solid solution in all their alloy compositions, because both types of atoms are very similar in size.

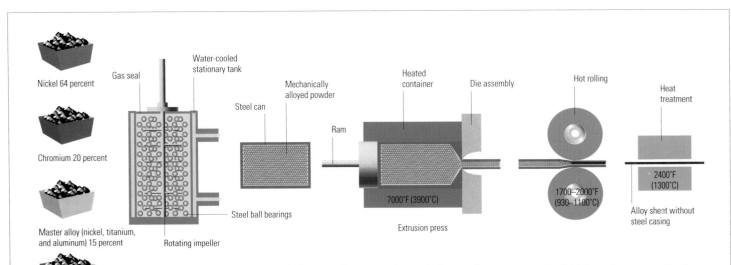

Nickel 64 percent

Chromium 20 percent

Master alloy (nickel, titanium, and aluminum) 15 percent

Yttrium oxide 1 percent

Gas seal

Water-cooled stationary tank

Steel can

Mechanically alloyed powder

Ram

Heated container

Die assembly

Hot rolling

Heat treatment

Rotating impeller

Steel ball bearings

7000°F (3900°C)

Extrusion press

1700–2000°F (930–1100°C)

2400°F (1300°C)

Alloy sheet without steel casing

Mechanical alloying may be used when an alloy cannot be made from molten components. A high-performance alloy for gas turbine blades is made by first blending the powdered ingredients in a ball mill, in which steel ball bearings grind the components together. The mixture is sealed in a steel can to protect it from contamination. The canned powder is extruded while hot and then hot rolled without melting to form the alloy. The steel casing is removed before the final heat treatment.

Interstitial solutions. If the solute atoms are much smaller than the solvent atoms, they can slip into the gaps that occur within the ordered array of solvent atoms. This is known as an interstitial solid solution (an interstice is a small gap or crevice). Interstitial solid solutions usually can only form with up to approximately 10 percent of solute. Beyond this percentage, the solute atoms cannot fit into the interstices without breaking up the metal structure and destroying the metallic nature of the alloy.

Intermetallic compounds. The components of an alloy may react together to form an intermetallic compound. One example is cementite, a compound between iron and carbon with the formula Fe_3C. This forms in steel alloys that contain at least 6.7 percent carbon, when regions of cementite form that are very different in properties from the surrounding steel. Like many other intermetallic compounds, cementite is very hard and brittle. When regions of cementite form in a steel, it hardens the material but makes it more brittle.

Multiphase alloys. Only a minority of alloys form solid solutions. Most metals have only a limited solubility in each other when solid and so do not mix completely. Their alloys tend to be a bit like fruit cake, with areas of different compositions, or phases. A phase is defined as a continuous state of matter—such as a solid, liquid, gas, or solution. If the metals were completely insoluble in one another, each phase would consist of pure metal. If, as is more common, there is some solubility, the phases are different solid solutions—all containing some of each component. In tin-lead alloys, for example, two phases are found. One of them (the alpha phase) is lead with 5 percent tin dissolved in it. The other (the beta phase) is tin containing 1 percent lead.

Physical properties

It is the distortion caused by the presence of two types of atoms that makes alloys stronger and harder than pure metals. In a pure metal crystal, the atoms are lined up in straight rows that form flat, two-dimensional arrays (arrangements), just as marbles do when tightly packed together on a flat tray. Another plane (layer) of atoms fits easily into the gaps of the first, and these planes stack up on top of one another in a regular, crystalline structure (see the box on page 64). If a sideways force is applied to the top layer, it can easily slide over the layer below. This is what happens when a sample of pure metal is subjected to a force. The layers of atoms slide over each other and the metal becomes deformed.

The property of being readily deformed by a stretching force is called ductility. In the case of copper, the ductile nature of the pure metal allows it to be drawn out into fine wire without breaking. In many cases, however, the ease of deformation of a pure metal makes it too soft for many uses. This is when the strengthening effect of a second type of atom becomes useful. If a few marbles of a different size are slipped into the neat layers of the earlier example, it becomes much more difficult for one layer to slip over the other, since the rogue marbles block the slippage. This is the situation with an alloy: the two different types of atoms resist the deforming forces and the alloy becomes harder. In steel, for instance, the addition of just 0.1 percent carbon increases the strength of iron by a factor of ten.

There is another way in which a pure metal can be strengthened by the alloying. When a pure metal solidifies, its atoms do not normally have time to order themselves into a perfect crystal. Instead, the metal solidifies as small areas of ordered atoms with

This clean room is used to exclude contamination in the preparation of high-performance alloys of titanium and specialist steels. Even the slightest trace of contamination is capable of changing the properties of the alloy.

dislocations (imperfect joins) between them. The spacing between atoms along these joins is not ideal for bonding to occur, and the joins act like weak points. If a deforming force is applied, the metal can break open along these boundaries, and as the rupture spreads into the body of the metal, the sample cracks open. The presence of a second type of atom can reduce the formation of crystalline regions, and since there are fewer dislocations, there are fewer paths of weakness to encourage cracking. Hence, the alloy is less brittle than the pure metal.

Heat treatment

Various forms of heat treatment can improve the properties of an alloy still further (see METALWORKING). If an alloy that can form an intermetallic compound is heated to a high temperature and then cooled very rapidly, it forms a supersaturated solid solution. That is, the intermetallic compound stays uniformly dispersed at a higher concentration than is soluble at the lower temperature. If the alloy is then heated again to a lower temperature than before and cooled again, the intermetallic compound forms into a precipitate of very fine crystals that are dispersed throughout the whole alloy structure. In this form, the compound forms a very effective barrier to slip and the movement of dislocations, the structural defects that can lead to crack formation. The whole process is known as precipitation hardening. It is widely used in magnesium, copper, and aluminum alloys as well as in some steels.

Quenching (rapid cooling) of steel leads to the precipitation of martensite—a hard and brittle form of carbon-in-iron solution. Martensitic stainless steels are used to make surgical instruments, cutlery, and jet engine parts. Further heat treatments can increase the ductility of martensitic steels.

The strength and hardness of alloys can be increased by rolling and hammering. This phenomenon, known as work hardening, occurs because the application of stresses causes the dislocations present in the metal to become randomized so that areas with large concentrations of dislocations, which would cause weak spots, are avoided.

Other properties

A further important advantage of alloying is corrosion resistance. Most metals are chemically reactive and are prone to attack by water, oxygen, and other materials in the atmosphere (see CORROSION). Alloying steel with 11 percent or more chromium makes stainless steel, which has good resistance to corrosion. Similarly, 10–15 percent chromium and 3–5 percent aluminum are commonly added to nickel- and cobalt-based alloys for use in heat-resistant components for jet engines, where corrosion could be catastrophic. Chromium and aluminum improve corrosion resistance by forming a stable film of their oxides (compounds with oxygen) on the surface of the alloy. This resists further attack by oxygen and protects the underlying metal from corrosion.

S. ALDRIDGE

See also: COMPOSITE; IRON AND STEEL PRODUCTION; METALS; NONFERROUS METAL.

Further Reading:
Amato, I. *Stuff: The Material the World Is Made Of.* New York: Basic Books, 1997.

SOME IMPORTANT ALLOYS: THEIR COMPOSITIONS AND USES

Alloy	Composition	Uses
Tool steel	95.40 percent iron 0.85 percent carbon 3.75 percent chromium	Drills, saws, lathes
Stainless steel (martensitic)	80.55 percent iron 0.7 percent carbon 17.0 percent chromium 0.75 percent molybdenum 1.0 percent manganese	Cutlery, bearings, surgical tools
Cartridge brass	70 percent copper 30 percent zinc	Wires, pipes, tubes, lamp fixtures, ammunition components
Pewter	90 percent tin 0–10 percent lead, copper, antimony, or bismuth	Tableware, drinking vessels
Invar	63.8 percent iron 36.0 percent nickel 0.2 percent carbon	Scientific measuring instruments

AMBULANCE AND EMERGENCY MEDICAL TREATMENT

Ambulances are vehicles designed to transport sick and injured people to hospitals as quickly as possible

In the time of the Roman emperor Julius Caesar (100–44 B.C.E.), organized transportation and care of the sick and injured were already part of the military scene. But back on the home front, emergency systems were historically slower to develop. Without centralized hospitals where advanced medical techniques could be available, there was little incentive to move a sick or injured person.

In the United States, it wasn't until the Civil War (1861–1865) that ambulance wagons came into use. In the early 20th century, these evolved into motorized vehicles. But early ambulances offered very little besides basic transportation. In fact, since the vehicles required had to be the right size to transport a person lying down, they were often supplied by funeral homes.

The modern emergency medical service (EMS) developed in response to the realization that advanced life-support techniques used in hospitals would be even more advantageous if they could be applied to the patient earlier. Laws were enacted to establish an EMS network with over 300 regional entities in the United States. Training standards were set up for professionals and volunteers, and communications systems linked ambulance services with hospitals, police stations, and firehouses. Today, EMS systems stand ready 24 hours a day to assist the tens of millions of people requiring emergency medical care each year.

First aid

First aid is the immediate care provided to a sick or injured person. In cases of serious illness or trauma (injury), obtaining professional medical assistance is one of the primary procedures of first aid. Others are to attend to life-threatening conditions; to minimize further injury and complications, including infection; and to make the patient as comfortable as possible within the circumstances.

When a serious condition arises, the person administering first aid activates (or has a bystander activate) the local EMS. In many areas of the United States, this can be done by dialing 911. The 911 system was set up to provide a universal telephone

An ambulance arrives at the entrance to a hospital's emergency room.

number for emergency services. The more advanced systems automatically record both the phone number and location from which the call is placed. Areas without the 911 service have local emergency telephone numbers. A dispatcher will take the emergency call, send the appropriate assistance, and instruct the caller on what to do until help arrives.

While waiting for the ambulance, the immediate priority for the person giving first aid is to see to the ABCs of emergency medical care. These are:

Airway. Open the airway if necessary, and see that it remains open.

Breathing. Provide artificial ventilation in case of breathlessness.

Circulation. Perform cardiopulmonary resuscitation (CPR) if there is no pulse, and control the patient's bleeding.

CPR is one of the most important elements in first-aid training. It is a method of using external chest compression combined with artificial (mouth-to-mouth) ventilation for a patient experiencing a

CORE FACTS

- Members of the general public trained in first aid can provide important assistance until medical help arrives.
- Ambulances are operated by trained emergency medical technicians and may be equipped with life-support apparatus, particularly for cardiac emergencies.
- Emergency rooms in hospitals are the portals through which all acutely ill or seriously injured patients are admitted and stabilized before receiving further medical care elsewhere in the hospital.

CONNECTIONS

● Paramedics can use **DIAGNOSTIC TESTS AND EQUIPMENT** and **MEDICAL MONITORING EQUIPMENT** to treat ambulance patients; meanwhile, they can communicate with a physician using **TELEMEDICINE.**

cardiac arrest. CPR can cause the heart to start beating again on its own. But whether or not this happens, it is imperative to keep oxygenated blood circulating to the patient's brain until medical help with advanced life-support techniques arrives.

Bleeding is generally controlled with pressure and elevation. An inflatable air splint is sometimes used over a dressing to create a pressure bandage. A tourniquet, tied to constrict circulation to a limb, was at one time commonly used to control bleeding, but it is now only used as a last resort, in cases such as hemorrhage from severed arteries. Incorrect use of a tourniquet may result in the loss of a limb due to gangrene (tissue death), which is caused by the complete absence of blood circulation in a limb, or permanent damage from crushing skin, nerves, and muscle tissue.

First-aid training is available to the general public from many institutions, such as schools and hospitals, often at nominal cost. In the United States, a number of states have passed Good Samaritan laws to protect people who give first aid from legal liability when they offer their assistance in good faith.

EMTs and paramedics

The health-care providers who arrive in response to a 911 call are called emergency medical technicians (EMTs). There are several levels of EMTs, based on the amount of training they have had and the corresponding scope of practice they are permitted. All EMTs can provide basic emergency care and life support, including administering CPR and oxygen, controlling bleeding, bandaging wounds, immobilizing fractures, and assisting at childbirth. EMTs generally work in pairs, one of whom is responsible for driving the ambulance. Their activities are guided by established protocols, and they can be supervised by a physician via either radio or telephone.

The most highly trained EMTs are known as paramedics, a term that originated in the Korean War (1950–1953), when medical specialists parachuted into remote locations. In addition to the EMT functions, paramedics can establish an IV (intravenous infusion, or drip, of drugs or life-saving fluids); dispense many medications; insert a needle into the chest to relieve pressure around a collapsed lung; and interpret heart monitor readouts—always under the supervision of physicians through radio or telephone contact. In some rural areas, paramedics may treat patients locally, without transporting them to a hospital, which may be too far away.

The certification program for paramedics requires up to 2000 hours of training, so most EMTs at this level are professionals. Paid EMTs include those working for hospitals or private ambulance services, and those who work in urban areas. Altogether, there are about 150,000 paid EMTs in the United States. However, many EMTs with basic certification, requiring up to about 120 hours of training, work as volunteers with rescue squads and fire companies.

Ambulances

The old hearse-shaped ambulances have today been supplanted by purpose-built vehicles large enough to accommodate the patient, perhaps a family member, at least two EMTs, and supplies and equipment. The smallest ambulances, often used in cities where maneuverability through crowded streets is vital, are modified vans. They are relatively inexpensive but

An early ambulance, run by the U.S. Ambulance Corps during the Civil War, transports dead and wounded soldiers from the battlefield in 1862. Compared to modern ambulances, these makeshift vehicles were extremely uncomfortable and ill-equipped.

have very limited interior space. Larger ambulances have boxlike patient compartments mounted on a van or pickup truck chassis. These are more expensive to purchase but often turn out to be very cost-effective in the long run, because when the chassis wears out, it can be replaced without having to replace the patient compartment as well.

Modern ambulances are equipped with first-aid supplies, medicines, and critical care equipment. Airway devices include tubes that can be inserted in the nose or mouth and connected to ventilators to support breathing. Mechanical ventilation can be used to provide full respiratory support for a patient who is not breathing or to decrease the work of breathing for a patient who appears to be in any kind of respiratory distress.

Electrocardiographs—machines that track the electrical signals in the heart—are used to monitor heart activity. A patient in cardiac arrest is in an extremely critical situation for which immediate intervention is the only hope for survival. In many cases, the cardiac arrest first manifests itself as ventricular fibrillation, with the pumping chambers of the heart feebly vibrating instead of working in rhythm to circulate the blood. An electric shock delivered across the chest while the heart is still in fibrillation will often get the heart beating again (see MEDICAL TECHNOLOGY).

EMTs are trained to use external defibrillators—machines with paddles that are placed on the patient's chest and deliver a shock of hundreds of volts for a fraction of a second. Most ambulances are equipped with automatic models, which check the rhythm of the heartbeat every two to four seconds. If their electrodes detect ventricular fibrillation, they sound an alarm and give the patient a shock at preprogrammed levels.

In addition to medical supplies and instruments, ambulances have features that are designed to make transportation of the patient to the hospital faster and easier. An ambulance must have a long wheelbase (so that the patient won't have to lie over the rear axle and experience a bumpy ride), a low center of gravity (to keep the vehicle from rolling when taking corners at high speeds), and a low floor (making it easier to load the stretchers). Many ambulances have four-wheel drive so that they can be operated safely in all kinds of weather. Adjustable hydraulic suspension systems allow the patient compartment to be lowered in order to get the stretcher in and out. Automatic transmission ensures smooth gear shifts, making the ride more comfortable for the patient and attending EMTs.

The most elaborate ambulances in the world are probably those run by the International Grand Prix Medical Service. These are present at auto races throughout Europe and, since racetracks may be far from any hospital services and the sport of auto racing can cause significant injuries, they need to be virtually self-sufficient mini-hospitals. Dust-free and air-conditioned, they are equipped with hydraulic lifts, refrigerated blood banks, battery-powered X-

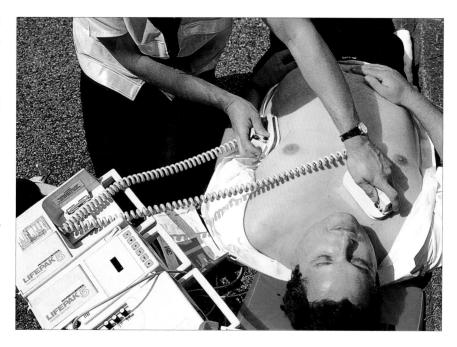

ray machines, electric generators, self-contained hot and cold water supplies and their own operating rooms. And, despite being 50 ft (15 m) long and weighing 24 tons (22 tonnes), these ambulances can be driven at up to 70 mph (113 km/h).

In some areas of the world, ambulances are equipped with traffic-signal control systems that cause traffic lights to turn green as they approach. Drivers of other vehicles are meant to stop and allow emergency vehicles using lights and sirens to precede them through an intersection, regardless of whether the signal light is green or red. Still, it is safer for everyone if the ambulance can control the system so that it is traveling in accordance with the signals.

In 1974, the U.S. Department of Transportation developed standards for the appearance of ambulances so that they would be easily identified on the roads and not be obstructed by other traffic. The specified color was white, marked with an orange

A defibrillator machine is used by an ambulance crew on a man who has just experienced a heart attack. The defibrillator gives the patient a controlled electric shock. The shock causes the heart to return to its normal rhythm after cardiac arrest has caused the heart's ventricles to fibrillate (when the individual muscle fibers of the heart's ventricles beat quickly and chaotically).

CALLING AHEAD

The advance of digital cellular telephony has expanded communications between the ambulance and the hospital beyond the simple relaying of instructions to allow exchange of data as well. Being able to provide diagnostic information to physicians while en route means that early-intervention drugs can be started sooner, increasing the patient's chance of survival.

With telemedicine systems, physicians can observe a patient's symptoms in real time, using videophones. Vital signs and blood analysis data can also be transmitted and displayed on the physician's computer screen. Since the drugs that dissolve clots and lessen the effects of heart attacks and strokes can only be administered in the first few hours, every minute that can be shaved off the initial evaluation time is crucial. Also, multiple ambulances can be serviced simultaneously, and physicians can log onto the system over the Internet, allowing ambulance crews access to specialists in their offices. Telemedicine systems are expected to be useful in many situations for which timely intervention is important, including trauma.

A CLOSER LOOK

During an earthquake drill in San Francisco, a fireman demonstrates CPR (cardiopulmonary resuscitation) on a simulated earthquake victim. Firemen and all EMTs (emergency medical technicians) are trained to give CPR when a person has experienced cardiac arrest and is therefore no longer breathing.

stripe, blue lettering, and the Star of Life (a five-pointed cross with a snake wrapped round a staff positioned along the vertical axis), adopted as a national symbol for the EMS. As fire departments began to run their own ambulances, they had them painted in other colors, in order to match the rest of their apparatus.

WHEN DISASTER STRIKES

All too often, natural disasters, explosions, or pileups on the highway result in large numbers of people being injured at once. Regional EMS systems have specific protocols to cover disasters, with neighboring services cooperating so that no area is left completely without means to deal with other emergencies that may also arise.

On the scene, EMTs evaluate patients and tag them in an initial triage step that determines their priority for transport to the hospital. Meanwhile, early treatment is provided to the patients while they wait (SEE ACCIDENTS AND DISASTERS).

News of the disaster is called in to one or more hospitals, and preparations are immediately begun. Every hospital is required to have a disaster plan and hold drills twice a year. When the plan must be implemented, available staff are summoned from throughout the hospital. Some prepare the hospital's existing operating rooms and rig improvised ones in the emergency room. Others stock treatment areas with the necessary supplies. Gurneys (wheeled stretchers) are taken to the door to wait for arrivals. If weather permits, a reception, triage, and waiting area is set up outside so that the entire emergency room area can be used for treatment. Most hospitals have a public relations officer on staff to act as a liaison with the press. Everyone is involved and has a specific job to do in the organized chaos that is an emergency department in action.

A CLOSER LOOK

The ambulance will transport the patient to the nearest hospital that offers an appropriate level of care. This is often the local community hospital, but regional medical centers offer specialized care for serious illnesses and injuries. If it would take too long to get to such a facility via ground transportation, either because of its distance or due to gridlocked traffic, air ambulances may be used.

Air ambulances

The first recorded air ambulance was a French fighter plane that evacuated a wounded Serb soldier during World War I (1914–1918). In World War II, many casualties were transported in cargo planes.

The helicopter, with its ability to take off and land in small spaces, dramatically reduced battlefield mortality, since wounded soldiers could be strapped to litters (stretchers) and quickly airlifted to field hospitals. Significant wartime use of the helicopter started with the Korean War (1950–1953), when more than 20,000 wounded soldiers were transported. In the Vietnam War (1956–1975), 800,000 wounded were evacuated by helicopter.

In civilian use, the helicopter can transport patients from the scene of an accident directly to the roof or parking lot of a trauma center. Helicopters and small, highly maneuverable airplanes are also used to provide transportation between medical facilities, such as when a patient must be quickly sent to a regional center for specialized care. Using an ambulance to take a patient to a medical center a few hundred miles away is time-consuming. It not only puts additional stress on the patient and delays hospital care, but it also ties up the ambulance, making it unavailable for local service.

Beginning in 1972 with a program in Denver, Colorado, increasing numbers of hospitals and agencies have set up air transport systems. By 1998, there were 160 programs operating across the United States. In-flight medical crews, generally consisting of a flight nurse and a paramedic, staff cabins so well equipped with advanced life-support systems that there is little lapse in quality of care during the interval between two hospitals' intensive care units.

The emergency room

Upon arriving at the hospital, EMTs place the patient's stretcher onto a gurney and roll it into the emergency room (ER). They provide the staff with as much information as possible about the patient's condition and the treatment already given. At that point, responsibility is transferred to the ER staff.

Of course, many patients arrive at the emergency room under their own power, with a broken arm or a cut requiring a few stitches. All patients are quickly evaluated by a nurse in what is known as the triage procedure. Emergency rooms are not first come, first served—otherwise, critically injured patients could be allowed to bleed to death while the sprained ankle of an earlier arrival is wrapped. Triage requires that first priority go to patients whose survival might depend on immediate treatment.

LIFELINE IN THE AIR

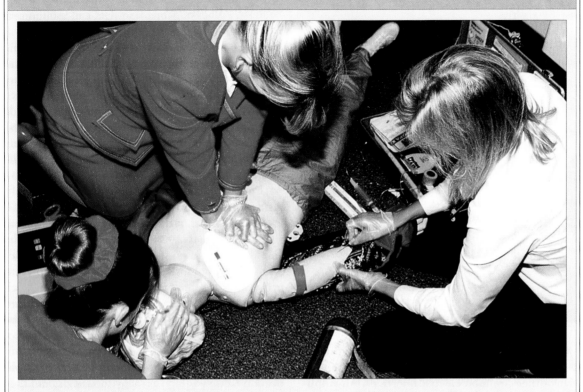

An airline crew practices applying CPR on a model, in the event a passenger goes into cardiac arrest.

An airliner in flight is not a good place to have a medical emergency. Even if there is an airport nearby, descending from cruising altitude (around 30,000 ft/9140 m) takes about twenty minutes. An intercontinental flight might be over the ocean, hours from any airport, when an emergency strikes. About 1000 people go into cardiac arrest and die on airliners every year, more than are killed in plane crashes. CPR is not sufficient to sustain cardiac arrest patients until help can be reached on the ground; they rarely survive more than 10 minutes without advanced life support.

To give cardiac arrest victims in flight a fighting chance, automatic external defibrillators are beginning to be installed on airliners, and flight crews are being trained in their use. The portable defibrillator kits can be set up in about half a minute. As is the general procedure in medical emergencies, the help of any physician on board is requested, but the crew is expected to handle the equipment on its own with a success rate comparable to that in ambulance care.

A CLOSER LOOK

In life-threatening emergencies, the patient must be stabilized before other treatment can begin. Several doctors and nurses will generally be involved. Again, the ABCs of airway, breathing, and circulation are evaluated. Blood pressure is monitored to ensure the patient isn't in shock. Once stable, the patient will probably be admitted to the hospital for observation, treatment, or surgery.

Although they are called emergency rooms, in fact, emergency departments generally have several rooms, including a waiting area, reception area, and a number of treatment rooms. Most emergency rooms separate life-threatening cases from those requiring routine care for relatively minor injuries. Others have special-purpose rooms, such as pediatric or cardiac care units.

Medical professionals working in the emergency room include physicians' assistants and nurse practitioners—professionals with degrees who are trained to perform a variety of procedures under the supervision of physicians. Teaching hospitals also have medical students, interns, and residents assigned to the emergency room staff. Attendants transport patients and prepare treatment areas for use. Receptionists, security guards, social workers, and clergy round out the team.

S. CALVO

See also: INTENSIVE CARE UNIT.

Further reading:
Bache, J. B. *Accidents and Emergencies*. Oxford, England; New York: Oxford University Press, 1994.
Beck, R. K. *Pharmacology for Prehospital Emergency Care*. Philadelphia: F. A. Davis, 1996.
Ross, A. D. *The Medicine of E.R. or, How We Almost Die*. New York: Basic Books, 1996.

ANESTHETICS

Anesthetics are medicines or other techniques used to stop pain during surgery, dentistry, and childbirth

These nurses are attending a postoperative patient who is recovering from an anesthetic.

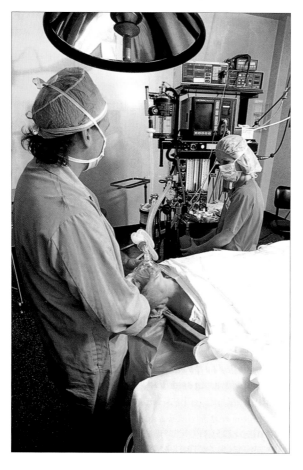

Skeletal remains and historical evidence suggest that rudimentary surgery has been performed by humans for thousands of years. Ancient skulls have been found that contain holes that had apparently been drilled to relieve fluid pressure on the brain. The cesarean section (surgically removing a child from the mother's womb) was named for Roman statesman Julius Caesar (100–44 B.C.E.), who it is believed was born in this way. With no way to mask the pain of the incising scalpel, surgery was performed only as a last resort to save the patient's life. Many patients died at the shock of such intense pain.

A good surgeon was a fast surgeon, and procedures were essentially limited to the hasty removal of teeth or gangrenous limbs. Physicians prided themselves on being able to perform amputations in less than a minute. Abdominal surgery was rarely attempted. Until anesthesia eliminated the terrible pain of surgery, conditions such as appendicitis were almost invariably fatal. The life-saving operations of today were impossible to imagine (see SURGERY).

Early pain relief
Throughout history there have been many medications used to relieve pain. Plants such as the opium poppy (*Papaver somniferum*), the coca leaf (*Erythroxylon coca*), the cannabis plant (*Cannabis sativa*), and mandrake root (*Mandragora officinarum*)

were used by herbalists and folk healers. The general depressant alcohol is another substance that dulls pain. In fact, some operations were attempted while the patient was intoxicated with alcohol. Occasionally surgeons even resorted to knocking their patients out with a blow to the head. To relieve mild pain, soothing ointments and lotions were manufactured from compounds that were contained within plants such as the camphor tree (*Cinnamomum camphora*) and peppermint (*Mentha piperita*). Bark from certain willow trees (*Salix* species) contains the active ingredient salicin. (A synthetic form of salicin known as acetylsalicylic acid—aspirin—was later made by German pharmaceutical manufacturer Bayer.) However, none of these substances were powerful enough to anesthetize a patient undergoing surgery.

Chemists experimenting with gases discovered that some had unusual and unexpected effects. For example, a sniff of nitrous oxide (N_2O) induced euphoria and fits of uncontrollable laughter. Ether ($C_4H_{10}O$) had similar effects. By the early 1840s, the effects that these gases had were being demonstrated at exhibitions, and nitrous oxide in particular was used as a recreational drug. Physicians and dentists occasionally observed that partyers under the influence of nitrous oxide who fell and injured themselves felt no pain, and they began trying nitrous oxide on animals and themselves. However, the medical establishment of the time frowned on their work. The idea of performing surgery on patients who were under the effects of ether or nitrous oxide was viewed as dangerous, and some early failures of public demonstrations fueled the image of the experimenters as quacks. However, due to the perseverance of those physicians and dentists the use of such substances was accepted. Indeed, by the time of the American Civil War (1861–1865), the use of anesthesia was common.

Blocking pain
Anesthesia was used for decades before anyone actually understood how it worked. The human nervous system consists of about 15 billion nerve cells, known as neurons. Scientists and physicians were not

CONNECTIONS

● Anesthetics are also used in **VETERINARY MEDICINE** to eliminate the pain animals would feel during **SURGERY**.

CORE FACTS

■ Gases, such as ether and nitrous oxide, were first used as anesthetics in the 1840s.

■ Anesthetics work by blocking the transmission of pain signals between nerve cells.

■ The human body can produce substances that have similar effects to those of anesthetic drugs.

■ Anesthetics are classified as local, regional, or general, depending on how they block the sensation of pain.

able to see these cells until sufficiently powerful microscopes had been developed. Neurons transmit information between the brain and other parts of the body, and then back again, by sending electrical impulses through the neurons. These signals are produced by chemical reactions mediated by substances called neurotransmitters. Some neurotransmitters can activate other nerve cells. Others serve to switch off another nerve cell's signals.

In 1973, scientists discovered that nerve cells have special sites on their surfaces that opiates, such as opium and morphine, can attach to. When the opiates lock on to these opiate receptors, the neurons that relay pain signals are turned off, and the neurons that block pain signals are turned on. Opiate receptors are located in areas of the brain that process pain signals. They are also found in other areas of the brain, which explains why using opiates disturbs breathing patterns, temperature control, and mood.

At first, scientists were puzzled as to why the body would have developed specific receptors for opiates. However, they soon found that electrical stimulation of neurons can also block pain. Similarly, drugs that counteract opiates also prevent the electrical stimulation from working. This suggests that the electrical stimulation acts by causing the body to produce opiate-like chemicals of its own. These chemicals, called endorphins, were identified in the 1970s as the body's pain relief system. Stress can cause endorphins to be released, which accounts for the "runner's high" and the ability of injured people to function in a crisis.

Types of anesthetics

There are three main types of anesthetics: local, regional, and general. Local anesthetics block sensation in a particular area of the body. They are generally synthetic drugs such as procaine hydrochloride (trademarked as Novocain), which is similar in structure to cocaine but is modified to preclude addiction. Local anesthetics may be applied directly to the skin or mucous membranes as creams, gels, sprays, suppositories, or lozenges. They may also be given intravenously. Since only small amounts of medication are used, recovery is immediate and side effects are rare.

Some drugs, for example lidocaine, cannot be taken intravenously as an anesthetic. This drug is only injected intravenously to treat cardiac arrhythmias (alterations in the rhythm of the heart) and can actually induce arrhythmias in healthy people. Because of this, when giving local anesthetics it is important not to inject them intravenously.

Regional anesthetics are delivered into the spine, blocking signals from the waist down. They are usually administered as an epidural, in which anesthetic is injected into the space around the membranes surrounding the spinal cord via a fine tube. The tube is left in place to allow further doses of the anesthetic. Regional anesthetics do not cause loss of consciousness, although a sedative such as diazepam is often used before the epidural procedure to relax the

The milky juice of this unripe poppy seed pod contains the drug opium.

WILLIAM MORTON AND OTHER PIONEERS OF ANESTHESIA

U.S. dentist William Thomas Morton (1819–1868) was born in Charlton, Massachusetts. He was the son of a shopkeeper. It is reputed that Morton graduated from the Baltimore College of Dentistry, although little is known of his early life and this is uncertain. During his partnership with Horace Wells, Morton arranged for Wells to demonstrate the use of nitrous oxide for a tooth extraction from a patient at Harvard University, where Wells had witnessed use of the gas at a "laughing gas party." Although Wells' patient fell fast asleep and later said he'd felt nothing during the procedure, he was heard to groan. The demonstration was judged a failure.

Morton was still hopeful that a way could be found to eliminate the pain that often frightened his patients into declining his services. U.S. physician and chemist Charles Jackson (1805–1880) suggested trying ether, which Morton successfully used to extract a tooth. In 1846, U.S. physician John Warren (1778–1856) used Morton's ether formulation to painlessly amputate the leg of a young woman. This success, in an operation that was normally horribly painful, marked the watershed for anesthesia.

Morton had used additives to color the ether and disguise its smell and patented it under the name Letheon. He attempted to keep its identity a trade secret and charged license fees to others who wanted to use it. However, Morton's attempt at entrepreneurship was a failure. To convince physicians to use Letheon, he was forced to disclose that it was simply ether, and his patent became worthless. Licensees demanded their money back, and legal battles pushed him deeply into debt. He also became involved in a feud with Jackson over credit for the invention of anesthesia; Jackson claimed that Morton had only carried out something that Jackson had suggested.

Wells, who conducted a few too many chloroform experiments on himself, became deranged and committed suicide. Morton died in 1698 a broken man, still raving about the iniquity of Jackson's claims. Today, the Smithsonian Institution in Washington honors Morton as the discoverer of surgical anesthesia.

PEOPLE

PAIN RELIEF WITHOUT DRUGS

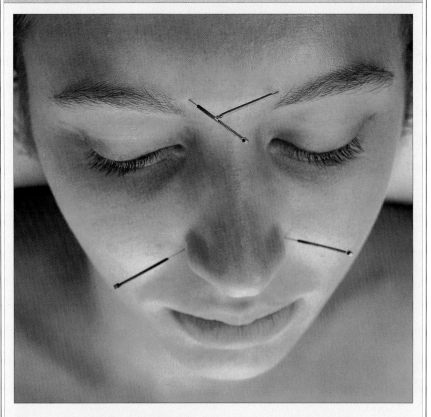

Acupuncture needles are inserted into a patient's face to treat hay fever.

A technique of Chinese medicine called acupuncture has been used for over 2000 years to relieve pain. In this process, very thin needles are inserted at the specific points on the body. Acupuncture is believed to work by causing the body to release endorphins. It is most widely used in relieving muscular pain and conditions of chronic discomfort. In some cases, heat or a weak electric current is used to increase the needles' effect. Researchers have even tried to replace the needles with laser light in the hope that more endorphins are released.

Pain relief without the use of anesthesia has been of particular interest in childbirth, due to the concern that drugs might affect the baby or interfere with the birthing process. In addition, while most women want pain control, they generally prefer not to sleep through such a significant event. Techniques that are used to relieve pain during "natural childbirth" include focused breathing exercises, hypnosis, and massage.

A CLOSER LOOK

patient making it easier for doctors to administer the delicate procedure. The effects of an epidural wear off within a few hours. Due to this relatively quick recovery period, childbirth and many operations on the legs and lower abdomen are now performed with regional anesthetics.

General anesthetics affect the whole body. They depress the nervous system, resulting in a deep sleep. Some, such as thiopental sodium, may be administered intravenously. The injected anesthetics work quickly and can be used alone for a short time. For longer procedures, however, doctors tend to use them in combination with an anesthetic gas. The amount of general anesthetic used depends on various factors, including the patient's weight, age, and the type of surgery. Usually a light anesthetic in combination with a muscle relaxant is used. With general anesthesia, effects on the patient may last for up to 24 hours.

During surgery

The person who administers anesthesia during an operation is called an anesthetist. The anesthetist may be a physician whose specialty is anesthesiology. The anesthesiologist does a three-year residency in the specialty and takes exams certified by the American Board of Anesthesiology. Some anesthesiologists specialize further in a field such as pediatric or obstetric anesthesiology. Specially trained nurses may also administer anesthesia. The certified registered nurse anesthetist works under the supervision of the surgeon or an anesthesiologist.

In addition to administering the anesthesia, the anesthetist is responsible for monitoring the overall condition of the patient during surgery. An anesthesia machine vaporizes a measured amount of the anesthetic gas, which is mixed with oxygen and delivered to the patient through a face mask. If the particular operation requires profound muscle relaxation, the patient will not be able to breathe on his or her own, so a tube is attached to the patient's windpipe and a mechanical ventilator is used.

Monitoring equipment is used to help the anesthetist record the patient's vital signs at every moment (see MEDICAL MONITORING EQUIPMENT). Three electrodes are fixed to the patient's chest with gel, and these allow continuous monitoring of the heart with an electrocardiograph. Blood pressure is taken every two to five minutes. A pulse oximeter uses a sensor clipped to the patient's finger or earlobe to monitor the oxygen level in the blood.

Future prospects

The discovery of endorphins explained the success of many nonpharmaceutical methods of pain relief. It also suggested research areas. Pain researchers have found that people suffering from chronic pain often have low levels of endorphins and those with high pain resistance have a high level. Biofeedback (a technique of making automatic body functions, such as blood pressure, detectable to the senses in order to gain voluntary control over the functions) is being explored to help patients train their bodies to block pain. In the pharmaceutical industry, anesthetic agents are continually being developed to provide pain relief, anxiety control, and relaxation with minimum side effects.

S. CALVO

See also: AMBULANCE AND EMERGENCY MEDICAL TREATMENT; DENTISTRY; INTENSIVE CARE UNIT; OBSTETRICS AND GYNECOLOGY; PHARMACOLOGY AND DRUG TREATMENT; SURGERY.

Further reading:

Anesthetic Toxicity. Edited by S. A. Rice and K. J. Fish. New York: Raven Press, 1994.

ANIMAL BREEDING

Animal breeding is the human control of the reproductive cycles of animals

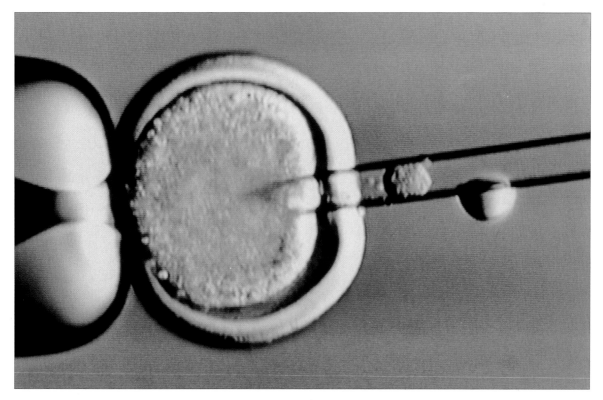

A light micrograph shows a sheep egg, magnified x 500, being injected with an embryonic cell during sheep cloning. In this process, the egg (at center) has had its own genetic material removed. A pipette (at left) holds the egg in place while a microneedle (at right) is used to inject the egg with an embryonic sheep cell. The egg is implanted, then stimulated to grow using a spark of electricity.

Many reasons exist for breeding animals, including breeding for utility (especially in agriculture), as pets, and for sports such as horse racing. Desirable characteristics vary greatly from the purely economic, such as a fast growth rate in pigs, to the purely aesthetic, such as conformity to a specified appearance in pedigree dog breeds. Breeders have encouraged different characteristics at different times and in different places, and many animal breeders place a strong emphasis on insuring genetic diversity. Improving the quality of an animal species is a dynamic process, not a constant progression toward a perfect set of preexisting qualities.

Whatever the animal and the nature of the improvement sought, the general requirements of animal breeding are the same. Every breeder must select the best animals, insure they breed and produce healthy offspring, and evaluate the results of the breeding process.

CORE FACTS

- Animals are bred for many reasons, but it is usually to improve their usefulness, vigor, or appearance.
- The central task for the breeder is to select the best animals to breed.
- Breeding generally seeks a balance between reinforcing desirable traits and preserving genetic diversity.
- Newer technologies, such as cloning and genetic engineering, will present new possibilities and dilemmas to the animal breeder.

A background to animal breeding

All domesticated animals originated from wild relatives. For example, dogs resulted from the domestication of wolves and other wild dogs; chickens have their origins in Asian jungle fowl. Animals were probably first domesticated by capturing and taming young wild animals. The most useful and docile captive animals would be allowed to breed, and as each generation passed, the animals became more distinct from their wild ancestors. Domestication was a crucial step in the development of agriculture (see AGRICULTURE, HISTORY OF).

The process of controlling animal breeding has constantly evolved throughout history. Great advances in breeding techniques were made in the 18th century in Europe, notably in England by farmer Robert Bakewell (see the box on page 80) and others, and the pace of change has increased since. The discoveries of the principles of genetics and evolutionary science in the late 19th and 20th centuries led to the development of a scientific basis for breeding. This process continues to the present day with techniques such as artificial insemination and cloning.

Genes and heredity

Genetics is the branch of biology that deals with the heredity and variation of organisms. The genetic material that determines these factors is called DNA (deoxyribonucleic acid). The units of heredity are called genes; these bits of information are located on the DNA-rich chromosomes in the cell nucleus (see GENETIC ENGINEERING).

CONNECTIONS

- **CLONING** is the highly controversial procedure by which genetic material from an animal embryo cell is inserted into the egg of another individual that has had its own genetic material removed.

- Researchers in **AGRICULTURAL SCIENCE** continue to look for improvements in animal breeding processes.

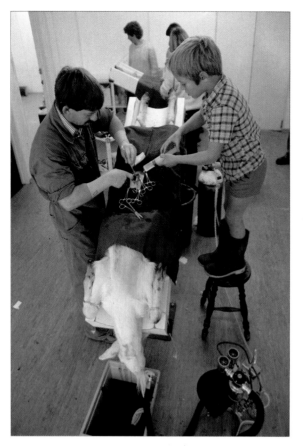

A veterinary surgeon and his young assistant transplant an embryo from a purebred Angora goat to a domestic goat in an operating room in New Plymouth, New Zealand.

Nearly all the cells in an animal's body contain a pair of chromosomes with their corresponding genes. However, an egg (female sex cell) or sperm (male sex cell) contains only one chromosome, or one copy of each gene. During breeding, egg and sperm combine to restore the paired state of chromosomes and genes in an embryo cell (fertilized egg). During the chromosome duplication and pairing process, however, genes are reshuffled, forming new, unique combinations in the embryo cell.

Classical studies of the mechanisms of heredity concentrated on characteristics that are displayed as one of several distinct types, such as the presence or absence of horns. These characteristics are generally determined by a single pair of genes with two or more separate forms called alleles. Different combinations of alleles produce different characteristics.

Most characteristics, however, have a more complex pattern of inheritance and are determined by several interacting genes, or polygenes, each with different alleles. Such characteristics are generally the most economically important traits in an animal's performance. Examples include the growth rate of meat livestock and wool yield in sheep.

Selecting the right animals

The primary task in animal breeding is to select the right animals to be mated. The general appearance of animals has traditionally been an important selection factor, especially for those that must conform to a certain breed standard. Appearance and other subjective judgments of animal value are still important, but more objective measurements of performance are also major selection criteria.

Parents with desirable traits do not necessarily produce offspring with the same qualities. The genetic mechanisms that determine how various characteristics are inherited are complex, and environmental factors such as diet and climate can greatly influence an animal's qualities. To address this problem, breeders use a concept called heritability, which is the proportion of the total variation observed in a trait due to genetic variation. Heritability is an estimate obtained by statistical analysis of a given set of animals and is expressed as a decimal fraction or percentage. For example, chicken egg size typically has a heritability of about 0.5, or 50 percent. Traits with high heritability (0.4 and above) offer the best potential for rapid improvement through breeding.

There are several ways in which animals are evaluated for breeding. The first is by examining the merits of individual animals, or mass selection. This involves identifying those animals that perform significantly better than the average. Mass selection is the most accurate evaluation for traits with high heritability that are evident before breeding age. The animals must be kept in strictly controlled conditions for an accurate assessment to be made.

A second method—pedigree selection—involves assessing the performance of an animal's ancestors. Detailed pedigree records continue to be maintained for various animals, most notably Thoroughbred racehorses. Pedigree selection has limited value on its own, and considering ancestors beyond two generations is rarely worthwhile—the genetic contribution of each ancestor is diluted with each generation. Pedigree selection is most useful with traits expressed later on in life, such as longevity, where the merit of ancestors may be the only guide. It is also considered important for breeding pets.

A third method, family selection, is similar to pedigree selection, except that the performance of siblings (brothers and sisters) is considered rather than that of ancestors. Family selection is most useful when there are large numbers of siblings to study.

Progeny testing involves judging an animal's breeding value from the performance of its progeny (offspring). Similar to family selection, large numbers of progeny give the most information, especially if they live in a variety of environmental conditions.

Progeny testing, pedigree selection, and family selection are all useful to test for sex-dependent characteristics, such as the prediction of milk yield in cows. The breeding value of a bull for this trait can be predicted by the milk yield of his sisters and female ancestors. Progeny testing is probably most widely used for the selection of bulls for dairy cow breeding.

In practice, a combination of some or all of these methods is used to test the breeding value of an animal, often with different methods used at different stages. For example, young male chickens may initially be selected to breed by pedigree selection; then by mass selection as their own qualities begin to show; then by family selection, from their sisters' egg-laying performance; and finally, by the progeny testing of their own offspring.

Statistical methods are increasingly important in the analysis of performance, giving more accurate, unbiased estimates of breeding value. As more ancestor, sibling, offspring, and performance standards are used to determine breeding patterns in animals, the more beneficial it is becoming to have statistical analyses performed by computers.

Once an animal has been selected for breeding, there are two systems that are used to take advantage of its high breeding value. Inbreeding is the mating of animals that are more genetically similar than the population average—that is, siblings. Outbreeding is the mating of animals less genetically similar than the population average.

Inbreeding

The purpose of inbreeding is to concentrate the degree of heredity for certain traits, thus producing visibly different individuals possessing these traits. As a result, inbreeding has been used to produce and maintain distinctive lineages, or purebred lines, such as the standard poodle.

Inbreeding has the disadvantage of concentrating the frequency of undesirable alleles in a population. This increases the incidence of genetical defects. Inbred lines also tend to show a decline in size, vigor, and fertility as a result of their low genetic diversity. As a consequence of this depleted gene pool, animal breeders tend to use inbreeding sparingly.

Outbreeding

Outbreeding, or crossbreeding, increases the genetic variation of the offspring. It typically involves breeding animals from different lines to produce crossbred offspring (hybrids). Outbreeding seeks to combine favorable traits. For example, Indian Brahman cattle, which are highly tolerant of heat and insect pests, have been mated with Hereford cattle, which produce high-quality meat. The resulting hybrids have better heat and insect resistance than Herefords and yield better meat than Brahmans. The hybrid cattle are useful as beef breeds for tropical regions.

Crosses can also be made between animals from different, but related, species. For example, the mule (a cross between a horse and a donkey) is an example of hybrid vigor, or heterosis. This is a long-recognized phenomenon where the offspring of a cross between parents of different breeds or species are more vigorous than either of the parental types, a result of the increase in genetic variety. The progeny of different breeds are usually also more fertile than their parents; the progeny of different species are usually sterile. The majority of agricultural animals are hybrids of different lines; for instance, most farmed pigs are crossbred.

Controlling mating

Selection is pointless unless mating is controlled. Many unselected animals will be slaughtered before they reach breeding age, and males not required for breeding are often castrated to avoid the possibility of them impregnating females.

A worker loads a mule's carrying bags with bricks at a brickyard in Peshawar, Pakistan. The mule is the result of outbreeding between a horse and a donkey. As with most inter-species hybrids, mules are strong and hardy, but sterile.

Traditionally, selected animals have been mated simply by putting them together in a field or barn during the breeding season. Males usually mate with several females. If a bull or ram is left to run with several females, patches impregnated with waterproof dye will be attached to his chest. These will indicate the females he has attempted to mate with, since he will leave dye marks on the females' backs as he mounts them. More controlled mating may be achieved by confining females in individual stalls and leading a male to her. This system is common for mating pigs and Thoroughbred horses.

Artificial insemination is very important in modern livestock breeding, especially for cattle (see ARTIFICIAL INSEMINATION AND FERTILITY TREATMENT). It enables a male of high breeding value to father thousands of offspring. Artificial insemination makes progeny testing much more valuable because of the huge number of offspring available for study.

Embryo transplantation

Embryo transplantation, used with cattle, goats, pigs, and sheep, aims to increase the number of offspring from a quality female. A highly rated female is given hormone treatment to cause her to produce more eggs than normal. The female is then mated with an equally prized bull. The eggs that have been

ROBERT BAKEWELL

An artist's impression shows Bakewell inspecting New Leicester sheep at his farm in Dishley, England.

British farmer Robert Bakewell (1725–1795) introduced great advances in livestock breeding in the 18th century that laid the foundations for modern breeding. From about 1760, he conducted extensive breeding trials with cattle, sheep, and horses on his family farm in Leicestershire, England. Bakewell carefully selected the best of local stock to breed, following the axiom "Like begets like," and recorded his successes and failures in detail. He also popularized the practice of hiring out prize males for breeding purposes.

Bakewell's work yielded impressive improvements in the size and quality of the animals that he bred. For example, he did much to develop and popularize the Longhorn breed of cattle, a large breed that yields high-quality meat. However, his greatest success was the development of the robust, well-meated Dishley Leicester breed of sheep. Most previous sheep breeds had fattened too slowly to provide meat economically and so were raised predominantly for wool; the Dishley Leicester made sheep farming for meat much more viable. Bakewell's fame spread widely, and his farm was considered to be at the forefront of successful management in its day.

PEOPLE

fertilized are surgically removed from the female, and each embryo is then transplanted into the womb of a recipient mother. This means that a highly rated cow, for instance, can typically originate 50 calves in one year, instead of the usual one. Embryo transplantation is generally successful, but its application is currently limited, because it is an expensive and extremely technical procedure.

There are various extra modifications of embryo transplantation that increase its flexibility. For example, the embryos can be frozen and put into short-term storage before transplantation. Similarly, eggs have been artificially fertilized in a laboratory (in-vitro fertilization). Additionally, embryos can be split at an early stage of development using microsurgery; each portion of the embryo can then be transplanted into recipient mothers, which will later give birth to identical twins. This procedure is called artificial twinning. Although most frequently used for livestock, artificial twinning may also prove useful for increasing the breeding success of endangered animal species in captivity.

Cloning

Cloning embryos to artificially produce genetic duplicates of an animal has also become possible (see CLONING). DNA is extracted from an animal embryo cell and is inserted into a host egg cell that has had its own genetic material removed. The modified embryo can then be implanted into a recipient mother and grow into a copy of the original embryo. In 1997, scientists in Scotland succeeded for the first time in cloning a sheep from an adult body cell rather than an embryo. Although this research is controversial, and the long-term vigor and fertility of such cloned animals is still unknown, cloning has much potential to change the practice of future animal breeding. In theory, a highly desirable beef bull could be cloned many times to rapidly produce numerous animals of identical high quality.

Genetic engineering

Direct manipulation and alteration of an animal's genetic material—genetic engineering—has the potential to produce even more drastic changes in animal breeding (see GENETIC ENGINEERING). By introducing DNA from unrelated organisms into another animal's DNA, new genetic combinations can be made that would never occur in nature.

Many new applications are possible with genetic engineering. For example, human genes for various blood proteins have been transferred into the DNA of cattle and sheep. The animals then produce the proteins in their own blood, which can be extracted for medical use. Some scientists believe that genetically engineered pigs may one day be able to provide compatible organs for emergency transplantation (xenotransplantion) into humans.

As with cloning, genetic engineering is likely to be at the forefront of future advances in animal breeding. However, there are ethical objections to some of the potential applications of these technologies and concerns about the welfare of the animals involved. There is also uncertainty over the long-term effects of creating genetically modified animals, and so any widespread application of genetic engineering to animal breeding is likely to be accompanied by debate and controversy. For example, there is particular concern with xenotransplants that humans may be exposed to lethal viruses from the organs they inherit, because it is a way of introducing viruses into hosts that would have otherwise never been exposed to them.

T. ALLMAN

See also: AGRICULTURAL SCIENCE; AGRICULTURE, HISTORY OF; ANIMAL TRANSPORT; ARTIFICIAL INSEMINATION AND FERTILITY TREATMENT; CLONING; GENETIC ENGINEERING; LIVESTOCK FARMING; VETERINARY MEDICINE.

Further reading:
Animal Breeding and Infertility. Edited by M. Meredith. Boston: Blackwell Scientific Publications, 1995.

ANIMAL TRANSPORT

Domesticated animals of many species have been used to transport people and property for thousands of years

This scene from the film Ben Hur is a reenactment of the famous chariot races that took place in Rome over 2000 years ago. Although the races were a spectator sport for the ancient Romans, chariots were also used for commerce, transportation, and war.

Animal transportation has broadened the horizons of humankind immeasurably. When people could travel only as far as they could walk, carrying food, supplies, and children, few went very far and none went very fast. On horseback or using carts, merchants could travel between communities for trade, carrying information along with their goods. Mounted warriors could not only move faster but also had a height advantage in battle. The war chariot—an animal chariot in which a warrior rides in a small cart behind a horse—was an integral part of the conquering empires of the ancient world.

The age of animal transport lasted almost 7000 years—until the development of the internal combustion engine (see INTERNAL COMBUSTION ENGINE).

Even today, animals are used in regions where motorized vehicles are not available or suitable for the terrain. Domesticated animals such as camels, elephants, and horses are still ridden for recreation and are used to pull vehicles as well.

The domestication of animals

About 12,000 years ago, humans began to interact with animals other than as predators or prey. Wolves, jackals, and wild dogs became domesticated. As hunter-gatherer societies started giving way to agricultural settlements, a variety of animals began to be raised for food. People started using pack animals around 5000 B.C.E., since farming introduced the need to pull plows and carry produce (see PLOW).

Which animals were raised as beasts of burden depended on what species were indigenous to the region, their ease of domestication, and the size of the loads that needed to be carried. The earliest pack animal was probably the ass in the Middle East. Asses can carry only about 130 lb (60 kg) though, so for heavier loads the domesticated camel was used. The camel—a hardy animal that can withstand long periods without food and water—eventually became indispensable in the desert regions, where they traveled the trade routes in long caravans (see the picture on page 82). Oxen and elephants were used in various regions of Asia, and llamas—relatives of the camel—were domesticated in South America. Horses were first tamed and used as pack animals by nomads of the central Asian grasslands.

CORE FACTS

- Pack animals were first used to carry food and other supplies around 7000 years ago.
- People started to ride horses about 3000 B.C.E. The distances they could travel greatly increased, opening new opportunities for communication and trade.
- Elephants were the "living tanks" of the ancient world. They were used by armies in Asia and the countries bordering the Mediterranean Sea.
- In developed countries, motorized vehicles have replaced animals for most transportation needs. However, horse riding is still a popular recreational activity in many parts of the world.

CONNECTIONS

● **HORSE-DRAWN TRANSPORT** developed from the invention of the spoked **WHEEL**.

● Since around 5000 years ago, animals have been used in **AGRICULTURE** to pull **PLOWS** and carry farm produce.

A camel caravan crosses the desert near the Giza Pyramids in Cairo, Egypt.

Wheeled vehicles were in use in Mesopotamia by about 3500 B.C.E., and domesticated animals were used to pull them. When the invention of lighter spoked wheels allowed vehicles to travel faster over a wider variety of terrain, simple wheeled carts developed into an array of carriages, wagons, and chariots used for transportation, commerce, and war (see HORSE-DRAWN TRANSPORT; WHEEL).

The mounted traveler

People first started to ride horses around 3000 B.C.E. The rider would sit on a cloth thrown over the horse's back and clutch a rope or leather thong tied around the horse's jaw. About 2000 years ago, the Chinese and Romans began using saddles. Metal stirrups helped ancient nomads from central Asia, called the Huns, establish their reputation as fine riders. These innovations made riding more comfortable and helped riders remain in their seats.

Horses were used in hunting, in sports, for general transport, for sending messages, and for military purposes. Other members of the horse family, especially mules (the offspring of a male ass and a female horse; see ANIMAL BREEDING), were also used for riding. In military campaigns, where speed was less important than intimidation, elephants were ridden into combat, terrifying opponents who had never seen them before and trampling anyone who stepped in their path. Elephants were used successfully by the Carthaginians and other ancient warriors, but they had their drawbacks. Elephants consume a huge amount of fodder, tire easily, and are difficult to control. They are especially well known for their tendency to stampede in the heat of battle. In Asia, they are still used as work animals—especially in remote forest areas for logging—and they also appear in religious ceremonies and processions.

Comfortable group-seating accommodations, called howdahs, complete with cushions and canopies, grace their high, swaying backs.

During the Middle Ages, knights in suits of armor had protective plates made for their horses, which they trained for battle by competing in jousts. Once guns were invented, however, the stronger armor required to resist bullets was too heavy to wear and was gradually phased out (see ARMOR). However, mounted regiments, called cavalry, continued to be an important part of most armies well into the 20th century. During World War II (1939–1945), traditionalists continued to advocate that mounted troops should remain the backbone of the U.S. armed forces, because they could travel off-road and live from the land. While millions of horses were used, the powerful German tank forces pushed the Allies to respond in kind, eventually eclipsing the cavalry (see CAVALRY AND CHARIOT).

Horse tack and horseshoes

The equipment used to ride a horse is called the tack, and although the exact type of tack varies with the requirements of the particular application, the basic components are the same.

The bridle is used to control the horse. Leather straps go around the face and are attached to the reins and the bit; the bit is placed behind the horse's teeth. The first bits were made of horn or bone, but metal bits were in use by the time of the ancient Greeks and Romans. The purpose of a bit is to steer or stop the animal by applying pressure to the horse's mouth so that the horse will turn its head in the desired direction. There are many different bits. One of the simplest is the snaffle, which consists of two short pieces of metal joined in the middle. The snaffle causes the horse to raise its head and is sometimes used in combination with a curb bit. The curb bit, which is controlled by a separate rein, is used to apply a pressure that makes the horse lower its head for quick turns or stops.

Saddles both stabilize the rider and protect the horse's back. The framework of a saddle is the tree, traditionally made of wood but now sometimes molded from fiberglass. The tree is padded, usually with foam rubber, and covered with leather. Stirrups hang from the saddle and provide support for the feet. Safety stirrups have rubber sections that can become detached from the saddle, preventing the rider's foot from twisting in the event of a fall.

The English saddle has a seat that holds the rider's weight forward. Variations of this saddle are designed for hunting, horse shows, polo, and general recreational riding. Specialized racing saddles are extreme versions of the English saddle, lightweight and shaped to encourage the rider to lean far forward along the horse's neck.

The sidesaddle has only one stirrup and is used by people who cannot sit astride the horse. Traditionally, women riders fell into this category for the sake of modesty when wearing dresses. Women generally used sidesaddles up until about the 1920s. Today, sidesaddles are mostly a thing of the past, but they still find some use among disabled people who have trouble riding astride the horse.

The Western saddle originated in Spain and was adopted by the cowboys and ranchers of Mexico and the Wild West. This saddle has a horn in front used to tie the end of a lariat (the long light rope made from hemp or leather and used with a running noose to catch livestock or to tether grazing animals), and a deep padded seat for comfort on the trail.

Horseshoes protect the horse's hooves from rough or hard surfaces and have been used for thousands of years. The earliest forms of horseshoes were made from leather and quickly wore out. Then the ancient Egyptians began nailing wooden shoes to horses' hooves. Eventually iron horseshoes were adopted, not unlike those in use today. Farriers are blacksmiths who shoe horses, carefully trimming the hoof before nailing on the shoe. Modern shoes are usually made of aluminum or steel and generally come ready-made; the farrier adjusts them for each individual horse. There are several types of horseshoes; the type used depends on the horse and the type of surface it is expected to encounter.

Recreational riding

In most developed countries today, the horse is primarily used for recreational activities. Many of these pursuits, such as hunting, polo, and Thoroughbred racing, arrived in the United States from Britain. Organized hunts are still held by many people in Britain and the United States. Polo is especially popular in Argentina. Thoroughbred racing is patronized by the British royalty and is popular all over the world. In the United States, harness races, in which the jockey rides on a light two-wheeled cart pulled behind the horse, are attended by thousands of spec-

ACROSS THE ICE AND SNOW

A team of huskies pulls a sled over the icy Arctic terrain of Alberta, Canada.

While large animals would sink into even hard-packed snow, dogs are light enough to run across its surface. The Eskimo dog breeds, including the husky and malamute, weigh from 50 to 100 lb (23 to 45 kg) and are extremely swift and agile, pulling sleds in teams of up to ten. Before the invention of snowmobiles, dogsleds were the only mode of ground transportation in many Arctic regions.

The wooden dogsleds are about 10 ft (3 m) long and 2 ft (0.6 m) wide, with wooden or metal runners. They are low to the ground and have space to strap supplies or to carry a passenger. The sled driver walks or runs behind the sled, occasionally jumping on for a ride.

Dogs are inherently social animals, and this fact is put to use on a dogsled team. One dog, chosen for strength and intelligence, is taught a few basic commands, and the other dogs follow his or her lead. The dogs may be hitched to the sled in single file, in pairs, in threesomes, or each on a separate line from the sled so that they can fan out over a larger area. The dog team can consistently pull a load twice its own weight at up to 5 mph (8 km/h).

A CLOSER LOOK

tators. Trail riding is enjoyed by many, while others prefer competing in shows and meets. Rodeos preserve the broncobusting (horse taming) and roping skills that were traditionally used to tame wild horses and accustom them to wearing a saddle and continue to be prized by cowboys and cowgirls.

S. CALVO

See also: AGRICULTURE, HISTORY OF; CAVALRY AND CHARIOT; HORSE-DRAWN TRANSPORT; ROAD TRANSPORT, HISTORY OF; SNOW AND ICE TRAVEL.

Further reading:
The Complete Horse Book. Edited by E. Edwards. New York: Dorling Kindersley, 1991.
The Whole Horse Catalog. Edited by S. Price. New York: Simon & Schuster, 1993.
Piggott, S. *Wagon, Chariot, and Carriage: Symbol and Status in the History of Transport.* New York: Thames & Hudson, 1992.

ANIMATION

In its simplest terms, an animated film is created one frame at a time

This still, from Nick Park's Academy Award-winning animated film The Wrong Trousers *(1993), shows some of his cleverly manipulated clay characters.*

CONNECTIONS

● Animators use **PHOTOGRAPHY** to record the stills that are linked together to make a complete film.

● Increasingly, **COMPUTER GRAPHICS** are used in animation.

In most people's minds, the word *animation* is associated with the classic feature-film fairy tales of U.S. film producer Walter (Walt) Disney (1901–1966). However, the animated film embraces many different forms and styles. Traditional motion pictures reduce moving images to 24 static photographs each second and then capture each image on a reel of film. After the images have been edited and collated, a projector casts the stills onto a movie screen in rapid succession to create the illusion of motion (see CINEMATOGRAPHY). Animators follow much the same method as the motion-picture maker, except they must form the individual images, often over a very long period, then photograph them one at a time. The same illusion of motion is created when the frames are projected onto a movie screen.

A brief history of animation

Some of the very first films involved animated techniques. French film director Georges Méliès (1861–1938) experimented with stop-motion special effects in his magical short films such as *A Trip to the Moon* (1902); French animator Emile Cohl (1857–1938) and U.S. animator John Bray (1879–1978) photographed stick-figure drawings by 1905; and U.S. cartoonist and animator Winsor McCay (1871–1934) starred with a theatrical comedy (known as vaudeville) called *Gertie the Trained Dinosaur* (1914). In the 1920s, Austrian animator Max Fleischer (1883–1972) and Walt Disney established animation studios producing weekly short cartoons with stars such as Betty Boop and Mickey Mouse. However, animation took a huge leap forward in 1937 with the release of Disney's first feature-length film, *Snow White and the Seven Dwarfs*. From *Pinocchio* (1940) to contemporary classics such as *Beauty and the Beast* (1991) and *The Lion King* (1994), Disney is seen as the father figure of feature animation—artistically and commercially.

The U.S. motion-picture corporation Warner Brothers produced shorts made by U.S. animators Chuck Jones (1912–) and Tex Avery (1908–1980) that demonstrated a surrealistic humor, especially suited for animation. In the 1950s, Universal Pictures Company showed that wit and imagination can substitute for dizzying action and beautiful backgrounds, as was confirmed by Matt Groening's *The Simpsons* in 1987 (see the box on page 85).

Other developments include the *manga* genre, which is characterized by bold use of colors and vivid imagery. Japanese animator Hayao Miyazaki (1941–) worked on the first *manga* film—*Puss in Boots* (1969)—and continues to produce startling work.

CORE FACTS

■ Some of the very first films were animated cartoons, but the form has continued to evolve for a century.

■ Cartoon animation involves numerous steps and much painstaking labor.

■ Animation includes cutout figures, movable puppets, and creations using sand, paint, clay, and other artistic media.

■ Computer-assisted animation has taken hold for the new millennium.

British film producer Nick Park (1958–) created the modelling-clay characters Wallace and Gromit for the short films *A Grand Day Out* (1989), *The Wrong Trousers* (1993), and *A Close Shave* (1995).

Cel animation

For a feature film made with cel animation, a team of animators, directors, editors, producers, and writers may spend a year or more developing the story, sketching model sheets for each major character, and producing storyboards depicting the whole film. With a finished script in hand, the team records all the dialogue tracks first and then times them on a cue sheet to determine the precise frame where each sound will begin and end. The musical score is usually recorded after the filming and editing.

The key animators (often one for each major character) may create just a few drawings in a sequence of an action, concentrating on the extreme points to suggest the flow of the action. For example, if Goofy were playing tennis, the animator might draw Goofy holding the ball, then a single drawing of him raising his arm, the ball in the air at its peak, then Goofy in his swing and finally Goofy with the racket around his ear. Then the animation assistants, called in-betweeners, finish all the other drawings in between these key drawings to complete the scene. Clean-up artists fine-tune the lines of the rough pencil sketches. Meanwhile, background artists paint elaborate scenery on heavy paper sheets.

The pencil sketches are back lit (mounted on an illuminated surface) and photographed. Originally, inkers would carefully trace the drawings onto 8-x-10-inch (20.3-x-25.4-cm) clear plastic sheets called cels. Later, the photocopier machine performed this arduous task. Today, cels are scanned on desktop scanners and digitally transferred onto computer. Opaquers (so-called because their paint obscures parts of the clear cels) flip the cels and paint the appropriate colors on the back, using the lines from the pencil sketches as guides and separators. Often several cels comprise a single frame to suggest a three-dimensional background or to avoid redrawing the entire figure for each successive frame. A moving arm, for example, might appear on a separate cel level while the rest of the figure remains stationary from frame to frame. Mouth movements are also often handled separately from the rest of the figure.

Finally, all the cels and backgrounds are carefully assembled. Up until recent years, an animation camera was used to photograph all the composites. This specialized camera has a glass plate that holds the artwork for each frame rigidly in place on the compound (a glass-covered rack). A series of computer-controlled gears allows the camera to pan across a background horizontally or vertically while the compound holding the artwork moves in the appropriate direction under the camera. Mounted vertically above the artwork, the camera (called a rostrum camera) can move up and down, simulating dollies (on which the camera tracks toward or away from the subject) and suggesting pans and tilts.

This animator is operating an animation camera. Mounted above layers of artwork, the camera can record the overall image of each cell onto film.

Once the photographic images have been acquired, they are edited to the required sequence and length. Today, most of this work is done on computer. After editing, the the musical score is recorded and edited to synchronize with the events in the film. The film score (music) is often an important part of the advertising and merchandizing package that accompanies a successful release.

Other animation techniques

Most of the animated films and cartoons that are made today are based on cel animation, but there are other ways to create animated images. Some are based on old devices such as zoetropes; others use the latest computer technology.

THE SIMPSONS

One of the greatest milestones in the history of animation occurred in 1987, when U.S. cartoon-strip writer and animator Matt Groening (1954–) conceived *The Simpsons* for Twentieth Century Fox's *The Tracey Ullman Show*.

Based in the fictional city of Springfield, *The Simpsons* provides a satirical view of life in North America through the lives of the Simpson family—Homer and Marge (the parents), Bart, Lisa, and Maggie the baby. The show combines biting commentary on social and environmental issues with guest "appearances" by a long list of film, TV, and music stars. The prestige of *The Simpsons* is such that many of these stars are happy to lend their voices to cartoon characters that are parodies of themselves.

By the start of its ninth series in 1997, *The Simpsons* had been honored with a Peabody Award, 10 Emmy Awards, seven Annie Awards, three Genesis Awards, three International Monitor Awards and three Environmental Media Awards.

A CLOSER LOOK

Virtual-reality computer animation is made using real people. Sensors are attached to various parts of an actor's body that enable a computer to detect the location of body joints. The computer subsequently uses this information to create a cartoon figure on the screen. The resulting animated character therefore has a very lifelike motion.

Cameraless animation. During the 19th century, artists created the illusion of a moving image for toys such as flip books (piles of sheets of paper, each with an image slightly different to the next, that would be flipped by running a finger rapidly from the bottom to the top of the pile). Scottish animator Norman McLaren (1914–1987) made dozens of films by painting images directly onto frames of clear film or scratching the emulsion (chemical coating) away from unexposed film. The film would then be run on a cinematographic projector (see CINEMATOGRAPHY).

Stop-motion animation. Stop-motion animation involves using puppets as the characters of the moving image. Just as filming a series of drawings can imitate motion, so can filming photographs of stationary objects. This technique's first great practitioner, U.S. animator Willis O'Brien (1886–1962), invented dinosaurs for the silent feature *The Lost World* (1925) and the beast in *King Kong* (1933). With the aid of an armature (a flexible wire frame under the figure), he positions his creatures, photographs a single snapshot with a motion-picture camera, then alters subjects slightly before exposing the next frame. Careful timing and meticulous precision perfects the illusion. O'Brien's assistant, U.S. animator Ray Harryhausen (1920–), improved the process in Sinbad's battle with the skeleton in *The 7th Voyage of Sinbad* (1958). Feature films, such as U.S. director Tim Burton's (1958–) *Nightmare Before Christmas* (1993), and numerous commercials have used this technique.

Clay animation's mixture of subtlety and realism has attracted filmmakers since animation's early days. U.S. animator Will Vinton (1947–) repopularized the form in many films, which he dubbed claymation, including his Oscar-winning *Closed Mondays* (1974). Nick Park took clay to new limits, winning Academy Awards for *Creature Comforts* (1990), *The Wrong Trousers* (1993), and *A Close Shave* (1995).

A stop-motion camera allows a series of images to be photographed on the release of a shutter. Stop-motion cameras can be used to create special effects with real people and objects. Between each release of the camera shutter, the actors move slightly. By sitting on the ground and scooting along between frames, it looks as if they are driving invisible cars. If the camera clicks a frame each time they jump off the ground, the projected result makes them seem to hover in the air.

The development of computer-controlled camera motion for *Star Wars* (1977), by U.S. film director George Lucas (1944–), showed that computers can repeat elaborate camera movements exactly. Indeed, most action features now involve the frequent use of stop-motion cameras and detailed models. Special-effects animators and model builders can make impossible visions seem credible. They also cost less than live-action shooting in terms of production.

Computer animation. While defying the definition of animation as a movie made one frame at a time, computer animation has advanced greatly since the early efforts of U.S. animators John Whitney (1917–) and Stan Van Der Beek (1931–1984). Once the animator completes the extremes, the computer takes over the labor-intensive work of the in-betweeners, inkers, and opaquers. With an artist in charge, the results can be satisfying and stimulating, as in the movies *Toy Story* (1995) and *ANTZ* (1998).

Virtual-reality computer animation. In virtual-reality computer animation sensors are attached to various parts of an actor's body. The sensors enable a computer to track the location and movement of the actor's joints. The computer subsequently uses this information to create a cartoon figure with very lifelike animated motion.

A rich variety

U.S. animator Winsor McCay made the first animated feature, *The Sinking of the Lusitania*, in 1918.

The 1970s saw an explosion in other media used for animation. U.S. animator Caroline Leaf (1946–) applied water-based ink and tempera (a paint containing egg yolk) with her fingers on a glass plate lighted from beneath to form translucent images for *The Street* (1976). Jacobus Willem "Co" Hoedeman (1940–) won an Academy Award in 1977 with sand as his medium in *Sand Castle*.

For time-lapse photography, a stop-motion camera with an intervalometer (timer) snaps a single frame at intervals. By projecting the resultant film at normal speed, a flower blooms in a few seconds or clouds rush across the screen in dancing rhythms.

M. CALLAHAN

See also: CINEMATOGRAPHY; COMPUTER; COMPUTER GRAPHICS; IMAGING TECHNOLOGY; PHOTOGRAPHY; SOUND RECORDING AND REPRODUCTION.

Further reading:
Blair, P. *Cartoon Animation*. Laguna Hills, California: Walter Foster, 1994.
Interactive Computer Animation. Edited by N. Thalmann and D. Thalmann. Englewood Cliffs, New Jersey: Prentice-Hall, 1996.

ANTENNA AND TRANSMITTER

A transmitter generates an oscillating electric signal that is converted by an antenna to an electromagnetic signal

Using electromagnetic radiation such as radio waves and microwaves to transmit signals through the air is one of the most important methods of communication. It is still the only practical form of instant communication over large distances that does not require laying down wire or fiber-optic cables (see ELECTROMAGNETIC RADIATION; FIBER OPTICS; TELEPHONY AND TELEGRAPHY).

An antenna, or aerial, is the device used to send out or pick up these electromagentic signals. An antenna consists of an electrical conductor such as a metal rod, which can be used to convert electromagnetic signals into electrical signals or vice versa. Transmitters are used to supply a transmitting antenna with the appropriate electrical signal.

Electromagnetic theory

In 1831, British scientist Michael Faraday (1791–1867) discovered that when an electric current flows in a wire, a magnetic field is formed around the wire. He also showed that a moving or changing magnetic field will cause an electric current to flow in a nearby electrical conductor. This effect, which allows magnetic signals to induce electrical signals and vice versa, is known as electromagnetic induction (see ELECTRICITY AND MAGNETISM).

In 1865, British mathematician James Clerk Maxwell (1831–1879) showed that a varying (oscillating) magnetic field moving through space causes, and is accompanied by, an equivalent oscillating electric field. In 1887, German physicist Heinrich Rudolph Hertz (1857–1894) demonstrated that radio waves, generated by an electrical oscillating device (an oscillator), can be transmitted over a distance and detected. Hertz's name is honored and remembered in the unit of frequency (speed of oscillation) known as the hertz. One hertz (Hz) is equivalent to one oscillation per second.

This microwave relay station in California uses a series of receiver and transmitter antennas to receive weak microwave signals and retransmit amplified signals.

CORE FACTS

- Transmitter antennas use electromagnetic induction to turn electric signals into radio signals. Receiver antennas use the same principles to turn low-level radio signals back into electrical signals.
- The operating frequency range of a particular antenna depends upon its size and configuration.
- The electric signal for transmitter antennas is supplied by a transmitter. Transmitters use a system called modulation to combine the data signal with a uniform carrier wave.
- Receiver antennas require amplifers to boost the tiny electrical signal that they produce.
- When a narrow beam is required, microwave antennas are used with dish reflectors that reflect the microwaves to or from the antenna.

The transmitter

A radio transmitter is a device for generating an oscillating electric current so that it can be applied to an antenna and produce a radiating electromagnetic field. Electric oscillations are voltages or currents that rise from zero to a peak in one direction and then reverse, return to zero, and continue to a peak in the opposite direction before returning to zero again. This sequence is called a cycle. If the electrical changes are smooth and regular, the wave produced is a sine wave.

Modern oscillators generate signals using a type of transistor, called an operator amplifier, that uses feedback in a resonant circuit to produce specific frequencies (see AMPLIFIER). Just as a guitar string will vibrate at a preferred frequency—its resonant frequency—that is determined largely by its length and tension, an electronic circuit will favor certain frequencies of electrical oscillation according to the combination of electronic components (such as resistors and capacitors) in the circuit. If the output from an amplifier is fed through a circuit that favors a particular frequency and then fed back to the amplifier input, the preferred frequency will be boosted relative to the other frequencies in the signal. After passing around the feedback loops a few times, the preferred frequency will be much stronger than any other. This is the basis of resonant-tuned circuits.

Many practical oscillators contain resonant-tuned circuits consisting of a resistor and a capacitor. For greater precision, a piezoelectric crystal may be included. Such crystals, which are also used in clocks to keep precise time, deform slightly if a voltage is applied to opposite faces and generate a small change in the voltage (see TIME MEASUREMENT). If they are included in the feedback path of an oscillator they produce an output of very stable frequency.

CONNECTIONS

- **GROUND STATIONS** use radio antennas to monitor and communicate with space vehicles such as **SATELLITES**, **SPACE STATIONS**, and **SPACE PROBES**.

Modulation

Transmitter oscillators produce a sine-wave current, which can be increased in amplitude (the height of the wave) by an amplifier. This sine wave is called the carrier wave and, by itself, carries no useful information. The information to be transmitted, such as a sound or a picture, must be converted into a signal (the modulation signal) and combined with the carrier wave in a process called modulation.

In amplitude modulation (AM), the high frequency carrier wave is caused to change in amplitude in accordance with the modulation signal. Receiver antennas that respond to amplitude modulation are liable to pick up electrical noise that also modulates the amplitude of the carrier wave. An alternative and better way of imposing information on a carrier wave is by frequency modulation (FM). In this method the amplitude of the sine wave remains constant but its frequency changes in strict accordance with the amplitude of the modulating signal. Other more complex methods of modulation include phase modulation and pulse modulation.

Frequency and wavelength

Types of electromagnetic radiation are characterized by their frequency. Because all electromagnetic radiation, including light, travels in air at the same speed of about 186,000 miles per second (300 million meters per second), the wavelength of any radio wave (the distance between two consecutive peaks) is the speed (measured in distance per second) divided by frequency (number of waves per second). This means that the higher the frequency, the shorter the wavelength (see WAVE MOTION).

The lowest radio frequencies used are about 10,000 Hz. Radio frequencies on the AM band range from about 500,000 Hz (500 KHz) to 1,500,000 Hz (1.5MHz). The FM band ranges from 88 million Hz (88 MHz) to 108 million Hz (108 MHz). UHF TV channels range from 470 MHz to 890 MHz. In all these cases the actual wavelength in meters, or fractions of a meter, can be found by dividing 300 million meters by the frequency. Thus the lowest radio frequencies have a wavelength of 30,000 meters (18.6 miles peak to peak). AM wavelengths range from about 600 meters to 200 meters, FM wavelengths from 3.4 meters to 2.7 meters, and UHF wavelengths from 0.63 meters to 0.33 meters. These dimensions are central to the design of antennas.

Antenna dimensions

The simplest antennas are merely rods of metal or other conducting material. To be most efficient, an antenna must be of such a length that it resonates electrically at the same frequency as the radio waves it is designed to transmit or receive. To resonate at a particular frequency, the physical length of an antenna should be half the wavelength of the radio waves that it is designed to transmit or receive. Antennas that are made to such dimensions are called resonant antennas; they radiate and receive signals efficiently at their resonant frequency. Resonant antennas only work effectively at a single frequency.

The antennas used in small transistor radio receivers work in a slightly different way because of the necessity to be small and to work over a range of different frequencies. These antennas use a coil of wire wound around a short rod of magnetic material called ferrite. The ferrite core increases the strength of the electric current induced in the coil by the radio waves at AM band frequencies.

The length requirements of transmitting and receiving antennas are exactly the same. However, transmitting antennas carry enormously larger currents than receiving antennas, because they transmit powerful radio signals to be received over large distances. Simple antennas can be connected together in complex arrays that function as one large antenna.

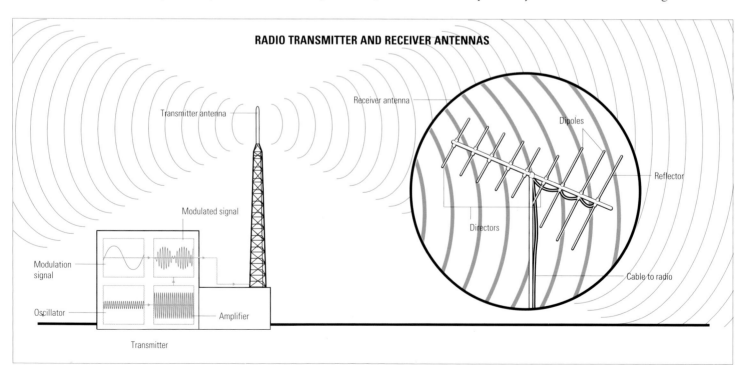

RADIO TRANSMITTER AND RECEIVER ANTENNAS

Receiver antenna

Transmitter antenna

Dipoles

Reflector

Modulated signal

Directors

Cable to radio

Modulation signal

Oscillator

Amplifier

Transmitter

Feeding transmitter power to antennas

The electrical output of a transmitter is carried along two conductors that may be parallel or coaxial (one conductor inside a hollow cylinder in the other). In both cases the two conductors must be insulated from one another (see CABLE, ELECTRICAL). At low frequencies, one conductor will be grounded (connected to ground or an object that will allow current to flow to the ground). The other conductor is connected to one end of a long antenna (it needs to be long because low frequency radio waves have long wavelengths). At higher frequencies, the antenna is usually cut in the middle and one conductor is connected to the inner end of each half, while the other is grounded as before. This arrangement is called a dipole. Antennas of this kind commonly have further conducting rods called parallel reflector elements behind the dipole and a sequence of ever shorter, closely spaced rods called director elements in front of it. These elements, none of which are electrically connected to the dipole, focus the radio waves on the dipole. This type of antenna, called a yagi, must be oriented carefully.

The familiar dish antenna for microwave transmission and reception is a dipole with a parabolic reflector behind it that, in the case of a receiving antenna, collects the signal and focuses it on the dipole. Microwaves behave very similarly to light, and the transmitting-dish antenna sends out a parallel beam of microwaves in much the same way as a searchlight sends out a beam of light waves (see LIGHT AND OPTICS). Careful orientation is also necessary for this type of antenna.

Receiving antennas

The resonant properties of receiving antennas are the same as those of the transmitting antennas, and the design of the antenna will determine the frequencies to which it is more sensitive. The electrical currents induced in an antenna by a radio signal are very small indeed and must be amplified in the receiver many times before their information content can be used. In some cases the received signal is so weak that losses in signal intensity in the leads from the antenna to the receiver would reduce the signal to below the background noise level. This low-level electromagnetic interference occurs all the time from sources such as electric motors and faulty ignition systems. In such cases where the received signal is particularly low, it is advantageous to fit a radio-frequency amplifier that can boost the signal to an adequate level in a small sealed box close to the antenna and away from sources of electromagnetic intereference (see RADIO RECEIVER).

R. YOUNGSON

See also: AIR TRAFFIC CONTROL; INTEGRATED CIRCUIT; MILITARY COMMUNICATIONS AND CONTROL; RADAR; SATELLITE; SEMICONDUCTOR AND SEMICONDUCTOR DEVICE; TELECOMMUNICATONS; TELEVISION; TELEVISION AND COMPUTER MONITOR; WIRELESS COMMUNICATION.

A biologist uses a directional antenna to track a leopard, which has been fitted with a small transmitter and antenna on a collar.

Further reading:

Smith, A. *Radio Frequency Principles and Application: The Generation, Propagation, and Reception of Signals and Noise.* New York: IEEE Press, 1998.
Stutzman, G., *Antenna Theory and Design.* New York: John Wiley & Sons, 1998.
Whitaker, J. *Radio Frequency Transmission Systems: Design and Operation.* New York: Intertext Publications, McGraw-Hill, 1991.

ELECTRONIC NEWSGATHERING

Artificial-satellite microwave communication, such as that provided by the International Telecommunications Satellite Organization (Intelsat), has made possible remarkable immediacy of on-the-spot television and radio news reporting. News reporters can use portable transmitter systems with small parabolic antennas to send narrow-beam ultrahigh frequency (UHF) TV signals to a satellite in geosynchronous orbit. These satellites can beam back the signals instantly to a large area of Earth's surface where they can be collected by the ground station that serves the reporter's television company or news agency (see GROUND STATION).

A geosynchronous orbit—otherwise known as a geostationary equatorial orbit, or GEO—is a circular orbit, directly above the equator, at an altitude of 22,200 miles (33,900 kilometers) above Earth's surface. The special characteristic of a GEO is that a satellite at this altitude will complete an Earth orbit in exactly the same time that it takes for one Earth rotation. Hence, a satellite orbiting in the same direction as Earth's rotation will remain over the same point on Earth's surface, making it easier for ground stations to maintain good communications with the satellite 24 hours a day.

During the Gulf War (1990–1991), the American public was able to watch daily broadcasts from Israel, Jordan, Saudi Arabia, and Baghdad. The Atlanta-based cable news network CNN relied heavily on the Intelsat satellite and electronic newsgathering technology in order to provide its 24-hour coverage of the conflict.

WIDER IMPACT

ANTIAIRCRAFT WEAPON

Antiaircraft weapons based on land and at sea are used to destroy enemy aircraft or missiles

The tracked rapier is an antiaircraft weapon used by the British Army and operated by a crew of three, who are housed in its armored cab. It has eight missiles, which are ready to fire within 30 seconds after the vehicle comes to a stop.

CONNECTIONS

● The evolution of antiaircraft weapons followed closely on innovations in **MISSILES** and **MILITARY AIRCRAFT**.

● Early antiaircraft weapons used a type of analog **COMPUTER** to improve their firing accuracy.

Antiaircraft weapons were developed to defend cities, ports, and military targets from attack by enemy aircraft and missiles. They consist of units of large guns or missiles that are set up on land and onboard ships, and they are usually controlled by radar and electronic systems (see RADAR). Antiaircraft weapons have existed from the time that aircraft were first used in warfare—in World War I (1914–1918)—and have had to develop in parallel with the airplane.

Weapons used to attack enemy aircraft call for far greater technological sophistication than weapons used against land or sea targets. Aircraft speeds and maneuverability have, therefore, been the main challenges in producing effective antiaircraft weapons.

Development of antiaircraft weapons

The earliest antiaircraft weapons evolved from guns used in land battles (surface-to-surface gunnery), such as rifles and machine guns. During World War I, a range of field guns, some as large as 3.5 in (90 mm) caliber, were converted for antiaircraft use. These weapons were crude and ineffective, however, because their aiming devices had not been designed for use against targets capable of rapid movement. The principal problem was to support the gun and track the target rapidly with it, at angles to the horizontal of up to 90 degrees. Initially, simple tripods were used with improvised mountings.

Between the world wars, as control of the air became a key factor in proving military might, great efforts were made to improve antiaircraft weapons. An elaborate form of early analog computer was developed to enable gun crews to rapidly calculate how far ahead of the enemy aircraft their guns should be aimed. These computers could also figure out the time-fuse setting of the shells.

The Bofors gun

One of the most effective antiaircraft weapons of World War II (1939–1945) was a quick-aiming weapon that could fire 120 rounds of a 2-lb (0.9-kg) shell per minute. This was the Swedish Bofors gun, used extensively on land and sea by U.S. and British forces, especially against dive-bombers (airplanes that fly high and descend steeply to drop their bombs). The Bofors guns could be rapidly elevated and traversed (rotated horizontally). Although it had a vertical range of about 2 miles (3 km), it was most effective against low-flying aircraft.

Antiaircraft artillery

Guns of up to 5 in (127 mm) caliber were designed specifically for use against high-altitude bombers between the wars and were extensively used in World War II. Many antiaircraft batteries (installations) were set up in Britain for use against German bombers during the civilian bombing campaign (called the Blitz) inflicted by Germany on London and other towns in 1940. As well as guns, the antiaircraft batteries included searchlights, listening devices, and predictors. A major improvement was the development of the proximity fuse, a miniaturized radar in the shell's nose that detected the nearest distance from the target before the charge was fired.

Surface-to-air missiles (SAMs)

Because proximity-fuse weapons were never particularly accurate or cost-effective, they became virtually obsolete soon after World War II. Their disuse was further prompted with the development in the 1950s and 1960s of surface-to-air missiles (SAMs) as a defense against high-altitude bombers. The U.S. Nike Ajax and the U.S. Nike Hercules are examples of SAMs. The earliest SAMs were tracked from the ground and guided by wires. These externally guided weapons were, in turn, superseded by more sophisticated missiles, capable of tracking the target by radar or by heat-seeking systems. Heat sensors in the missile enable it to home in on the target, and the warhead in the missile tip destroys it. Some types of antiaircraft weapons, such as the U.S. Redeye and Stinger types, are portable and can be launched from the shoulder. Hawk and Patriot missiles are radar guided; Patriots were particularly successful in intercepting Iraqi Scud missiles during the Gulf War.

R. YOUNGSON

See also: ARTILLERY; STRATEGIC DEFENSE SYSTEMS; TRANSDUCER AND SENSOR; WEAPONRY: SPECIALIZED SYSTEMS.

Further reading:

Blakelock, J. H. *Automatic Control of Aircraft and Missiles.* New York: John Wiley & Sons, 1991.

ANTIBIOTICS

An antibiotic is a drug that kills or stops the growth of bacteria or fungi

A hundred years ago, it was very common for people in the United States and in Europe to die from bacterial infections; an infected wound or a sore throat could be fatal. In the 20th century, the discovery and manufacture of antibiotics saved the lives of millions of people who would have died prematurely of infectious diseases in previous times.

The history of antibiotics

As long ago as 1683, Dutch physician Antoni van Leeuwenhoek (1632–1723) discovered bacteria, but not the link between bacteria and disease. The theory that microorganisms cause disease was first expounded by Italian microbiologist Agostino Bassi (1773–1856), whose work preceded the germ theory of great French chemist and microbiologist Louis Pasteur (1822–1895), published in 1868. Bassi discovered, in 1835, that a disease affecting silkworms, muscardine, was caused by a fungus. Pasteur, whose studies in fermentation led him to produce his germ theory, continued the work of Bassi. British surgeon Joseph Lister (1827–1912) also indirectly discovered the link between bacteria and disease when he began to use phenol to sterilize wounds. He found that many patients could survive postoperative infections.

German chemist Paul Ehrlich (1854–1915), found that certain chemicals could kill microbes (bacteria and fungi). In 1909 he announced the first antibiotic drug, Salvarsan, which was effective against the bacteria (spirochetes) that cause the disease syphilis, a sexually transmitted infection.

In 1932, German pathologist Gerhard Domagk (1895–1964) announced the discovery of the dye Prontosil Red, a powerful antibiotic that was the forerunner of today's sulfonamide drugs. In clinical tests, it saved the life of Domagk's own daughter, who was ill with blood poisoning. In 1939, Domagk was awarded the Nobel Prize for medicine but could not accept it until after World War II.

Scottish microbiologist Alexander Fleming (1881–1955) made a major breakthrough when he discovered penicillin in 1928 (see the box on page

A technician inspects a vessel that supports the fermentation of microorganisms, such as the mold used in the production of antibiotics.

92). The drug was used by the U.S. armed forces from 1943 to treat injured soldiers. However, it was not until 1946 that this antibiotic became available to the general public.

After penicillin, streptomycin was discovered by Ukrainian-born American chemist Selman Waksman (1888–1973) in 1943. Streptomycin was effective against tuberculosis, one of the most feared diseases of the time. Waksman found streptomycin in a common soil bacterium called *Streptomyces griseus*. Later it was found that the *Streptomyces* genus is a rich source of antibiotics, producing hundreds of different compounds. Molds are also a major source of antibiotics. Microbes produce antibiotics in order to kill off other species that might compete with them for food. By the mid-1950s, most of the naturally occurring antibiotics in use today had been discovered.

Types of antibiotics

There are three major types of antibiotics: natural, synthetic, and semisynthetic. The natural ones are derived from molds and fungi by a fermentation process. In a typical fermentation, a sample of the microbes is mixed with a nutrient solution in a big stainless steel tank. The microbes grow and multiply, producing lots of antibiotic. This is then extracted from the liquid in the tank by being dissolved in a solvent. The solvent is then removed by evaporation, and the antibiotic is purified (see BIOTECHNOLOGY). Synthetic antibiotics, such as the sulfonamides, are

CORE FACTS

- Antibiotics may act only on bacteria and fungi, not on viruses.
- Penicillin and streptomycin were the first successful antibiotics to be discovered.
- The use of antibiotics worldwide has meant many infectious diseases that were once fatal became treatable in the second half of the 20th century.
- Antibiotics work by attacking some aspect of the microbe's life cycle.
- Antibiotic resistance is becoming a serious public health problem.

CONNECTIONS

● Fungi from which antibiotics are produced are also used in the production of bread and other foods in the **BAKING INDUSTRY** and in the production of alcoholic **BEVERAGES** in the **BREWING INDUSTRY**.

THE DISCOVERY OF PENICILLIN

Penicillin was discovered by chance by British bacteriologist Alexander Fleming (1881–1955) at St. Mary's Hospital in London, where he was investigating the antiseptic qualities of tears and saliva. He was working with bacteria that formed visible colonies on a glass dish. A mold (*Penicillium notatum*) happened to land on an uncovered dish, and Fleming noticed that the colonies of bacteria were wiped out. From this accidental discovery emerged penicillin. Fleming then grew a pure culture of the mold, but he could not purify the bacteria-killing substance from the culture. It was not until 1939 that Australian pathologist Howard Florey (1898–1968) and German biochemist Ernst Chain (1906–1979) were able to purify penicillin and make sufficient quantities of it.

Florey and Chain discovered that penicillin worked by blocking bacterial cell division, and that the amounts prescribed and the duration of the dosage were crucial to its effectiveness. Researchers in the United States developed large fermenting tanks used to grow the fungus in order to treat wounded soldiers in World War II, where it saved thousands of lives and limbs. By 1945 it was clear the drug could destroy bacteria in a dilution of one molecule per 50 million molecules of water and that it could be made in very large quantities. Shortly after the war, the drug came into general use in the United States and Europe.

Sir Alexander Fleming, the discoverer of penicillin, photographed in 1951.

A CLOSER LOOK

made by chemists in a factory. The semisynthetics, of which ampicillin is an example, are a blend of the two; that is, a natural antibiotic is made by fermentation and later modified by chemical synthesis.

Different antibiotics tend to have different uses (see the table below). An antibiotic that is active against a wide range of bacteria is known as a broad spectrum antibiotic. Many antibiotics are given in tablet form; however, some of them break down in the stomach, so these must be added directly into the blood by an injection. Antibiotics are also used to prevent illnesses in farm animals. However, overexposure to antibiotics in this way is believed to be driving the evolution of resistant strains of microbes.

How antibiotics work

Antibiotics work by interfering with some aspect of the microbe's life cycle. For instance, penicillin and similar drugs stop bacteria from making their cell walls. Since human cells do not have walls, only the microbes are harmed. Other antibiotics, such as the group known as tetracyclines, block a microbe's ability to make any proteins. The sulfonamides work by stopping the microbe from making DNA, its genetic material. Microbes produce proteins and DNA in a different way than the infected animal and so only the microbes are affected by the antibiotic.

The drawbacks of antibiotics

Antibiotics cannot kill viruses, so they do not work against infections such as influenza. Furthermore, antibiotics are now losing their power as microbes develop resistance to their action. Among a population of microbes, some will always be more sensitive to the drug than others. When the microbes are exposed to an antibiotic, the more sensitive ones die first. This leaves a population of more resistant microbes. Over time the microbes become collectively more resistant. The overuse of antibiotics —using them when the immune system could deal with an infection unaided, for example—has caused resistant microbes to emerge even faster.

S. ALDRIDGE

See also: BIOTECHNOLOGY; PHARMACOLOGY AND DRUG TREATMENT.

Further reading:

Dixon, B. *Power Unseen: How Microbes Rule the World.* New York: W. H. Freeman and Company, 1994.

SOME WIDELY USED ANTIBIOTICS

Antibiotic	Type	Use
Ciprofloxacin	Broad spectrum	Traveler's diarrhea; urinary tract infections; skin and joint infections
Amoxicillin, Ampicillin	Penicillin antibiotic	Chronic bronchitis; middle ear and urinary tract infections
Erythromycin	Penicillin alternative	Throat infections; pneumonia; Legionnaires' disease
Metronidazole	Antibiotic, antiprotozoan	Infection with amoebas; protozoan infections; vaginitis
Tetracyclines	Broad spectrum	Chronic bronchitis; fungal infections of the mouth and genitals; acne

ANTISEPTICS AND STERILIZATION

Antiseptics are chemical agents that destroy microorganisms; sterilization is the process of destroying them

In 1865, renowned British surgeon Joseph Lister (1827–1912) wondered whether the microorganisms that French chemist and microbiologist Louis Pasteur (1822–1895) had found to cause putrefaction were responsible for the wound infections that were killing so many of his patients. Lister knew that sewage odors were often neutralized with a solution of carbolic acid, also called phenol, and reasoned that this worked because it killed the microorganisms that caused the odor. So he tried soaking his surgical instruments in phenol and used phenol spray while operating. The infection rate among his patients immediately plummeted. By the end of the 19th century, aseptic or germ-free surgery was standard procedure (see SURGERY).

Microorganisms are bacteria, fungi, and protozoa. Many biologists also consider viruses to be microorganisms, although there is some debate over whether they are extremely simple forms of microorganisms or extremely complex molecules. Viruses are very small—they are invisible to an optical microscope—and although they can replicate (multiply) only within living cells, they can be the hardest to destroy. Aseptic (germfree) conditions are achieved through the use of sterilization procedures to kill all microorganisms. Disinfection is the destruction of harmful microorganisms; resistant bacterial spores may remain after disinfection. Antiseptics, or disinfectants, are chemicals that act against microorganisms. The term *antiseptic* is generally used only in the context of application to living tissues. Antibiotics differ from antiseptics in that their destructive action is specific to certain bacteria (see ANTIBIOTICS).

Sterilization

Sterilization may be accomplished in several ways. The method used depends on what is to be sterilized and what sort of treatment it can withstand. Autoclaves are used in hospitals to sterilize surgical instruments, swabs, and linens. The autoclave works like a pressure cooker. When water is boiled in a closed vessel so that the steam cannot escape, the increase in pressure raises the boiling point from

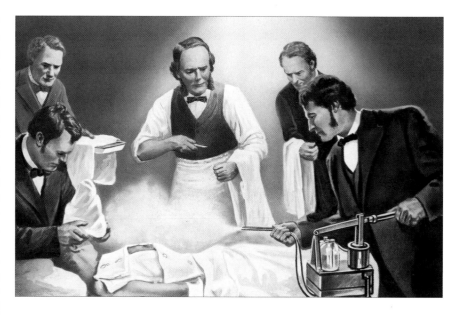

This painting depicts British surgeon Joseph Lister using carbolic acid spray in one of his earliest antiseptic surgical operations.

212°F (100°C) to about 260°F (127°C). Boiling the items at the higher temperature helps to kill even bacterial spores, which can survive immersion at water's normal boiling point. The autoclave is generally run about an hour at a time, so that the boiling water can penetrate into the linens.

For powders and oils, which cannot be immersed in water, dry heat may be used, but this requires hotter temperatures for longer periods of time. Two hours in an oven at 350°F (180°C) will kill bacterial spores. Instruments can be soaked in a chemical sterilizing solution or exposed to an open flame. Waste products can be incinerated to kill microorganisms.

High-intensity ultraviolet light can also be used to destroy microorganisms, since it causes permanent genetic damage and prevents them from multiplying. Ultraviolet light does not penetrate solids, but it may be used to sterilize surfaces, air, and transparent liquids. It is sometimes used to sterilize hospital air ducts.

Higher-energy X rays or gamma rays can be used to sterilize materials such as foodstuffs that would suffer from either soaking or heating. Typically the substances to be sterilized are sealed in airtight bags and moved on a conveyor belt past a cobalt-60 radioactive source. The high-energy radiation from such a source kills microorganisms within seconds. This method has been rather controversial partly because of the unfounded fear that it makes the food itself radioactive.

Killing microorganisms is not the only way to achieve aseptic conditions; in some cases the organisms may also be removed by filtering. For liquids, filters made of fused glass, diatomite, or cellulose ester membrane can remove bacteria, but filter pore sizes small enough to eliminate viruses have not yet been achieved. High-efficiency particulate air (HEPA) filters can remove 99.9 percent of particles

CORE FACTS

- The introduction of aseptic conditions greatly reduced the infection rate in surgery.
- Sterilization is the process of destroying microorganisms by heat, radiation, or other means.
- Disinfectants work by disrupting microorganisms' cell membranes or destroying the proteins that the cells need to function.
- Many different types of chemicals may be used as disinfectants.

CONNECTIONS

- The use of effective antiseptics has greatly increased the safety of **SURGERY**.

- Early antiseptics contained heavy **METALS**, such as mercury, which later proved to have toxic effects.

A technician opens up an autoclave containing sterilized materials to be used in the preparation of injectable medicines. The airtight suit prevents the technician from contaminating the freshly sterilized materials.

greater than 0.3 micrometers. Again, the filter pores are much larger than viruses, but airborne viruses often travel on far larger particles of dust or mucus. Consequently, HEPA filters work effectively against these viruses as well.

Disinfectants

Some disinfectant chemicals are surface-active, disrupting the membranes of microbial cells. Others destroy or denature the proteins necessary to the cells' biological processes. A disinfectant's effectiveness varies with temperature, concentration, time, and the pH (acidity) of the environment. Efforts

should be made by those concerned to choose the least toxic disinfectant that would perform best in each particular circumstance.

Many types of chemicals work as disinfectants. Organic solvents both disrupt cell membranes and denature proteins. They include isopropyl alcohol, which is commonly used as a skin disinfectant, for example in swabbing the skin before an injection. It cleanses as well as disinfects, and it has the advantage of evaporating without leaving a residue.

Heavy metals have an antiseptic effect. Mercury-based antiseptics were once popular for treating cuts and scrapes, but they are seldom used today. With mercury, many preparations are quite toxic, and the milder ones, such as Mercurochrome (merbromin) and Merthiolate (thimerosal), are not very effective.

Lister's original antiseptic, phenol, is no longer used in hospitals in the developed world in its concentrated form because it is toxic, corrosive, and has a strong smell. However, dilute solutions are still used, for example in throat disinfectants, and compounds related to phenol are used in household disinfectants and antibacterial skin washes.

The halogens are a group of elements that can be used as disinfectants because of their chemical reactivity. Halogen disinfectants include chlorine (used in bleach and in swimming pools) and iodine. Tincture of iodine (a weak solution of iodine in alcohol) was once a popular household antiseptic. It has now been largely supplanted for use on skinned knees by antiseptics with less sting. But iodophors, molecular complexes of iodine with soaps or detergents, are commonly used in hospitals as preoperative skin washes; they are also present in antibacterial soaps.

Too much of a good thing?

Many scientists are concerned that in our enthusiasm to destroy harmful microorganisms, we are allowing stronger germs to evolve that are tougher to control. Bacteria multiply quickly, and when we kill off the specimens most susceptible to a particular disinfectant or antibiotic, the most resistant strains are left to take over. Publicity about microbial food poisoning has made bactericidal household cleansers and hand soaps very popular. The result is an environment awash in antiseptics, and the bacteria adapt. As a result, stronger weapons must be found to fight the next disease outbreak, and the cycle continues. Already there are some strains of bacteria causing outbreaks of infection in hospitals; these new "superbugs" are resistant to all known antibiotics.

S. CALVO

See also: CLEANING AGENTS; PHARMACOLOGY AND DRUG TREATMENT; SURGERY.

Further reading:

David, J., and Zimmerman, B. *Killer Germs: Microbes and Diseases that Threaten Humanity.* Chicago: Contemporary Books, 1996.
Youngson, R. *The Surgery Book.* New York: St. Martin's Press, 1993.

HOUSEHOLD DISINFECTANTS

Disinfectants used in the home may not have to be quite as powerful as those used in a hospital or industrial environment, but they have many other requirements levied upon them. Toxicity must be minimized, strong smells are frowned upon, and corrosive products will not be suitable for use on most household surfaces. Cleansing properties are desirable, so that a single product may serve to both clean and disinfect (see CLEANING AGENTS).

Fortunately, strong disinfectants are not really necessary for general cleaning. Ordinary detergents and soaps wash away about 90 percent of the microorganisms on a surface. When a disinfectant is required, phenolics may be used, but weaker acids such as lemon juice or vinegar may suffice. Pine cleaners are also considered disinfecting if they contain at least 20 percent pine oil. Ammonia is an alkaline disinfectant; detergent complexes with ammonium chloride are the active ingredient in many household disinfectant cleansers.

The alkalis also include trisodium phosphate, once a common ingredient in household cleaners but now somewhat out of favor because of concerns about phosphates causing excess algae growth when they are rinsed into the environment. Chlorine bleach is effective against mildew (mold), but it must not be used together with ammonia, because combining them causes a chemical reaction that produces poisonous chlorine gas.

A CLOSER LOOK

AQUACULTURE

Aquaculture is the farming of aquatic plants and animals

Aquaculture is the fastest-growing form of agriculture in the United States. It is being taken up by farmers trying to diversify their operations, commercial fishers whose catches are dwindling, and national or multinational corporations searching for expanding sectors in the food industries. Coastal pollution, overfishing, and world population increases are creating a worldwide market for farmed fish. The main expansion has come in high-priced fresh fish species, such as crayfish, oysters, prawns, salmon, shrimp, and trout. The two most heavily farmed fish in the United States are catfish and crayfish, which are raised mainly in the southeastern states. Hawaii has an extensive and diverse aquaculture industry that is deeply rooted in the traditional aquaculture of Asia. Like Japan, Hawaii farms large amounts of seaweed. Algin, agar, and carrageenan—used as thickening or gelling agents in drugs, food, and other products—are all important substances that are derived from seaweed.

The life cycles of farmed fish are strictly controlled by fish farmers. Selected fish, usually the healthiest and meatiest, are allowed to spawn, often with the aid of hormone injections. Most fish are cultured in tanks or ponds with carefully controlled environments. The fry (juvenile fish) are then taken to shallow tanks or ponds and, as they grow, to larger, deeper tanks or ponds. Fish farmers usually harvest, package, and sell the final product.

Pond culture

Some fish farming, especially of fish raised for recreational fishing, is done in natural ponds. Recreational-fishing ponds are often on small farms and may also be used to provide water for livestock, for irrigation, or for swimming. As a result, the water quality is lower than in other forms of fish farming. However, the natural pond environment often produces healthier fish and requires less maintenance than artificial tanks, since fish have adapted to their ecosystems over centuries and it is difficult to replicate the same conditions artificially. Fish for recreational fishing are likely to stay outdoors all year, reproducing naturally and being restocked as necessary. In cool climates, fish can remain over the winter if the ponds are deep enough and the water is well circulated.

A seaweed harvester attends to her work at a plantation on the coast of East Africa. The seaweed is planted and harvested in a three- to four-week cycle throughout the year and much of the preparing, planting, and collecting is done at low tide.

Raceways

Raceways are rectangular troughs made from concrete and pitched to allow constant flow of a shallow stream of water. Because their design ensures good oxygenation of the water, raceways can support larger numbers of fish in the same area than ponds can, so fish harvesting and disease treatment are made easier. Raceways are especially popular for raising trout, which need cold, well-oxygenated water.

Net-pens

Salmon and trout are sometimes raised in submerged net enclosures placed in lakes or salt water near the ocean. These pens may either be fixed to pilings driven into the bottom of the lake or ocean or allowed to float from an anchor in deeper waters. The advantage of using net enclosures to farm fish is that areas that have little other function can be farmed intensively. The fish are easily observed and harvested, and the nets take up little space. However, disease is difficult to control, and the fish are subject to the action of waves, predators, and other unpredictable events.

Recirculation systems

When fish are raised in tanks, some or all of the water may be reused. The water can be purified by passing through settling tanks and filters that remove dead organic matter. However, such systems are expensive to set up. An alternative is to use the water to irrigate greenhouse plants: the soil acts as a natural filter and the water is collected for reuse.

Shellfish culture

The traditional method of farming oysters and mussels is to capture wild larvae and plant them on poles or trays in relatively sheltered ocean locations. When

---

CORE FACTS

■ Fish may be raised in ponds, tanks, net pens, raceways, or complex recycled water systems.

■ Shellfish are raised from wild larvae that are planted on poles or in trays in sheltered ocean locations.

■ Sport fish, such as hybrids of bream or striped bass, are raised in natural farm ponds.

CONNECTIONS

● Improvements in **DEEP-SEA AND DIVING TECHNOLOGY,** have caused oyster and sponge farming to become far less dangerous than it was in the past.

● Developments in the techniques used in **HYDROPONICS** has aided methods of plant cultivation in the field of aquaculture.

Fish are trapped and stored in this submerged net enclosure in a lagoon in Takaroa Atoll on one of the Tuamotu islands of French Polynesia.

half grown, they are taken to safer places until they are ready to sell. In Japan, farmers have perfected the art of producing pearls from oysters. A fragment of shell is inserted under a piece of living oyster tissue, around which the oyster then grows a pearl. Clam larvae are harvested from the beach; prawns, shrimp, and crayfish are raised by catching wild, egg-bearing females and keeping them in ponds or tanks until the juveniles hatch. The hatchlings are kept in separate tanks until they are sufficiently adult to move to the main tanks. Farmers in Minnesota and Kentucky are experimenting with raising crayfish in rice paddies.

Breeding

Today, farmers have shown much interest in the scientific breeding and genetic engineering of fish and shellfish. Breeding has improved some strains of fish for recreational fishing, such as hybrids of bream or striped bass. Other fish are being bred for their ability to thrive in crowded conditions and to grow faster. In the northern United States, efforts are under way to breed walleye that will thrive in captivity. Similarly, flounder are being bred to acclimatize to domestic conditions and to fresh water. A sterile variety of oyster has been developed that can be grown and sold all year round. At the moment, work is also under way to produce genetically engineered prawns (see GENETIC ENGINEERING).

M. COBERLY

See also: FISHING INDUSTRY; ORGANIC FARMING AND SUSTAINABLE AGRICULTURE.

Further reading:

Ackefors, H., Huner, J. V., and Konikoff, M. *Introduction to the General Principles of Aquaculture.* New York: Food Products Press, 1994.
Aquaculture and Water Resource Management. Edited by D. J. Baird et al. Boston: Blackwell Scientific Publications, 1996.
Koch, F. K. *Mariculture: Farming the Fruits of the Sea.* New York: Franklin Watts, 1992.
Lee, J. S., and Newman, M. E. *Aquaculture: An Introduction.* Danville, Illinois: Interstate Publishers, 1997.

ENVIRONMENTAL PROBLEMS CAUSED BY AQUACULTURE

Although there are many advantages to using aquaculture to breed fish, there are also disadvantages. For example, nonnative fish or organisms shipped with fish sometimes escape into the wild. A good example is the European green crab, a voracious shellfish-eater that has destroyed the soft-shell clam industry in Maine. Another disadvantage is problems with disease and pollution. For example, oyster farms must be monitored for paralytic shellfish poisoning, which results from a type of toxin-secreting plankton the oysters eat. Humans may be poisoned after eating contaminated oysters.

Coastal shellfish farms are often threatened with contamination from humans through nearby sewage systems. Bacteria that are helpful in human intestines can be pathogenic (disease-causing) when they enter fish and are then eaten by humans. Oysters off the coasts of Long Island and Rhode Island have been unsafe to eat since the 1960s. In 1993, heavy rain caused the Charlotte, North Carolina, storm drains, which contained human waste, to overflow. Nearby shellfish were close to harvesting when high levels of fecal coliform bacteria such as *E. coli* were found in the seawater. Oyster beds off the coast of Florida were closed for the same reason in 1995 and 1997. As fish consumption grows, it is vital to educate people to cook seafood thoroughly to avoid toxins and parasites.

The often crowded conditions of a hatchery are an ideal breeding ground for fish diseases. Since hatcheries play an important role in restocking wild fish populations, they must be carefully managed to prevent diseases that develop in the hatchery population from causing problems in the wild. The whirling disease spread among wild Colorado trout and myxobolus among wild fish in Utah were caused by hatchery errors. Also, the irresponsible use of antibiotics to cure disease in confined fish can lead to higher antibiotic resistance in bacteria (see POLLUTION AND ITS CONTROL).

WIDER IMPACT

ARABLE FARMING

Arable farming is the use of land suitable to grow crops for human and animal consumption or other purposes

Wheat fields surround a farm in Condon, Oregon. U.S. farmers grow about 71.2 million tons (64.6 million tonnes) of wheat each year. The United States is the second biggest wheat producer in the world, after China.

The cultivation of crops provides most of the world's human food supply. Indeed, significant areas of land are devoted to it in countries all over the world. It is estimated that about 10 percent of Earth's total land surface is devoted to arable farming; about 15 percent of the total area of the United States is cropland. Traditionally, arable farming has been part of a mixed agriculture, with some of the crops grown used as livestock feed. Today, arable farming tends to be more specialized, and farmers often grow large amounts of a limited number of crops for specific purposes.

MODERN CEREAL FARMING

Cereal grains, such as barley, buckwheat, millet, corn, oats, rice, sorghum, and wheat, are the most important and widely grown crops in the world. In developing countries, over 80 percent of the human diet consists of cereal grains alone. In developed countries, however, much of the cereal grains are used as livestock feed.

Modern cereal farming, such as the cultivation of wheat in the Great Plains area of the United States, is highly mechanized and intensive agriculture. Wheat is a versatile crop, and it can be grown in a variety of climatic zones. To insure a successful harvest, however, the wheat must be grown in a nutrient-rich soil.

Preparing the soil

Soil preparation is a crucial step in successful wheat cultivation. The physical manipulation of the soil to improve it as a medium for cultivation is called tillage. In certain conditions, draining or irrigating the land may be necessary to control soil water levels before any tillage can be done (see IRRIGATION AND LAND DRAINAGE).

The main function of tillage is to change the soil structure so that it is better aerated, incorporate residue and soil amendments, and provide a good seedbed for plant germination and growth. Tillage is performed using a range of mechanical implements; the treatment chosen, and hence equipment used, will depend on the climate, soil type, and which crop is to be grown. Plowing is often the first stage in tillage, and it has the greatest impact on soil structure (see PLOW). Other tillage machinery falls into three broad types: subsoilers, harrows, and rollers. Subsoilers are used to break up compacted or

CORE FACTS

- Crop farming is the origin of most of the world's supply of food.
- Modern arable farming is a highly mechanized and intensive process.
- Successful harvests depend on the year-round management of crops.
- Many factors must be considered to insure the successful cultivation of crops, such as soil quality, climate, pests, disease, and weeds.

CONNECTIONS

- Modern **AGRICULTURAL** methods require **HARVESTING MACHINERY** to gather crops efficiently and cost-effectively.

- Today, **PRECISION FARMING** methods use **SATELLITES** to determine the precise application of **SOIL** amendments and even planting rates.

A CLOSER LOOK

MINIMAL TILLAGE SYSTEMS

Repeated tillage damages the soil structure in the long term by disrupting microorganisms in the soil, causing surface crusting, and increasing the possibility of topsoil erosion. The compaction caused by the continual passage of heavy machinery increases this damage. For this reason, some land is managed with the minimum possible disturbance of the soil.

Minimal tillage has the additional advantage of lower equipment and fuel costs, and planting preparation time is also reduced. Weeds can be controlled by herbicides or by mulching—piling up crop residues such as straw around crop bases to smother weeds, retain soil moisture, and provide a layer of dead plant material that provides protection from erosion.

Minimal tillage is now practiced on nearly a third of the total cropland in the United States. The main disadvantage of such methods is the higher use of herbicides, and it is not successful for heavier, more compacted soil types that require deeper tilling to ensure adequate drainage.

A tractor pulls a chisel disk across the remnants of harvested wheat, called wheat stubble, in Illinois.

hard ground below the soil surface to improve drainage and root penetration. The subsoiler consists of a wheeled frame under which a number of cutting legs are attached. As the subsoiler is pulled across the surface of the soil, the cutting blades pierce through the soil, typically to a depth of 2 ft (0.6 m). Like all modern tillage equipment, the subsoiler is pulled along by a tractor (see AGRICULTURAL TRANSPORT AND MAINTENANCE MACHINERY; TRACTOR).

Machines called harrows, or cultivators, are the most common tillage tools. A harrow is a tractor-drawn frame from which spikes or long teeth called tines project down through the soil as the machine is pulled along. The oldest design still used in arable farming is the chain-link harrow, which consists of an open flexible framework of chain-gauge metal, with spikes at each link. This is a light tool, used to complete the tillage process or to cover seed after sowing. The spike-tooth harrow is similar to the chain-link

harrow but has a heavier, more rigid frame and larger spikes. Other rigid-framed cultivators have long, curved tines made from tensioned steel; these flex slightly as they are pulled through the soil, increasing the penetration power. Such cultivators are used to break up lumpy soil and to remove weeds.

The chisel disk is another popular tillage tool. Several sets of saucer-shaped, rotating metal disks are arranged on a frame so that they slice into the soil as the harrow is pulled. Chisel disks are used to break up heavy soil and to cut up the remains of previous crops after they have been harvested. They are generally used as the second tillage after plowing.

Nearly all modern harrows are powered by a tractor. This increases control over the machine, since the working power can be varied directly by the operator, rather than depending on the rate at which the machine is pulled across the ground. Most tractor-powered harrows are of a rotary type, with a tined or bladed shaft that can turn at speeds of up to 500 revolutions per minute.

Rollers are used to break up clods of earth and to create a firm surface. They may be flat or ribbed and can cover a width of over 25 ft (7.5 m). A variation is the furrow press, consisting of a row of spaced rings, designed to roll plowed furrows but leave the ridges between furrows untouched. Rollers are often incorporated onto the back of harrows to give a combination of tillage effects from a single machine.

Sowing the crop

When the soil has been tilled, the seeds can be sown. Wheat may be planted either in the late fall or early spring, depending on climate and crop variety. Wheat farmers may purchase seed of a particular variety or sow seed saved from their last harvest. In either case, the grain is usually treated with pesticides to deter pest attacks both during storage and after planting (see PESTICIDE AND HERBICIDE).

Traditionally, sowing is done by hand-scattering the seed onto the ground. Alternatively, various simple ·distribution tools are used to insure a more regular spread of·seed. These can be pushed by hand or pulled by a horse. In intensive agriculture, planting is mechanized, and sowing is achieved by one of two methods: broadcasting or drilling.

Broadcasting means that the seed is distributed over the surface of the soil. It is faster than drilling and is fairly independent of soil conditions. However, the distribution of the seed is less uniform than by the drilling process. Tractor-drawn grain distributors, called hoppers, may hold large quantities of seed. As the hopper is pulled across the field, seed passes into a distribution device at its base. The seed is then distributed onto the ground at a predetermined rate. Quite accurate distribution is possible using this technology, especially with modern electronically controlled distribution devices that can be monitored from the tractor cabin. For very large land areas, seed is broadcast from light aircraft. After broadcasting, the soil may be lightly harrowed to cover the seed.

If the drilling method is used to sow the seed, the farmer has more control over the depth and position of grain placement. Consequently, drilling is the more popular method in modern cereal farming. Seed drills are similar to harrows, but they are equipped with narrow blades at the open end of a seed-dispensing tube. As the drill is pulled along, the blade cuts a narrow furrow of a preset depth into which seeds drop; wheat is usually sown in lines about 4 in (10 cm) apart. Most drills have light wheels, called press wheels, or chains behind the dispensers that push the soil back over the seed. The planting density of the seeds is controlled either by a mechanical feed mechanism, such as a grooved roller that determines the rate at which grain can flow to the dispenser tubes, or by a pneumatically driven metering device that blows grain into the tubes at a certain rate. Some drills can dispense granular fertilizer along with the seed.

Some drills, such as the cultivator-drill combination, prepare the seedbed and sows the seed at the same time. These machines are basically harrows with a drill attachment and are used on land that requires light tillage only. Another device, the direct drill, does not involve any tillage at all. It is similar to a conventional seed drill but has much more powerful blades. Direct drilling can be done only on suitable soil types and in certain weather conditions, but it is a simple and rapid method, particularly applicable to minimal tillage systems (see the box on page 98).

Caring for the crop

The period between sowing and harvest is an extremely busy time for the wheat farmer. The basis of good crop care, or husbandry, is frequent inspection of the growing crop to check its progress and identify problems such as diseases or infestations at the earliest possible stage. If a problem is found, the farmer then attempts to manipulate as many factors as possible to minimize the problem and provide the optimum growing conditions. Some factors, such as the weather, cannot be predicted, but responding to changes in climate is essential to a successful harvest. The need for water is paramount, and in many areas irrigation (usually applied by sprinkler) must be provided during dry periods.

Providing sufficient nutrients to meet the needs of the crop is often the first concern, and manure or other fertilizers are often incorporated into the soil before planting (see FERTILIZER). Chemical fertilizers may also be applied to growing crops. In some regions, plant growth regulators are also applied. Similar to hormones in animals, these regulators are substances that have a marked effect on plant growth and development, even when present in minute quantities. For wheat cultivation, the most important role of these substances is to control stem elongation, insuring stronger, more wind-resistant stems. Successful use of growth regulators depends on careful dosage and timing of application, and performance can be inconsistent. Plant hormones

are used infrequently in modern arable farming. Increasing the scope of these substances may be the subject of future research (see AGRICULTURAL SCIENCE; PLANT HORMONE).

Weeds are plants that grow in places where people do not want them. They may compete with crops for light, nutrients, and water and reduce crop yield. Good husbandry is essential to eliminate this threat, because crops provided with the best conditions for growth will compete with weeds more successfully. In wheat farming, one approach is to destroy any standing weeds that are growing in the same area of cultivation as the wheat. This is achieved by an initial vigorous tillage before sowing the seeds. However, this practice may also help the germination of some of the weed seeds. Insuring that equipment is free from the seeds of unwanted plants is also very important, as is the practice of crop rotation (see the box on page 100).

This picture shows a tractor-pulled hopper distributing grain in southern Minnesota. The hopper holds large quantities of seed in a container that allows fixed quantities of the seed to pass into distribution devices (shown yellow). The seed is then scattered onto the ground at a rate that is determined by adjusting the distribution device.

TERRACED AGRICULTURE

Arable farming is easiest on flat land, especially if machinery is used. However, flat, nutrient-rich land is in short supply in many places, and agriculture has had to adapt to farming on slopes. Besides the physical difficulties of cultivating sloping land, the main problem is the likelihood of soil erosion. Tilling a slope will loosen the soil, and loosened soil can be washed away in large amounts by rain. Therefore, the key to farming on slopes is the creation of flat terraces.

Constructing terraces is extremely labor intensive. Terraces are made by building a wall of brick or earth along a contour of the slope and then remodeling the soil so that it forms a flat space between the main slope and the wall. This flat terrace can then be cultivated without erosion, provided that the terrace is well drained and the wall is maintained. Because the space is confined and difficult to access, animal and human power is often the only way to till a terrace.

Extensive terraces can be seen in many parts of the world. For example, the hillsides of many parts of western South America are farmed in terraces, some of which were built by the Incas in the 15th century.

A CLOSER LOOK

The most efficient way to eliminate the threat of weeds is to spray them with weed-killing herbicides (see PESTICIDE AND HERBICIDE). These substances can be applied even if there are no standing weeds in the area of cultivation; this eliminates the threat of germinating weed seeds emerging. This treatment is often done at a fairly early stage of crop growth, because this is when the competition is most damaging. Different herbicides are available that are designed for specific weeds or situations. In all cases of herbicide use, care must be taken to prevent herbicide spray from drifting and affecting wild plants or polluting water bodies. Consequently, herbicides (and pesticides; see below) have strict labeling requirements for their use and the plants for which the are used (see CROP SPRAYING AND PROTECTION).

Large wheat fields provide ideal conditions for the spread of diseases and pests. Many bacteria, birds, fungi, invertebrates, mammals, and viruses may inflict damage. If left unchecked, these organisms can lead to significant losses of yield, and, in the worst cases, completely ruin a crop. As with weed control, prevention of infestation is the key to eliminating such a threat. Measures such as growing disease-resistant wheat varieties, removing plants that act as hosts to pest insects, and using explosive bird scarers can all help. The use of a biological control may be appropriate in certain circumstances (see BIOLOGICAL CONTROL). The preferred approach is therefore one of integrated pest management that seeks to reduce opportunities for pests in every aspect of crop management.

Chemicals are also widely used to combat pests and diseases, and they may be used as a preventative measure if the risk of infestation is high. Pesticides can be applied to crops using sprayers mounted on all-terrain vehicles or by spraying the crops manually with backpack sprayers. Nearly all pesticides are potentially toxic to other organisms, including humans, and the environmental effects of pesticide usage must always be considered. All pesticides and herbicides should be used with extreme care. Fungicides are the most widely used class of pesticides in grain farming, because fungi cause the most prevalent grain diseases. Nearly all intensively grown wheat is sprayed with a fungicide at least once during growth. Most fungicides are effective, although over recent decades some molds have become resistant to certain types. For this reason, crop farmers avoid the prolonged use of a single chemical.

CROP ROTATION

Owl's clover is a pink-flowered legume that increases nitrogen levels in the soil.

Repeatedly growing the same crop on the same land every year is called monoculture, and it can severely deplete the soil of nutrients and provide conditions where pests will thrive. As a result, monocultures require high inputs of fertilizers and pesticides. Since this is also damaging to the land, an alternative is crop rotation, where different crops are grown on the same piece of land in different years.

Crop rotation has been a feature of agriculture for centuries. In medieval Europe, a three-course rotation was common. Wheat would be grown in the first year, beans or barley in the second, and the land would be left fallow (uncultivated) in the third year. This was later superseded by the Norfolk four-course rotation, developed in eastern England in the 18th century. Here, wheat would be followed in successive years by a root crop (usually turnips), then barley, and finally clover. Root crops were important because the soil could be vigorously weeded around them, thus cleaning the soil. The four-course rotation also eliminated the unproductive fallow year.

Most rotations incorporate a legume crop, such as clover or beans. These are important because they increase soil levels of the essential nutrient nitrogen, thus improving soil conditions for the next crop (see the picture above). Often a quick-growing legume will be included in a rotation for this purpose, and then plowed back into the soil as a "green manure" to further enrich it. Many rotation systems are possible and are still very important in modern agriculture to control weeds and pests, and to maintain soil quality.

A CLOSER LOOK

Harvesting

Wheats can be broadly grouped into winter wheats and spring wheats, according to the climate in which they grow best. Winter wheats, grown in milder climates than spring wheats, are planted in the fall and harvested the following spring or summer. Spring wheat is planted in the spring and harvested in the same year. Modern farms harvest wheat and other grains with a combine—a machine that collects the wheat as it passes through a field and separates the grain from the husks and stems in a beating process called threshing. In much of the developing world, grain is cut with hand tools (see HARVESTING MACHINERY). After harvest, the grain is dried and stored.

OTHER CROPS

The cultivation of most crops requires the same intensive management as is needed for wheat cultivation. However, there are some differences due to the particular requirements of each crop.

Rice

Rice is an extremely important grain, especially in Asia. Most is grown in flooded fields called paddies. Rice is usually sown into damp seedbeds and then

ARABLE FARMING IN THE TROPICS

A farmer sprays the plants on a banana plantation in New South Wales, Australia.

Tropical areas present particular agricultural problems. Annual precipitation levels are usually high, although many areas have distinct dry and wet seasons. Many soils, being thin, prone to erosion, and with low levels of stored nutrients, are unsuitable for frequent cropping. Weeds, pests, and disease organisms all flourish in hot, damp tropical conditions.

Intensive agricultural practices developed in temperate zones do not usually transfer well to tropical regions. Tractor-drawn implements have often proved unsuitable for tropical conditions—especially since replacement parts may be difficult to obtain—and mechanization can lead to unemployment and poverty if its introduction is poorly managed. Agricultural areas are often remote, and transporting expensive agrochemicals to them is difficult. Heavy tillage can quickly erode tropical soils. Large areas of monoculture plantations have been established in many tropical countries, especially for exported crops such as bananas. However, these are generally established on nutrient-rich soils, with better transport links, and financed by large corporate capital inputs. Their profitability relies largely on the low cost of local labor and the availability of simple mechanical tools.

Much tropical production is by traditional methods on relatively small farms, where a diverse mixture of crops are grown together (intercropping) to reduce the opportunities for pests, provide a year-round food supply, and spread the risk in case of failure of any one crop. Human and animal labor are very important.

A CLOSER LOOK

transplanted by hand in clumps of three to six seedlings into flooded fields when they are about six weeks old. The paddies are kept flooded until they are drained for harvesting, unless there is a severe weed infestation, in which case it may be necessary to drain and weed the fields and then flood them again. Since successful irrigation is crucial to the effective cultivation of rice, drought may be the biggest threat to the crop. Most operations are performed manually in the developing countries, but rice farming is highly mechanized in the southern parts of the United States and other places where intensive agriculture is common.

Root crops

Many plants are grown for their roots, either for human consumption or as animal fodder. Root crops generally require well tilled soil and accurate spacing of seeds to avoid overcrowding the plants. Often seedlings are raised in greenhouses and transplanted into the field (see HORTICULTURE). Potatoes must be planted using special machines (seed potatoes are much larger than the seeds used for other crops). Row planting also requires the spaces between rows to be kept weed-free; this can be done by using various cultivating machines, whose tines can be adjusted for various spacings between rows. Harvesting root crops presents extra problems, as the roots must be lifted from the soil undamaged, the leafy tops removed, and excess soil cleaned from the root.

T. ALLMAN

See also: AGRICULTURAL TRANSPORT AND MAINTENANCE MACHINERY; AGRICULTURE, HISTORY OF; AQUACULTURE; FARM STORAGE; GENETIC ENGINEERING; HYDROPONICS; PLANT BREEDING AND PROPAGATION; PRECISION FARMING; SOIL SCIENCE; TRACTOR.

Further reading:
Plaster, E. *Soil Science and Management*. 3rd edition. New York: Delmar Publishers, 1997.
Smith, C. *Crop Production: Evolution, History, and Technology*. New York: John Wiley & Sons, 1995.

ORGANIC FARMING

Organic farming seeks to eliminate the use of synthetic chemicals in agriculture. Instead, organic farmers make use of naturally occurring substances, such as animal manures for fertilizer and certain plant derivatives as pesticides. Emphasis is also placed on traditional techniques, such as crop rotation, mulching, and weeding by hand.

Organic farming has gained popularity due to the environmental and health impacts of agrochemical use. Although organic yields are usually lower than those obtained by conventional agriculture, organic agriculture is often more efficient in terms of the ratio of crop yield to the consumption of resources (such as tractor fuel and synthetic chemicals). Since organic produce often fetches a higher price than its conventionally grown counterpart, organic methods can also be commercially competitive (see ORGANIC FARMING AND SUSTAINABLE AGRICULTURE).

A CLOSER LOOK

ARCHAEOLOGICAL TECHNIQUES

An aerial view of an archaeological site on the Greek island of Naxos.

CONNECTIONS

● **RADIATION DETECTION** from airplanes and **SATELLITES** can find various structures buried underground.

● Scientists are experimenting with **ULTRASONICS** to locate artifacts both in the water and underground.

Scientific techniques are vital in archaeology for finding historic sites and gaining knowledge about them

Aerial photography

One very useful way to get a large-scale view of an area of archaeological interest is by aerial reconnaissance. Photographs taken from low-altitude airplanes or balloons show the overall layout of sites. When the camera is pointed straight down, there is no perspective distortion, so the resulting images are convenient to use for mapping. Alternatively, the photographs can be taken at an oblique angle, which sharpens contrast and facilitates the discovery of new details in the terrain.

Subterranean features can often be discerned by the way they affect the appearance of the soil or vegetation above them compared with the surrounding terrain. For example, crops will generally grow more sparsely over a buried wall, producing a pale line as seen from the air.

Remote sensing data from orbiting spacecraft generally cover too large a swath of Earth in each image to be of much use to archaeologists. However, images from the LANDSAT satellites are higher resolution and have been used in the study of large-scale features such as agricultural settlements, irrigation systems, and villages linked by networks of roads (see SATELLITE).

Sensors and signals

Many of the tools developed by geophysicists to find underground mineral and water resources have been put to use by archaeologists. Magnetometers can point out materials that have been made weakly magnetic from exposure to heat. This includes not only hearths and ovens, but also artifacts which are fired before use, such as pottery and bricks. Resistance meters can locate building foundations, that are better electrical insulators than the surrounding soil. Also, ground-penetrating radar beams radio signals to Earth from airplanes and satellites; differences in the way the signals bounce back hint at buried structures such as walls and roads (see RADAR).

The popular image of an archaeologist as someone who is seeking high adventure and priceless historic objects with a pick and a spade is a modern myth. Archaeologists aren't treasure hunters; they are scientists studying the physical remnants of settlements and civilizations to illuminate humanity's past. They use modern technologies both in the field and in the laboratory.

FINDING THE PAST

An archaeologist chooses a site to excavate after very careful study, in order to make the best use of the limited amounts of time and money available. The slow, careful digging necessary in archaeology means that a trench the size of a grave may take days to excavate. The more scientists can learn about a potential site beforehand, the less time will be wasted. Having found an area of interest, archaeologists will want to find the best places to dig test pits and to learn as much as possible about the site while minimizing cost and the disturbance to the area.

CORE FACTS

■ Excavation is a destructive and expensive process; it must be done as efficiently as possible, and often within a very limited span of time.

■ Remote sensing and geophysical testing techniques can be used to locate buried structures and artifacts before a site is excavated.

■ Archaeological sites are studied in layers, with each underlying layer older than the one above.

■ Artifacts are useless without information about where they were found, because knowing the location and grouping of artifacts is essential for dating them and their surroundings, and for learning about the ways in which they were used.

However, these techniques can only give an inferred description of the content of a site based on a variety of physical properties: they do not have the immediacy of a clear image or an artifact in hand. Improved signal-processing techniques, as well as cumulative experience with using the sensors, are bringing continued progress to the field. Yet despite such improvements, these techniques are not particularly well suited to prehistoric archaeology. Prehistoric shelters were often built using the local soil and vegetation, so they are difficult to distinguish from their surroundings; and tools and other artifacts may be too small for the sensors to find.

New techniques

Techniques for locating and identifying buried objects are often derived from techniques that were originally developed for unrelated applications. For example, ultrasound-SONAR technology—first developed as a defense tool for use in torpedo warfare—is being adapted for surveying archeological sites. The results are displayed in a visual format, rather like the images generated by an ultrasound scan of a fetus in a mother's womb.

Another technique, called nuclear quadrupole resonance, exploits a physico-chemical phenomenon that originated in research chemistry. The nuclei of certain elements absorb and emit radiation at frequencies that are characteristic of their immediate chemical environment (see SPECTROSCOPY). For example, calcium in bones gives a signal that is different from the signal produce by calcium in limestone because the type and configuration of other ions around each calcium ion is different in the two cases. Hence, traces of bone can be told apart from other calcium-containing debris.

To help in developing new sensors and to learn to recognize the signals of prehistoric habitation, researchers from the U.S. Army's Construction Engineering Research Laboratories and the University of Illinois established the world's first archaeological test bed, called the Controlled Archaeological Test Site (CATS), in 1998. At CATS, bones, the remains of cooking fires, burial mounds with interred pig carcasses, packed earthen floors, and other simulated prehistoric finds were seeded at locations recorded within a millimeter, allowing sensors to be tested in controlled conditions. Grids were established with artifacts placed at different depths to establish instruments' ranges and effectiveness.

It may someday be possible to answer many questions about archaeological sites without digging at all. This is especially important for culturally sensitive sites, such as human graves, or in areas where subsequent building, which may itself be ancient, has made excavation impossible.

EXCAVATION

Where it is feasible, excavation is still central to field archaeology because of the reliable evidence it provides. The purpose of excavation is not merely to dig up artifacts, but to place them and other features

surrounding them in context, based on their location. An artifact removed from its context is not only robbed of information about itself, but it has become useless for providing any clues to its surroundings. And since excavation of an area destroys most of the evidence, it cannot be repeated—excavation has to be done right the first time.

Surveying and sifting

Excavation sites are first surveyed and laid out in numbered grids (see the picture above). Generally, a sampling strategy is used by the archaeologists to learn the overall layout of the site and to determine where digging would be most useful. Large screens are used to sift through the excavated soil for small artifacts. On discovery, each artifact is tagged with a number, which is then listed in a catalog, and the progress of the dig is then recorded in field note-

The settlement of Isabela, in the Dominican Republic, was the first one founded by Italian explorer Christopher Columbus (1451–1506) on his second voyage to the New World in 1493. It was abandoned in 1496 after a series of epidemics and famines ravaged the population. This picture shows the remains of the settlement, now an excavation site, which is divided into sections by grids.

AHEAD OF THE BULLDOZERS

As more of Earth is covered by roads, houses, and farms, archaeologists often find themselves scrambling to study an area before access to it becomes more difficult. Most governments now have agencies that control their archaeological resources and regulations requiring archaeological surveys to be carried out before any new construction. In the United States, such regulations apply mainly to construction on federal lands or that which is federally funded. The Archaeological and Historic Preservation Act of 1974 authorized funds to record and preserve archaeological resources when threatened by construction in these areas. In some cases, development plans have been changed when important discoveries have turned up.

Much of the urban archaeology that takes place is performed under "rescue" conditions, working around existing buildings and infrastructure. In heavily settled areas, it is impossible to clear large areas for archaeological excavation. A key task for urban archaeologists is to be aware of the window of opportunity available between demolition and development.

A CLOSER LOOK

This surveyed underwater site is the remains of the Glass Wreck, a ship that sank in the Aegean Sea off the coast of Turkey in Serçe Limani Bay in the early 11th century. Divers continue to search the site, 111 ft (34 m) below sea level, for artifacts such as these well-preserved pottery vessels.

books. Efforts are being made to standardize the recording of information so that it can be easily exchanged between computer databases.

Processing and analysis

After the excavation, processing and analyzing the artifacts can take longer than the dig itself. Deciding when to clean them is also important, because while dirt and soil may cover up the clues that make identification and classification of the artifacts possible, they may also provide important information, such as the residues of the contents of vessels.

Classification

Artifacts are generally classified by decoration, shape, and material, and similar objects are grouped together in a process known as typology. Groups of artifacts and building types seen at a particular time and place are called assemblages, and groups of assemblages are called archaeological cultures. Standardized recording methods allow archaeologists to compare large numbers of artifacts at once, so they can discover associations between them.

Underwater sites

Archaeological sites located underwater can be found by using methods similar to those used for land sites. Photographs taken from airplanes may show the outlines of sunken buildings. Submarines can photograph these sites more closely. Divers, using underwater cameras and metal detectors, can also discover sites and objects of archaeological interest. Sonar is particularly useful for mapping underwater archaeological sites. A method called sonar scanning pinpoints objects from the reflection of sound waves. However, getting to these areas and retrieving artifacts can be much more difficult; divers must descend to the sites in submersible decompression chambers and use buoyancy tanks to lift large objects to the surface for further investigation (see DEEP-SEA DIVING AND DIVING TECHNOLOGY). Their efforts are often well rewarded, however, as materials such as wood and cloth are far better preserved in water than in dry soil.

DATING TECHNIQUES

One of the most important things archaeologists want to know about the archaeological sites and artifacts they find is when they were created and used. There are two basic categories of dating methods. Relative dating is the ordering of a group of events in sequence and attempting to determine the amount of time between them. Absolute dating anchors such a floating time line to a specific period, whether it is to an approximate century or a particular day, month, and year.

PUTTING IT ALL TOGETHER

When choosing an excavation site, archaeologists often combine different types of information. For example, a topographical map showing the slope of the ground might be combined with maps of stream locations and soil composition data; the areas where relatively large, flat surfaces of good soil are near a water supply might be good places to seek the remains of a farming settlement. Traditionally, the stacking of data was done manually, using charts plotted on transparent sheets that were laid one over another.

Modern studies frequently use GIS (geographic information systems) to superimpose different types of data. The use of GIS makes more detailed analysis possible using a variety of sources and giving more accurate results with less effort. The data produced are also easy to manipulate, transmit, and share.

HISTORY OF TECHNOLOGY

Relative dating

Until about 50 years ago, relative dating methods were the only ones available to archaeologists. Stratigraphy—looking at the arrangement of Earth's strata, or layers—takes advantage of the fact that the present is literally built upon the past. Ruins are covered by shifting sands, encroachment of vegetation, and other natural or human processes. Newer structures are erected in their place. The result is a stack of layers, with the newest layers closest to the surface and the deeper ones dating from farther back in the past. To dig down is to dig backward in time.

Artifacts found in the same layer are said to be associated in time. But in order to make this determination, the site's stratigraphic structure must be carefully evaluated. Many human activities, such as excavation of subterranean chambers, can disrupt layers and cause confusion. Artifacts may be used for centuries and appear in a more recent layer than their origin would suggest. And pits dug for waste disposal cause other items to be buried deeper than expected.

One way to clarify an item's date is by studying changes in the types of artifacts found as technologies and decorative fashions changed and innovations spread to surrounding areas. Tracking pottery styles is an important example of this technique, which is used successfully by archaeologists throughout the world. Pottery is durable in the sense that it does not decay. Therefore, even when broken, it remains part of the archaeological record. It is also portable, so it is easy for influences to spread, which can provide evidence of migrations and trade routes. And pottery styles change often enough to provide useful information when fixing the date of such an item.

Stone tools, on the other hand, remained fairly static over millenia, so this technique is of limited use in prehistoric archaeology, which makes more use of other techniques, such as tracking climate data from ice cores and pollen studies. Chemical dating of bones—a chemical analysis of bone material that measures the depletion of its nitrogen content and its absorption of fluorine and uranium from groundwater—cannot provide absolute dates because environmental factors, such as temperature, moisture, and soil composition, affect the rate of change. However, bone dating can determine whether remains found in the same stratigraphic layer should really be associated in time. This technique was used in 1953 to expose the famous early-19th-century Piltdown man—billed as the "missing link" between man and ape—as a hoax: it had been planted in a Stone Age gravel pit.

Fixing a relative chronology to a known point in time can be tricky. One way is to use known historical events. People often kept ancient calendars that made reference to the reigns of kings and dynasties. However, a great deal of research must be done to establish the list of rulers with the lengths of their reigns and to link the list to our own calendar through contemporary records and inscriptions. Then artifacts carrying dates or kings' names can be used to date their surroundings.

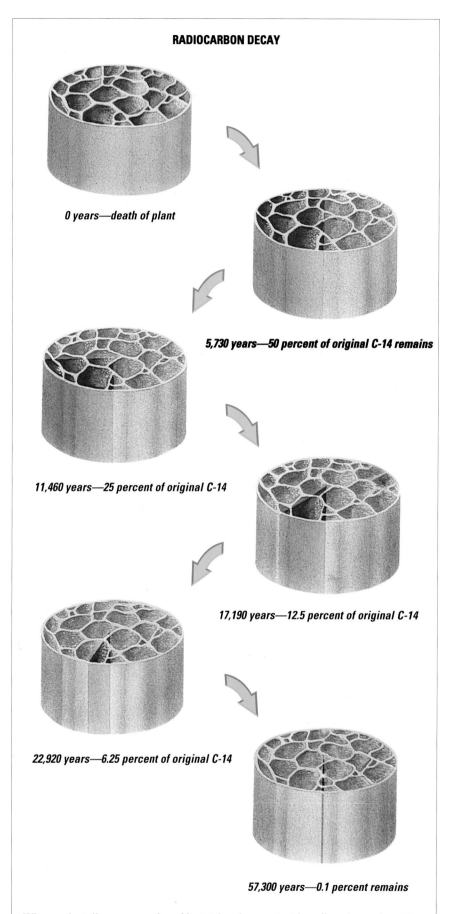

RADIOCARBON DECAY

0 years—death of plant

5,730 years—50 percent of original C-14 remains

11,460 years—25 percent of original C-14

17,190 years—12.5 percent of original C-14

22,920 years—6.25 percent of original C-14

57,300 years—0.1 percent remains

When a plant dies, a proportion of its total carbon content is radioactive carbon-14. This isotope slowly changes to nitrogen and the quantity of C-14 remaining reduces by half every 5,730 years. The quantity of C-12 remains unchanged and the age of the plant is revealed by the C-14 : C-12 ratio. The process was developed by U.S. chemist Willard F. Libby (1908–1980) in 1947; for which he won the Nobel Prize in 1960.

Dendrochronology, the science of assigning dates to tree rings, is an archaeological dating technique. Each concentric ring of the tree corresponds to a year of its life, and the tree's age can be calculated by counting the exact number of rings.

Absolute dating

Dendrochronology—the study of tree rings in relation to time—is an important method for absolute dating. Trees produce new wood in annual rings that can be seen in cross section. The rings vary in thickness depending on fluctuations in climate. The pattern for a given time period will generally be similar for the same species of tree growing in the same area. By matching sequences in trees with overlapping life spans, a long-term master sequence can be built up working backward from the present, and timber in structures of interest can be dated by comparing its ring structure to the master sequence.

Dendrochronology has been instrumental in the calibration of modern dating technologies such as radiocarbon dating, which is now one of the most common techniques used in archaeology. All lifeforms have molecules containing carbon. Most carbon is in the form of carbon-12, an isotope with six neutrons in each atomic nucleus. However, cosmic radiation hitting the atmosphere converts a certain amount of atmospheric nitrogen into carbon-14, which has eight neutrons. The carbon-14 isotope is radioactive, or unstable, and decays at a known rate. While an organism is alive, it continually absorbs carbon-14 through carbon dioxide, which plants absorb in photosynthesis and pass on to animals along the food chain. The result is a uniform concentration of carbon-14 in living organisms. After death, no more carbon-14 is absorbed, so the concentration decreases as the isotope decays, and the age of the specimen can be determined using a Geiger counter to measure the radioactive carbon-14 that remains.

In samples older than about 50,000 years, there is so little carbon-14 left that it becomes extremely difficult to measure. Also, this method can only date substances derived from plants or animals and is useless for such artifacts as pottery or flint tools. Long-lived radioisotopes of potassium and uranium are used as radioactive clocks, analogous to carbon-14 in life-forms, and can provide information over much longer timescales—even millions of years back to the earliest humans.

ARCHAEOLOGY ON THE INTERNET

The Internet is becoming an increasingly important tool for archaeological research. Since the Internet's inception, researchers have used it to exchange data, text files, and images, as well as to share news of ongoing projects with colleagues and the public.

Virtual-reality models can conceivably be made that would allow people to walk through anything, from an active excavation site to an ancient city in its heyday. Computer-aided design (CAD) tools have been used for some time to model archaeological sites as they are now or as they were in their own time. But with the virtual reality modeling language (VRML), three-dimensional "worlds" may be described in a way that allows them to be browsed over the Internet. Virtual museums on the Internet have flourished as a way to increase public awareness of archaeological projects and the artifacts and information they reveal.

S. CALVO

See also: FORENSIC SCIENCE; POTTERY; PREHISTORIC TECHNOLOGY; RADIATION DETECTION; SOIL SCIENCE, TRANSDUCER AND SENSOR.

Further reading:

Burial Archaeology: Current Research, Methods and Developments. Edited by C. A. Roberts, F. Lee, and J. Bintliff. Oxford, England: B.A.R., 1989.
Computer Applications and Quantitative Methods in Archaeology, 1994. Edited by J. Hugget and N. Ryan. Oxford, England: Tempus Reparatum, 1995.
Fagan, B. *In the Beginning: An Introduction to Archaeology.* New York: HarperCollins College Publishers, 1994.

HISTORY IN A PRIVY

Before the invention and popular adoption of the water closet, many households would use a privy—an excavated pit that would be used for the disposal of sewage and refuse. While most people would go out of their way to avoid stumbling upon the remains of an old privy, archaeologists delight in them. Once identified, generally through analysis of soil structure and composition, privies provide many clues to life in the communities they served.

Privy pits were often the final resting places of broken dishes, utensils, and other household trash. Since there were often laws or customs regulating the distance between outhouses and other buildings, privies can aid in mapping out the site. Also, careful analysis of the privy contents can sometimes identify heavy metals or other indigestible substances used in patent medicines, such as the mercury used to treat venereal diseases and other ailments in the early 19th century. In many cases, the use of such medications is mentioned in dated documents, and these chemical traces can help date an encampment and distinguish genuine, old privies from ordinary garbage pits.

A CLOSER LOOK

ARMOR

Armor has been used in fighting from prehistoric times to the present to protect the body from injury

Armor is a type of military clothing designed to protect the wearer against weapons—from swords to bullets and shell fragments.

The earliest types of armor were probably worn before recorded history—early soldiers wore leather helmets, back plates, and breastplates to protect their heads and upper bodies from attack. Other types of armor consisted of quilted fabrics of wool or linen. These types of armor were surprisingly resilient, tending to absorb the force when struck by a blow. However, improvements in metallurgy led to the use of, initially, softer, easily worked metals, such as bronze and, later, iron. At first, small, overlapping metal plates were sewn onto fabric jackets. The age of metal armor, however, is usually associated with the ancient Greeks and Romans.

Chain mail

After leather and fabric armor came chain-mail, which was probably first used by the Romans. Chain mail consisted of interwoven rings of iron and, later, steel. Later examples of chain mail might consist of a three-quarter-length bodysuit, as worn by Norman knights in the 11th century, or it might just cover particularly vulnerable parts of the body. For example, later Roman legionnaires wore a chain-mail shirt to protect the upper body. Chain mail was also used to protect the head and neck, usually under a leather and metal helmet, and the hands. However, chain mail was expensive, as well as very labor-intensive to make, and it was usually only affordable to knights and nobles. And although it was strong and resilient enough to absorb the impact of a slashing stroke from a sword, it was less effective in stopping thrusting weapons, because blades could penetrate between the iron or steel links.

Plate armor

Chain mail remained the chief form of armor until the 13th century, after which it was gradually superseded by plate armor. Plate armor, originally made from iron and, later, steel, comprised iron or steel plates joined together by rivets and leather fastenings. Chain mail was frequently worn under plate armor to protect jointed parts of the body, such as

A man dresses in chain mail and scale armor, the historic clothing of an 11th-century Norman soldier, at a reenactment of the Battle of Hastings in Sussex, England.

the elbows and knees, which could not be encased in the less flexible plate armor without making the wearer virtually immobile.

Strong and reasonably flexible, and not as cumbersome to wear as popularly imagined, plate armor made the wearer virtually invulnerable to most weapons, except close-range missile fire from, for example, the longbow or crossbow. Again, its expense made it the preserve of the wealthy and it was seen as a status symbol. However, ordinary foot soldiers did acquire pieces, usually from dead enemies on the battlefield. In the medieval period, the armored knight mounted on an armored warhorse was the dominant battlefield weapon.

Plate armor was made by casting sheets of iron and steel, cutting and beating them to shape, and piercing them to be riveted together. Full suits of armor contained dozens of sheets carefully fitted to an individual's shape, much in the way that the cloth for a tailored suit might be. Gauntlets (gloves) alone contained large numbers of small sheets, thereby allowing the hand to be clenched and unclenched. Although plate armor is most associated with the medieval period, it was first used by the ancient Greeks and Romans. The Greeks, for example, wore metal helmets, breastplates, and greaves (lower-leg

---

CORE FACTS

- Armor has been made from leather, quilted fabric, a variety of metals, and human-made fibers.
- Most commonly used in the medieval period, armor declined in importance with the widespread use of effective gunpowder weapons whose projectiles could penetrate armor at increasing distances.
- A commonly used form of modern armor is the upper-body jacket.

CONNECTIONS

- **METALS** such as bronze and iron have been the most popular materials for armor, and **LEATHER** was used in early armor.

- Plate armor was sufficient **BODY PROTECTION** against the **BOW AND ARROW**, but it became useless with the development of **FIREARMS**.

- Armor is used to protect soldiers engaged in **LAND WARFARE** from **BOMB, SHELL, AND GRENADE** attacks.

South Korean riot police are wearing protective shields in readiness for civil protest.

Metal helmets and upper-body armor continued to be worn until the late 19th century.

Armor for infantrymen (foot soldiers) became defunct even more rapidly: armored infantrymen—equipped with cutting or thrusting weapons for close-quarter combat—had worn helmets, upper-body armor, and thigh armor until the mid-17th century. Thereafter, armor-wearing infantrymen were seldom used. This again was due to improvements in firearms, which made close-quarter battle increasingly rare. However, for a time, a type of vestigial armor did remain, not for protection but as a badge of rank. For much of the 18th century, officers wore gorgets—small, ornamental pieces of armor—around their necks.

Modern body protection

Armor did not, however, entirely disappear. At the end of the 19th century, troops were going into battle in soft caps, which offered no protection to the head—particularly from air-burst artillery shells or shrapnel. Head wounds were common and frequently lethal. In World War I (1914–1918), all the warring nations introduced pressed steel helmets. Such helmets, although in some cases made of lighter-weight composite materials, are still used today (see COMPOSITE).

In the second half of the 20th century, armor was still being worn, chiefly to protect the upper bodies of troops or security forces in antiterrorist operations, such as hostage-rescue missions or bomb disposal. They are also used in situations that threaten to be particularly violent, such as public protests and riots. Some modern body armor consists of alloy steel plates fitted or stitched into a vest to protect the chest and groin. Other materials used in such protection include fiberglass or layers of nylon fiber. These are strong, flexible, and lightweight. They are capable of stopping bullets, bomb fragments, and knife thrusts but allow the wearer the freedom of movement to carry out any required task (see FIBERS AND YARNS).

I. WESTWELL

See also: ARTILLERY; CAVALRY AND CHARIOT; HAND WEAPONS; IRON AND STEEL PRODUCTION; METALWORKING.

Further reading:

Bishop, M. C. *Roman Military Equipment: From the Punic Wars to the Fall of Rome.* London: Batsford, 1993.
Boyne, W. *Weapons of Desert Storm.* Lincolnwood: Publications International, 1991.
Byam, M. *Arms and Armor.* New York: Knopf, 1988.
DeVries, K. R. *Medieval Military Technology.* Peterborough, Ontario, and Lewiston, New York: Broadview Press, 1992.
Michaels, G. J. *Tip of the Spear: U.S. Marine Light Armor in the Gulf War.* Annapolis, Maryland: Naval Institute Press, 1998.
Yue, C. *Armor.* Boston: Houghton Mifflin, 1994.

protectors). Later, Roman legionnaires wore sections of plate armor to protect their upper bodies and shoulders.

The 16th century saw the greatest flowering of the armorer's art. Never had plate armor been so technically complex, so ornate—or so costly. However, the value of armor on the battlefield was beginning to decline. This was due to the development of firearms. Although early firearms were not powerful enough to penetrate the best armor at anything other than close range, gradual improvements in the quality of gunpowder and firearms themselves meant that armor could then be penetrated at increasing ranges.

The decline of armor

Armorers at first tried to make armor heavier and thicker to offset improvements in gunpowder weapons, but they could never keep pace with these improvements. Knights became less and less mobile because of the weight of armor that, in effect, offered them little or no protection against firearms.

The insufficient protection offered by this bulky and heavy armor soon began to be less important than mobility on the battlefield. The process was gradual, but cavalrymen started to give up their full suits of armor. By the middle of the 17th century, arm and leg protection had generally disappeared, leaving mounted soldiers with just gauntlets (soon replaced by leather gloves), back plates and breastplates worn over leather jerkins (short, sleeveless jackets) to protect the upper body, and helmets.

ARTIFICIAL INSEMINATION AND FERTILITY TREATMENT

Fertility treatments, including artifical insemination, assist people who are having difficulty conceiving a child

For those who want a child, few things are as painful as the inability to conceive. Historically, the problem was automatically ascribed to the woman; men would claim to have several "barren" wives in succession. Now we know that both males and females can be infertile, and research into how these difficulties affect conception has made it possible for new helpful techniques to be developed.

Causes of infertility

There are many factors that affect the ability of a man and a woman to conceive. In women, these include egg production (ovulation), the successful journey of eggs from the ovaries through the fallopian tubes to the uterus, and an environment in the uterus that allows a fertilized egg to implant and develop. In men, healthy, active sperm must be produced and delivered by the ejaculate so that it makes its way through the women's cervix, the entrance to the uterus. Problems in any of these areas can result in difficulties with conception. About 20 percent of infertility cases involve both partners, though many cases of infertility have no diagnosable cause.

In recent years there has been a perception of an "epidemic" of infertility. Certain changes in lifestyle appear to have affected people's ability to reproduce. Fertility declines as women age, and over the past few decades people in advanced industrial countries have tended to start families later in life. Sexually transmitted diseases can cause reproductive tract scarring, as does the long-term use of the older type of intrauterine devices for birth control. Men and women may produce antibodies against the man's sperm, and this is more likely if a long, varied sexual history preceded attempts at conception. Older prospective parents are more likely to be taking medication that lessens fertility, and some people born in the 1950s have reproductive abnormalities caused by the drug diethylstilbestrol, used by their mothers to prevent miscarriage. The good news is that more techniques are available to overcome infertility.

Artificial insemination

If a man's sperm count is low, or his sperm cells are not active enough, artificial insemination is often tried. After the sperm is collected from the man, the dead or inactive sperm are filtered out, allowing

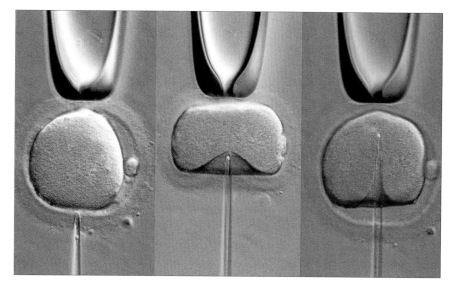

Three separate human sperms are being injected into each of three eggs. A pipette (top) holds the eggs (middle) in place while a microneedle (bottom) is used to inject the egg with the sperm. This is one of the steps in micromanipulation fertility treatment.

a concentrated sample of the healthiest sperm to be used for insemination. The sperm may be placed in a tiny cup, which is then fitted against the cervix, or it may be inserted at the cervix or directly into the uterus via a catheter. By timing the procedure to coincide with ovulation, this insemination technique is successful about 10 to 25 percent of the time.

Some conditions result in a complete or near complete absence of sperm in a man's semen. Often these are structural problems that can be repaired surgically. In other cases, the problem is a treatable hormone deficiency. If the situation is permanent, a couple may consider artificial insemination with donor sperm. Donor insemination is also an option for women without a male partner.

Reputable sperm banks offer the frozen sperm of donors who have been carefully screened to be free of sexually transmitted diseases and genetic defects. They limit the number of pregnancies per donor to reduce the likelihood of half-siblings later meeting as strangers and marrying. As a further safeguard against this eventuality, sperm banks generally maintain permanent confidential records of donors and will release nonidentifying information to adult offspring if requested. Since donor sperm samples are from men without fertility problems, the success rate is higher—about 40 to 80 percent.

Fertility treatment for women

Female infertility is often caused by hormone problems. In polycystic ovary syndrome, an excess of the male hormone androgen prevents ovulation. Fertility drugs such as clomiphene can be used, with a success rate ranging from about 30 to 70 percent. Multiple births are a common result of these drugs, because the stimulated ovaries often produce more than one egg in a cycle. In fact, multiple births occur in 10 percent of clomiphene treatments, and this figure increases with other drugs such as Lupron.

CORE FACTS

- There are many causes of infertility in both men and women.
- Artificial insemination is often used in cases of male infertility.
- Test-tube fertilization techniques can bypass the blockages that often cause infertility in women.

CONNECTIONS

- Recent developments in **OBSTETRICS AND GYNECOLOGY** have led to a better understanding of the female reproductive system and therefore to important advances in fertility treatment.

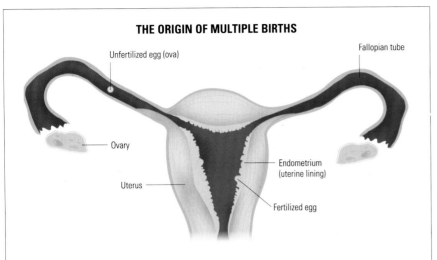

THE ORIGIN OF MULTIPLE BIRTHS

Unfertilized egg (ova)

Fallopian tube

Ovary

Uterus

Endometrium (uterine lining)

Fertilized egg

Two eggs are attached to the lining of the uterus, with a third on its way. If all three eggs are fertilized, the result could be triplets. This situation—the departure of more than one egg from the ovaries during one cycle—can occur in fertility treatment

In women whose fallopian tubes have become blocked by scar tissue or other obstructions, surgery known as tuboplasty may correct the problem. The surgery is done using a laparoscope, a fiberoptic tube inserted in the abdomen through a tiny incision while the patient is under anesthetic.

Bypassing fertility problems

The many new techniques that aid the conception process are referred to as assisted reproductive technologies. Which technique is most appropriate depends on the specific reasons for the infertility. If the fallopian tubes are blocked, in vitro fertilization

(IVF) may be a solution. In this procedure, fertility drugs are used to stimulate the production of several eggs. Using an ultrasound-scan image of the abdomen for guidance, a surgeon retrieves the eggs and places them in a dish with a sperm sample. If fertilization takes place and cellular division begins, three or four embryos are placed in the uterus in the hope that at least one will implant and be carried to term. The first baby conceived by in vitro fertilization, was Louise Brown, born in England in 1978.

Gamete intrafallopian transfer (GIFT) may be used when at least one fallopian tube is open but when infertility results from antibodies or other incompatibilities that prevent the sperm from passing through the cervix. GIFT is similar to IVF except that, instead of being combined in a dish for fertilization, the sperm and egg are mixed in a syringe and inserted immediately into the fallopian tube, well away from the the antibodies at the cervix. In zygote intrafallopian transfer (ZIFT) the egg is transferred after fertilization but before cell division—at the zygote stage. In tubal embryo transfer the embryo is inserted after cell division has proceeded for 48 hours. Variations of these techniques include the use of sperm or eggs from donors. Embryos not used can be frozen for up to three years before insertion.

Another category of techniques used to conceive a child involves surrogacy, in which a woman carries a child for someone else. The child may be conceived through artificial insemination, if the surrogate is to provide the egg, or via a procedure such as IVF.

Ethical issues

New reproductive technologies have sparked many debates about how far society should go to aid conceptions that cannot happen naturally. Donor eggs allow women past menopausal age to have children, and many people wonder how 55-year-old mothers of infants will fare when the children are teenagers. Some people argue against artificial insemination on the basis that infertility is a mechanism of natural selection that is being bypassed by these techniques.

The use of donor eggs and sperm has also led to questions as to what, exactly, defines parenthood. Highly publicized custody battles have centered around surrogate children and frozen embryos.

The situation is not likely to become simpler as these technologies become even more varied and new developments—such as micromanipulation techniques allowing the injection of a single sperm into an egg, and even cloning (see CLONING)—appear. Medical ethicists will be kept busy and cases will be tried in court. But, meanwhile, many formerly infertile people will be able to have the children they have yearned for.

S. CALVO

ARTIFICIAL INSEMINATION IN ANIMALS

Farmers, ranchers, and horse breeders have long known that they could improve their stock by controlling which animals reproduce. They were also free to experiment with fertility techniques without the constraints of the social mores that govern such activities in humans. Artificial insemination techniques for animals were developed about 100 years ago. Today, almost half the dairy cattle population is bred artificially, and artificial insemination is also important in the breeding of horses and sheep. An industry has grown up around the distribution of semen from high-quality animals.

The mechanics of artificial insemination are somewhat different in animals than in humans, because human participation is voluntary. It perhaps goes without saying that collection of semen from a 2000-lb (900-kg) bull or stallion requires great care on the part of the veterinarian. The most common method is to use a female animal to attract the male, and then intercede with a receptacle at the crucial moment. Another unique feature of artificial insemination in animals is the use of semen extenders, such as egg yolk or milk, to dilute semen samples. Thus diluted, a single ejaculate from a bull can inseminate up to 1000 cows.

In addition to its extensive use in livestock breeding, artificial insemination has become important in the preservation of endangered species. The sperm of dozens of rare species have been frozen and stored for use in breeding programs all over the world. This reduces the necessity of transporting animals between zoos and conservation facilities for breeding purposes, and makes it possible to breed animals that show a reluctance to mate (see ANIMAL BREEDING.)

A CLOSER LOOK

See also: BIOTECHNOLOGY.

Further reading:

Rosenthal, M. *The Fertility Sourcebook.* Los Angeles: Lowell House, 1995.

ARTIFICIAL INTELLIGENCE

Artificial intelligence is the computer simulation of human reasoning and behavior

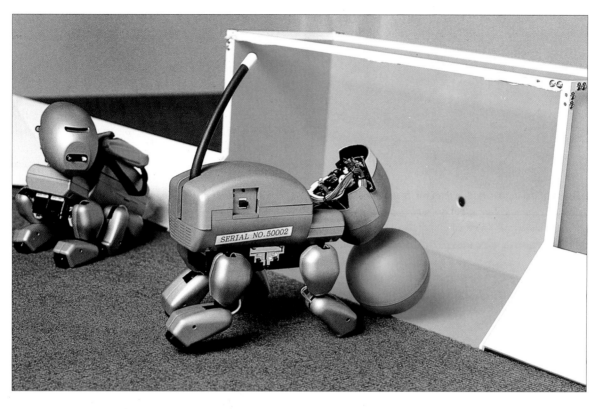

These robot dogs are competing in the 1998 World Robot Soccer Championship held in Paris, France. Competing robots require rudimentary artificial intelligence in order to recognize the ball and to play cooperatively with other team members.

Computers are programmed by breaking tasks up into ordered sequences of simple steps (algorithms). Tasks involving large numbers of repetitive calculations lend themselves well to this approach, and computers often perform these tasks much faster and more accurately than humans do. By examining all the possible moves that they and their opponent can make over the next part of a chess game, chess computers are now able to beat even expert players. However, most human reasoning cannot be easily reduced to a series of simple calculations and still remains far beyond the capabilities of the most powerful computers invented to date.

Human reasoning

To illustrate the complexity of even the most mundane tasks the human brain has to perform, consider the sequence of events when you encounter another person. First you interpret signals from your sensory organs to recognize that the object approaching you is a human. Further interpretation of these signals may tell you that it is a human with whom you are familiar. You may evaluate facial expression, tone of voice, clothes, or other cues to predict how the person is going to behave, then you plan how you are going to react. You communicate using a language in which similar-sounding words may have different meanings, and in which many different words may mean the same thing. If a few of the words are mumbled by the other person, you mentally fill in the blanks based on context. If obstacles are in your path as you approach, you step around them without letting them interrupt your thoughts.

All these functions are addressed in the various areas of artificial intelligence research. Some of the general or mundane skills in which humans currently outperform computers include pattern recognition, natural language processing, prediction and planning, and the ability to interact physically with the world in an intelligent way. Artificial intelligence (often referred to as AI) also includes expert tasks, in which decisions and actions are based on a body of specific knowledge about a subject. Ironically, the specialized expert tasks, such as diagnosing the symptoms of a doctor's patient, are generally easier to automate than mundane tasks, such as recognizing a person's face. This is because mundane tasks often involve a much larger range of potential circumstances.

The more we understand how we perform a complex task, the more chance we have of being successful in programming computers to perform the

CORE FACTS

- Artificial intelligence addresses both general reasoning and response to situations and also the manipulation of expert knowledge.
- Artificial intelligence researchers aim to build computer systems that can operate more autonomously and effectively in handling complex tasks.
- Disparate fields such as psychology, philosophy, neuropsychology, linguistics, mathematics, and computer science contribute to the field of artificial intelligence.

CONNECTIONS

● Computer systems that help doctors to diagnose medical conditions are a new development in the field of **MEDICAL TECHNOLOGY**.

● One possible use of artificial intelligence is to create "agents" that research information on the **INTERNET**.

These scenes are from the 1997 tournament in New York between state-of-the-art chess computer Deep Blue and chess grand master Garry Kaparov. The final score was 3.5–2.5 in favor of Deep Blue.

same task. For this reason, studies in neuropsychology and linguistics have a bearing on artificial intelligence. The very question of how far it is possible to go in simulating our mental processes brings artificial intelligence up against some of the basic questions of philosophy.

Artificial intelligence research can help shed light on the way humans think, and allow computer systems to be built that can operate more autonomously and effectively in handling complex tasks. Expert systems—computer systems that are tailored to specific tasks—can act as assistants where no human expert is available, or help in navigating a sea of possibilities such as in diagnosis and troubleshooting. Ever-increasing computer speeds and processing power are providing the resources for more complex AI experiments and to further explore the boundary between calculations and thought.

The Turing test

In 1950, at the dawn of the computer age, British mathematician Alan Turing (1912–1954) proposed an experiment that has become known as the Turing test. Any machine being evaluated for intelligence would be placed in one room, and a human control subject in another. The experimenter, in a third room, would communicate with both, using only a computer terminal or some other method that would mask the physical differences between the human and the machine. If, after asking questions typed in on the computer terminal and reading the answers given, the experimenter was unable to distinguish between the computer and the human, then the machine would be considered intelligent.

Many experts feel that the test has certain limitations. Evaluating only behavior that can be evidenced by questions and answers ignores aspects of human intelligence such as perception and manipulation. Furthermore, the assumption the test is based on—that intelligence is demonstrated only insofar as it imitates human response—is problem-

atic. For example, in order to masquerade successfully as a human, the machine would have to purposely make mistakes if asked to do complicated arithmetic. More fundamentally, John Searle, a philosopher at the University of California at Berkeley, made the argument that following a set of rules to generate an expected response is not the same as actually understanding the question. However, the Turing test provided a vital focus to a heavily philosophical, interdisciplinary field.

Early development

In 1955, the first artificial intelligence program, Logic Theorist, was developed at the RAND Corporation in Santa Monica, California, by Herbert Simon, Allen Newell, and J.C. Shaw. Logic Theorist proved theorems by using rule-based judgments (heuristics) to decide which alternatives were likely to prove fruitful. In implementing the program, the RAND group introduced innovative "list-processing" techniques for handling "symbolic" information, rather than using existing programming languages like FORTRAN, which were designed for numerical computation (see SOFTWARE AND PROGRAMMING). Some of the ideas of this early language, Information Processing Language (IPL), were adopted by artificial-intelligence researcher John McCarthy, then at the Massachusetts Institute of Technology (MIT), for the computer language LISP (LISt Processing), which was announced a few years later. LISP was soon adopted as the standard computer language of the artificial-intelligence world.

A 1956 conference at Dartmouth College, New Hampshire, united a group of researchers that came to dominate the field for decades. The conference founded the discipline of artificial intelligence, gave it its name, and crystalized its founding hypothesis: that the human mind does not physically touch the world but interprets and manipulates information passed to it by the senses, and similar manipulation of information can be performed by a computer.

Given the breadth of artificial intelligence, it is perhaps inevitable that the field diverged into several schools of thought. McCarthy, having moved to Stanford University, continued along the paths of formal logic. MIT's Marvin Minsky and Seymour Papert became interested in perception and pattern recognition. Frank Rosenblatt, at Cornell University, pioneered the use of neural networks. These are arrays of individual computational units, which are used in an attempt to model the workings of the human brain. These disparate efforts all contributed to growth and progress in the field.

The representation of knowledge

In order to construct computer programs that can manipulate knowledge intelligently, an effective way to represent that knowledge symbolically must be found. In all the methods used, the general mechanism for evaluating information and drawing conclusions is kept separate from facts, rules, or data that is specific to an application. This allows the method to be applied to a wide range of situations. There are three main ways of representing knowledge in artificial intelligence: predicate logic, frames, and rule-based systems.

Predicate logic. Predicate logic is a formal system in which mathematical symbols are used to describe propositions and the conditions under which they are true or false. Predicate logic is mechanical. This means that expressions are treated as strings of characters and rules are employed to manipulate them, regardless of any sense of their meaning. This method is well suited for computer programs and for applications like theorem-proving in which it is necessary to adhere to a rigid procedure. Predicate logic is a fundamental method that is often cited in discussions of artificial intelligence and its concepts. However, it is not the best way to implement what we think of as common sense or to deal with areas of uncertainty.

Frames. A more natural way to represent knowledge is to structure it into frames. Frames are data structures that represent classes of objects, concepts, or situations and also define their relationships. Subclasses may take the basic frame, inherit its properties, and tailor them for a particular need.

For example, a frame called *room* might be used to represent a generic room. The room would consist of only the essential floor, walls, and ceiling. A specific type of room such as a bedroom would be a particular instance of the frame called *room*. The bedroom might contain objects—such as a bed and a bedside table—themselves represented by other frames called *bed* and *table*. Characteristics of the specific bed and table can be represented by further frames. In this way, complex situations can be represented by a number of frames.

Frames are rich in descriptive abilities, but defining complex conditions under which something is true is more difficult than in predicate logic.

Rule-based systems. Knowledge may be represented in rule-based systems. A rule-based system consists of a set of facts and a number of IF-THEN rules, which are applied to incoming information in light of the known facts to generate a decision or conclusion. However, the rules are not applied sequentially, like the IF-THEN statements in a traditional computer program. Instead, the artificial intelligence program decides which rules are applicable to the given input. Rule-based systems may be either forward-chaining or backward-chaining. Forward-chaining systems are driven to some undetermined conclusion by the data they receive. Backward-chaining systems start with a goal, or a statement to be proved, and look for a combination of rules and facts that would account for it. Backward chaining may be more efficient when only a few of the possible conclusions are of interest. Rule-based systems are often used in expert systems (see the box on page 114).

Natural language processing

One of the active areas of artificial intelligence research is natural language processing. Although most human toddlers manage this with relative ease,

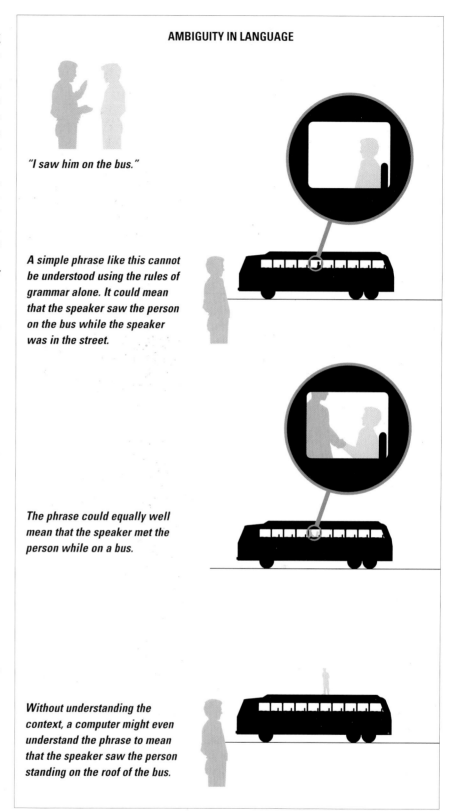

AMBIGUITY IN LANGUAGE

"I saw him on the bus."

A simple phrase like this cannot be understood using the rules of grammar alone. It could mean that the speaker saw the person on the bus while the speaker was in the street.

The phrase could equally well mean that the speaker met the person while on a bus.

Without understanding the context, a computer might even understand the phrase to mean that the speaker saw the person standing on the roof of the bus.

it is very difficult to automate. It involves many tasks, each rife with ambiguities. Yet the idea of being able to converse with a computer is a fascinating one, and even limited voice recognition is convenient for many applications.

Human speech can be electronically split into its various frequencies. These patterns can then be compared to the basic sounds of language (phonemes). Phonemes are combined to make words. However, they can be combined in different ways in a word, depending on the speaker's accent, the next word in

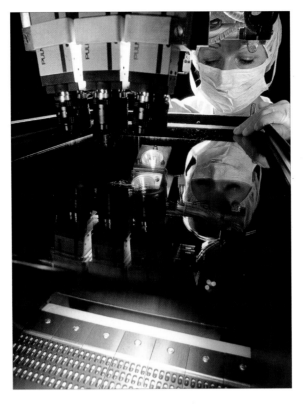

This technician is preparing a machine that uses a series of cameras to inspect the shape of drug capsules being produced in a factory. The control computer is programmed to interpret the information from the cameras and reject misshapen capsules.

the sentence, the speed at which the word is spoken, and many other factors. Speech recognition systems to employ statistical analysis and language rules to produce a "best guess" at what words were actually said (see VOICE RECOGNITION AND SYNTHESIS).

Once the words to be processed have been established, whether they were spoken or simply typed into a keyboard, the syntax (grammatical elements) must then be analyzed to discern meaning. Many sentence structures are unclear. Consider, for example, the sentence *I saw him on the bus.* Does the speaker mean that he or she was also on the bus, or did the speaker see the person through the bus window from the street? Might the speaker even mean that the person was sitting or standing on top of the bus for some reason? Both grammar and contextual rules must be applied to select the right meaning.

Natural language generation systems must deal with the same issues in reverse. In deciding what to say, they must consider the goal of the communication. Most drivers who stop their car to ask where they are would not expect to hear the answer "At a gas station," even if this answer was correct. For a computer to give accurate answers to a question is not enough; the response must also be relevant.

Another aim of artificial intelligence researchers in this area is to design systems that can translate from one human language to another. Merely to translate a sentence by looking up each word in a translation dictionary is not enough. Translation requires an understanding of the rules of grammar and the context and sense of each sentence.

Machine vision

Many homes and offices now contain equipment such as video cameras, digital cameras, and scanners that can scan images and other visual information into computer files (see IMAGING TECHNOLOGY). A much greater challenge is getting the computer to make sense of the visual information it has received. Digital images are broken down into a matrix of tiny points of color and brightness called pixels (see COMPUTER GRAPHICS). Image recognition systems determine the amount of change in color and brightness, enabling simple features such as lines and edges to be identified. Shading and understanding of perspective are used to determine how the scene would look in three dimensions. Often the features in the image are compared against model data in order to identify specific objects (see PATTERN RECOGNITION).

Machine vision systems are now used in industrial applications, particularly on assembly lines. They can help to position components for automatic assembly by robots and also assist in quality control monitoring (see PRODUCTION ENGINEERING AND PROCESS CONTROL; ROBOTICS). Autonomous vehicles equipped with machine vision may someday roam dangerous, unexplored territory, avoiding obstacles, choosing paths of interest, and reporting what they find. This has already begun to happen with the development of unpiloted vehicles that explore distant planets' surfaces and computer-controlled submarines called autonomous underwater vehicles (see DEEP-SEA AND DIVING TECHNOLOGY).

S. CALVO

See also: COMPUTER; STRATEGIC DEFENSE SYSTEMS.

Further reading:
Artificial Intelligence. Edited by M. Boden. San Diego: Academic Press, 1996.
Cawsey, A. *The Essence of Artificial Intelligence.* New York: Prentice Hall, 1998.

EXPERT SYSTEMS

Expert systems are computer systems that are tailored for use in a particular field. They analyze and make decisions about situations based on the knowledge of an expert in the particular field. Expert systems are used in many fields, including medicine, electronics, business, and law.

The PROSPECTOR system, developed at Stanford in the late 1970s, uses geological information to predict the type and location of deposits of mineral ore likely to be found on a particular site.

The clues in the geological data can indicate good places to look for copper or molybdenum, but like a human expert, PROSPECTOR cannot make predictions with absolute certainty. Instead, it relies on analysis of probability. Probabilities are defined numerically. A probability of zero indicates that an event cannot possibly occur. A probability of one is a certainty. The probability of getting "heads" in a fair coin toss is 0.5. In expert systems, it is important to consider the probability of some event or outcome based on the evidence, or known data.

In building a knowledge base, it is often necessary to work backward. For example, in developing PROSPECTOR, knowledge engineers used data on the prevalence of certain geological features in areas where the various minerals had been found in the past. Using this method, PROSPECTOR has predicted ore deposits in commercial quantities at several sites.

A CLOSER LOOK

ARTILLERY

The term *artillery* was in use long before the cannon was invented. It referred to various throwing engines, such as catapults. As a result, it is difficult when viewing history, particularly the history of the Middle Ages, to decipher exactly when the word ceased to mean exclusively engines and began to include cannon.

The earliest reliable reference to cannon was in 1326, in the city records of Florence, Italy, which mention the provision of cannon and shot. The first picture of a cannon appeared in England the same year, and from this it is known that the first cannon were of cast bell metal or bronze and were shaped like a vase with a slender neck and a thickened portion around the rear end. A vent hole was bored into the rear of the barrel and loaded with a charge of gunpowder. An arrow, wrapped in cloth to fill the bore, was the projectile, which was fired by applying a hot iron to the gunpowder in the rear hole. Yet there was no way of accurately aiming the cannon.

This primitive start was soon improved upon. Although casting was expensive—and demanded skilled craftsmen and special metals—the common technique of coopering (making barrels for wine or water) could be applied to making a cannon. By building up a series of strips of iron around a pattern, and then heating and hammering the strips into shape, a serviceable gun would emerge (which is why the operative part of a gun is still called the barrel). The padded arrow was replaced by stone balls. Stone was used because it could be easily worked and chipped into shape. Also, it weighed enough to do damage when it struck—but not as much damage as iron or lead balls. These, due to their weight, needed a larger charge of powder to move them, which caused the earliest guns to burst open.

Guns, mortars, and howitzers

By the 15th century, the technique of casting iron had been perfected. Machinery was developed that bored the cast barrel smooth and internally concentric, which made it easier for the guns to be shot accurately. The power and conformity of gunpowder also improved, and iron cannonballs, which could be cast cheaply, were developed. At the Siege of Constantinople in 1453, Mehmed II, unable to fire his cannon directly at the ships of his enemy, fired

An M-198 howitzer, with a 6.1-in (15.5-cm) bore, is being fired by soldiers of the Third Field Artillery during a multinational joint service exercise called Bright Star '85, in Egypt, in 1985.

them into the air over the tops of the intervening buildings, dropping the balls onto the ships from above—and thus inventing the mortar.

Eventually, three basic types of cannon came to be recognized: the gun, which fired at low angles of elevation and with high velocity against targets that could be seen; the mortar, which fired heavier projectiles up into the air so as to drop down behind any intervening protection (the mortar barrel was set at a permanent angle of elevation, usually about 70 degrees, and the range was varied by varying the charge of powder); and the howitzer, which could be elevated from 0 to 45 degrees and could fire at any angle so that it covered the roles of both gun and mortar, though with a heavier projectile that fired at a lower velocity than the gun. Within these groups, the different sizes of cannon were given exotic names—culverin, demi-cannon, cannon extra, basilisk, saker—to distinguish one from the other.

Mobility and reliability

The earliest guns were laid on the ground, wedged up with a block of wood, and fired. Later, rough timber supports were built for them, although the gun and its support still had to be moved on wagons and assembled where they were needed. Then came the wooden carriage, consisting of a pair of wheels and a wooden trail running from the axle to the ground, which held the gun barrel. The barrel was cast with two short, round stubs of metal called trunnions. These rested in hollowed-out grooves on the top of the trail. The gun could be moved up and down by means of wedges beneath the breech end (behind the barrel), so as to throw the shot to the desired range. As technology improved, guns became less heavy and it became possible to pull them with a small team of horses, keeping up with the army as it moved.

CORE FACTS

- There are three basic types of cannon: the gun, the mortar, and the howitzer.
- Modern artillery can hit the target with the first shot without the firing trial shots that could alert the enemy.
- The major branches of specialized artillery are coastal defense, antiaircraft, and antitank artillery.

CONNECTIONS

- The development of iron **CASTING** led to improvements in cannonballs and barrels by the 1400s.

- By the end of World War I, **MILITARY VEHICLES** such as **TANKS** had entered the battlefield, and artillery had to be invented that could pierce their armor.

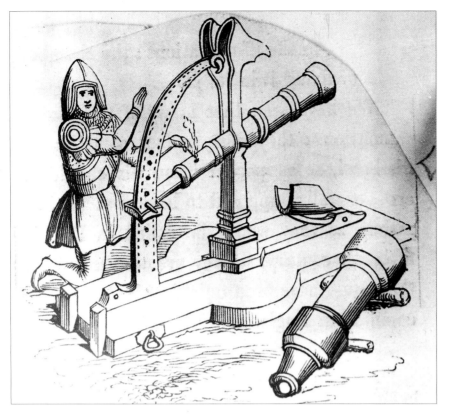

A drawing of one of the earliest cannons, first used in the Hundred Years' War by the English under Edward III against the French under Philip VI at the Battle of Crécy in 1346. Two cannon barrels of different sizes—the one in use and the other resting on the ground—could be fitted on the same mounting.

Although the intervening centuries saw much technical improvement in the manufacture and detail of cannons, there was nothing about a cannon from 1800 that would have baffled a gunner from 1400. However, all that was about to change—largely as a result of the Industrial Revolution.

Breech-loading and built-up guns

The Industrial Revolution of the 18th and 19th centuries generated new machinery, new technology, and a new breed of engineers. One such engineer was William Armstrong (1810–1900). During the Crimean War (1853–1856), he was astonished to find that a gun firing an 18-lb (8-kg) shot actually weighed over 3 tons (2.7 tonnes). So he set out to invent a new gun. The excessive weight of guns had been necessary up until this time, because the gun's barrel had to be thick in order to withstand the pressure of the gunpowder cartridge exploding inside it. Since a thick-cast iron gun barrel was very heavy, it also needed a huge timber carriage to transport it. Armstrong designed a gun that was built up from several thin wrought-iron tubes, which were heated and shrunk so as to compress upon each other, thus providing the desired strength without excess weight. He also rifled the gun (cut spiral grooves into the interior of the barrel) and loaded it from the breech (the rear end), not from the muzzle (the open end). He designed an elongated shell coated with lead, which bit into the rifling grooves and spun the shell as it left the barrel (the spinning motion stabilizes the orientation of the shell in flight).

In contrast to rifled guns, smoothbored guns had the disadvantage that the ball had to be appreciably smaller than the barrel, so that it could be rammed down without trapping air behind it. When it shot through the barrel, the ball bounced from side to side, and the direction it finally took depended upon which side of the barrel it had last bounced from. For this reason, accuracy was only moderate. Moreover, the weight of the shot or shell fired by a smoothbore was rigidly governed by the diameter of the ball. It was impossible to have any other size or shape, because an elongated shot or shell would simply tumble through the air and there would be no chance of any accuracy at all.

A spinning shell, however, is stabilized by the same laws of physics that control the gyroscope, and it flies accurately (see GYROSCOPE). Within limits, the shell can be either long or short. Lengthening it produces a heavier shot than a smoothbore could fire and, because the spinning of the shell guarantees that it flies point-first, it is possible to fit a nose fuse that detonates the shell when it hits the target.

The British adopted the Armstrong gun in large numbers, but other nations waited to see the long-term results of the gun's performance in battle. France adopted rifling but stayed with the muzzle-loading gun, placing soft metal studs on the shell so that it rode down the grooves when rammed inside and ran up the grooves again when fired. In Germany, ironmaster and munitions manufacturer

By the early 19th century, the cannon had become a reliable and fairly accurate weapon. The barrel was smooth internally and fired a round ball, which could be either solid or hollow. The hollow ball was filled with gunpowder and fitted with a burning fuse, which caused it to explode in the air over the target. The two-wheeled carriage could be moved by horses or by oxen. The gunpowder was placed inside prepared cartridges of cloth, which were then rammed down the cannon's barrel, followed by the shot. The cannon was fired by a goose quill filled with gunpowder, which was inserted into the rear vent hole and ignited with a flaming match.

ENGINES OF WAR

Engines fell into two classes: catapults (for throwing missiles) and crossbows (for shooting arrows). The earliest catapult was the mangonel, or onager—a wooden frame with a windlass (winch) on each side, joined across the frame by strips of rawhide through which a long wooden arm was pushed. The arm, secured to the frame by a rope, had a spoon-shaped end into which a stone was placed. Then the windlasses were turned, twisting the rawhide so that it became a powerful spring. When the rope was cut, the arm flew into the air and launched the stone.

The ballista was a bow consisting of a stout wooden post with a hole, into which an arrow was placed. A springy plank behind the post was pulled back by a rope and then released to hit the end of the arrow and drive it out.

Finally, in about the 10th century, the trebuchet was developed. This was similar to the mangonel, only instead of a rawhide spring, it had a long arm pivoted close to its lower end. The lower end carried a large basket full of stones, while the upper end carried a sling. The arm was pulled down to the horizontal by ropes, a stone placed in the sling, and the arm released. The heavy weight on the short end drove the top forward at high speed and the sling ejected its stone.

A CLOSER LOOK

Alfred Krupp (1812–1887) experimented with guns bored from solid steel blocks and developed another system of breech-loading. In Britain, engineer Joseph Whitworth (1803–1887) developed yet another way of loading from the breech and rifling a gun: he made the interior of the bore six-sided and twisted it. The shell was also six-sided and followed the twist, causing it to emerge from the muzzle spinning. However, sometimes it would jam inside the gun and blow it up. Many Armstrong and Whitworth guns were sent to the United States during the Civil War, yet smoothbore muzzle-loading guns were in use during the greater part of that war.

Curbing the recoil

Once the rifled breech-loader had become the standard armament, artillery was able to become more powerful. However, this brought with it a new technical problem. When a gun is fired, the exploding cartridge drives the shell out of the muzzle. At the same time, it causes the gun to recoil backward. Until then, gunners merely stood clear while the gun fired, waited until it stopped moving, and then pushed it back to its firing position, ready for the next shot. But if guns were to get bigger and more powerful, this method could not be tolerated.

After trying a number of devices to control the moving gun carriage, a solution was found. A hydraulic brake was put between the gun barrel and the carriage. As the gun recoiled, it pulled on a piston inside a cylinder full of oil. A valve in the cylinder allowed the oil to pass through it, but the restriction on the flow acted as a brake, absorbing the

recoil energy. At the same time, the gun also pulled on a second piston, which compressed a spring. On firing, the energy of recoil would mainly be absorbed by the oil buffer; some energy would be taken up by compressing the spring. After firing, the spring would expand to its original size, pulling the gun back into its proper place on the gun carriage. This system was then improved by using compressed air or nitrogen instead of the spring. As the gun recoiled, it placed the air or nitrogen under greater compression. At the end of the recoil, the gas expanded to its former volume and drove the piston back, thereby pulling the gun "into battery."

This image shows the Armstrong gun being manufactured in 1862 in "The Beehive"—a factory room in Woolwich, England. The Armstrong cannon fired 150-lb (68-kg) shells and had an 8-in (20-cm) bore.

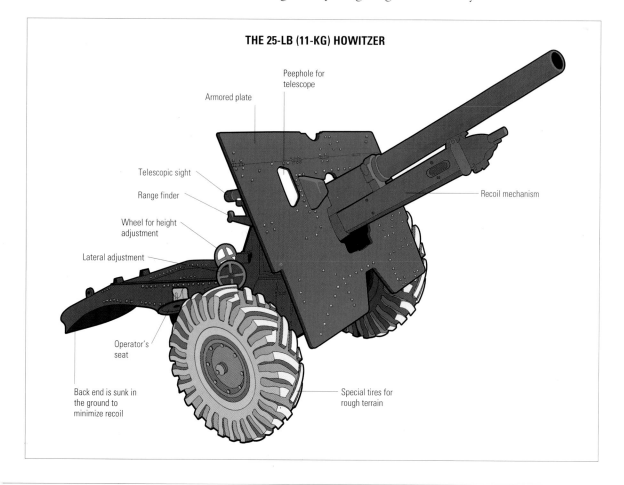

THE 25-LB (11-KG) HOWITZER

Peephole for telescope

Armored plate

Telescopic sight

Range finder

Wheel for height adjustment

Lateral adjustment

Recoil mechanism

Operator's seat

Back end is sunk in the ground to minimize recoil

Special tires for rough terrain

SUPERGUNS

Big Bertha, a German gun used to bombard Paris in 1918, had an 11-in (28-cm) bore.

Building guns to fire exceptionally heavy shells or to fire across incredibly long distances presents problems, but the general principles remain the same. One problem is that the enormous temperature and pressure of the huge cartridge can melt away ordinary rifling and driving bands, and the shell needs to be made with ribs that engage with specially deep grooves in the gun. Another problem is to allow enough barrel length for the cartridge to deliver all its power before the shell leaves the muzzle.

Perhaps the most famous supergun was the Paris Gun of World War I, developed by Germany. This fired a 220-lb (100-kg) shell 8.5 inches (21 cm) long to a target 68 miles (109 km) away. the Paris Gun had a barrel 43 yds (39 m) long and weighed 145 tons (131 tonnes). It had to be specially braced to prevent it from sagging under its own weight. The cartridge weighed 335 lbs (150 kg) and gave the shell a muzzle velocity of 6510 ft (1984 m) per second.

A German railroad gun of World War II, the Gustav, was a supergun with a caliber of 31.5 inches (80 cm). It fired a 7-ton (6.4-tonne) shell over 24 miles (38 km). The entire gun and its carriage weighed 1250 tons (1134 tonnes) when assembled, a task that took about three weeks.

A CLOSER LOOK

Specialized artillery

As the 20th century progressed, artillery was divided into specialized branches. The first major branch was coastal defense, which coincided with the emergence of fortress guns in the latter half of the 19th century. Their job was to defend ports and naval bases against attack by hostile ships. These guns later became specialized into two main types: heavy guns for firing on ships out at sea, and fast-firing light guns for attacking high-speed small torpedo boats intent on raiding harbors.

Another type of artillery appeared before World War I (1914–1918): antiaircraft artillery, devoted to the task of shooting at aerial targets. This was a difficult challenge: for the first time, guns had a target that moved at much higher speed and at a greater distance than previous targets—the target could cover a great distance in the time the shell took to reach it after firing. The gun operator had to guess how far in front of the target the gun had to be fired to have a chance of hitting the moving target (see ANTIAIRCRAFT WEAPON).

In the last months of World War I, the first tanks entered service, and new artillery emerged to deal with them. Guns had to be capable of rapid direction changes and of firing shot at high enough velocity to punch holes in tank armor. In the period between World War I and World War II, horses— formerly the principal means of moving artillery in the field—were replaced with motor vehicles that could tow guns at high speed. Old wooden wheels and solid axles were replaced with pneumatic tires and spring suspension. In World War II, various armies fielded tens of thousands of guns of all sizes, massed in formations.

Present-day artillery

Immediately after World War II, military strategists envisaged the use of battlefield nuclear weapons in warfare (see NUCLEAR WEAPONS). However, it soon became apparent that such weapons were too powerful to use. Therefore, artillery remained a vital component of land forces, and some of the electronics technology developed in the 1960s began to be used for artillery (see ELECTRONICS).

The first electronic systems for artillery—developed during World War II—were used as a means of directing antiaircraft artillery. These systems provided instructions for directing guns at unseen targets. Later, electronic fuses were developed that detonated shells at the optimum distance for inflicting damage on their targets. Computers were built that took high-speed calculations to assess the effect of wind, air temperature, air density, and other factors on the flight of the shell, thereby increasing accuracy (see COMPUTER). Previously it had been necessary to fire trial shots to ascertain the exact distance to the target. Now this can be calculated by computers, and complex corrections can be applied in seconds, so that the first shot strikes the target. For moving targets, advanced missile-guidance technology has been applied to artillery shells to steer them to their intended point of impact (see MISSILE). The artillery forces of World War II would never have survived the aerial precision-bombing and guided-missile attacks typical of modern warfare.

I. HOGG

See also: BOMB, SHELL, AND GRENADE; FIREARMS; FORTIFICATION AND DEFENSE; HAND WEAPONS; LAND WARFARE; SIEGE WARFARE.

Further reading;

Dastrup, B. L. *The Field Artillery: History and Sourcebook.* Westport, Connecticut: Greenwood Press, 1994.
DeVries, K. R. *Medieval Military Technology.* Lewiston, New York: Broadview Press, 1992.
Gudmundsson, B. I. *On Artillery.* Westport, Connecticut: Praeger, 1993.

AUTOMOBILE

The automobile is a vehicle used for transport and is made of many integrated mechanical and electrical systems

Automobiles are an integral part of modern society and many people's main means of transportation. The proliferation of automobiles has, for better or worse, created societies in which far-flung suburban communities radiate outward from commercial centers. These, in turn, disperse in an ever-widening sprawl, often leaving urban centers to disintegrate. At the same time, automobiles have given people a great deal of freedom to travel very large distances whenever they require. This serves to broaden the choices of exactly where they work, live, and play.

The key invention that made the automobile possible was an engine capable of replacing the horse in pulling a passenger carriage (see HORSE-DRAWN TRANSPORT). But an automobile is more than an engine on wheels topped by a seat. Many systems are required to deliver the engine's power, move the automobile, start it and stop it, control its speed, and steer it. As people spend more and more time in their cars, they have begun to expect that a car should provide all the comforts of home: safety, comfortable seating, a controlled climate, an entertainment system, and sometimes a telephone. All these systems, wedged into a vehicle small enough to be conveniently maneuverable, must work together smoothly and be easily operated by a driver whose eyes are on the road.

Body and frame

There are two main types of automobile construction. In body-over-frame construction, a steel frame is used as a base, and sections of the body are then bolted directly onto it. In unibody construction, there is generally no frame. Instead, the body sections themselves serve as the structural elements.

Suspension system

Imagine using a toy construction set with interlocking plastic bricks to build a model car. The last pieces to be attached would probably be the wheels, with their axles fitted right onto the bottom of the toy car. A short test run on a bumpy driveway, however, would demonstrate a major drawback of this design: the forces on the wheels would quickly shake the model apart. The suspension system prevents this from happening in a real automobile and also provides the driver and passengers with a journey that is relatively comfortable.

Most suspension systems consist of springs that support the body or frame on the wheel axle. Hydraulic shock absorbers help to prevent the body from bouncing up and down on the springs. Ball joints and stabilizers allow the correct degree of play between the wheel assemblies and the body. Modern automobiles may have computer-controlled active suspensions that adjust the car to particular types of

CORE FACTS

- Automobiles are powered by the internal combustion engine, which burns gasoline in order to do mechanical work.
- In each cycle of the engine's pistons, a controlled burning is sparked by the ignition system.
- In order to work properly, the engine must be kept lubricated with oil and operated in the appropriate temperature range.
- The control of exhaust emissions, safety, and comfort have become increasingly important in modern automobile design.

CONNECTIONS

- The particular **AERODYNAMIC** shape of an automobile is important in reducing drag forces from the atmosphere.

- Automobiles are the biggest source of **POLLUTION** in cities and are a massive drain on natural **ENERGY RESOURCES**.

- **ELECTRIC ROAD VEHICLES** that are powered by **ELECTRIC MOTORS** may one day replace more conventional automobiles.

driving conditions. The suspension functions so that the automobile can drive long distances over a variety of road conditions without being shaken to pieces (see SUSPENSION SYSTEM).

Wheels and tires

Automobile tires are mounted on wheel rims made of steel, aluminum, magnesium, or other materials. The shape of the rim is intended to hold on to the tire even if it bursts while the car is moving. The tires themselves are designed to cushion the bumps in the road and to provide traction. The surface that touches the ground—the tread—and the sidewalls are made of natural and synthetic rubber. The interior structure of the tire, which holds in the pressurized air and provides stiffness to the treads, consists of layers of concentric belts supported by cords of steel wire, fiberglass, or heavy-duty textiles such as Kevlar. Most modern tires are of radial construction, in which the cords are at approximately right angles to the belts (see TIRE; RUBBER; WHEEL).

Engine

An engine is a machine that converts the heat energy obtained from burning a fuel into mechanical energy (see ENGINE). In an automobile, the fuel is usually gasoline—a highly flammable, refined petroleum product that contains additives to improve performance (see GASOLINE). The gasoline is burned by a series of controlled explosions in an internal combustion engine (see INTERNAL COMBUSTION ENGINE). Inside the engine, expanding gases from the burning fuel cause pistons to move down in cylinders. After combustion, the gases are released and the piston is forced back up by the crankshaft, which also converts the linear motion of the piston into a rotary motion which can be used to turn the wheels.

The internal combustion engines used in most automobiles operate in a four-stroke cycle. The fuel is mixed with air to provide the oxygen required for combustion. It is then drawn into the top of each cylinder through its intake valve as the piston moves down in the intake stroke. As the piston comes back up in the compression stroke, the intake valve closes, and the mixture of fuel and air is compressed so as to generate a more powerful explosion when the gas is ignited. Once this happens, the piston is forced down by the force of the gases in the power stroke. The exhaust stroke pushes the burned gases up and out through the cylinder's exhaust valve, and allows the cycle to begin again. The opening and closing of the valves in the proper sequence is controlled by a camshaft, which has a series of contoured surfaces called cam lobes.

Automobile engines are often classified by the arrangement of their cylinders. Many four-cylinder engines are of the in-line type, in which the cylinders are lined up one beside the other. The slant design, in which the cylinder block is inclined to one side, is a variation that allows the engine to fit under a lower hood. The V-type engine has two rows of cylinders placed at an angle to each other. V-6 and V-8 engines (with six and eight cylinders respectively) are the most common, but V-10 and V-12 engines are also used occasionally.

Engine size, which may be given in cubic inches, cubic centimeters, or liters, refers not to the physical dimensions of the engine but to the total displacement of the cylinders: the change in volume between the top and bottom of the pistons' strokes (piston volume is a determining factor in the power output of the engine). Another important engine parameter is its power (or horsepower). This is a measure of the rate at which the engine performs work.

Ignition system

In order for the engine to start burning its fuel, a spark must be provided. This is the task of the ignition system. Each cylinder has its own spark plug, which creates a spark by applying a voltage difference between two electrodes separated by a tiny gap. The voltage required across the gap is thousands of times higher than the 12 volts provided by the car's battery. After the ignition switch is activated by means of the ignition key, the current passes from the battery through an ignition coil. This is a transformer that can increase the voltage from the battery to up to about 100,000 volts (see BATTERY; TRANSFORMER). In most engines, the voltage is supplied to the various spark plugs at the correct time by a revolving device called a distributor. Newer ignition systems without distributors are computer controlled and use multiple ignition coils.

To keep steady power coming from the engine, the ignition system must fire the cylinders smoothly, one after the other. Each cylinder must receive its spark in turn, just at the moment when the piston reaches the top of the compression stroke. The timing of many automobiles can be monitored with a stroboscopic timing light. Newer models may be timed with a magnetic timing meter. If the timing is off, it can be adjusted by a mechanic. A tune-up, in which spark plugs and wires may be replaced and the timing adjusted, can result in a significant improvement in a car's performance (see IGNITION SYSTEM).

Fuel supply

Gasoline used to run the engine is stored in a fuel tank with a capacity of anything between 9 gallons (34 liters) and 41 gallons (155 liters). Some automobiles run on diesel fuel, which combusts spontaneously when it is compressed in the cylinder and requires no spark plugs. The location of the fuel tank depends on the design of the car, but it should be somewhere protected from road debris and accidental rupture. Since the fuel tank is generally lower than the engine, a fuel pump is necessary to move the gasoline out of the tank. Fuel filters are used to screen out rust and sediment that may have condensed in the tank. In order for efficient combustion to take place, a constant ratio of fuel to air must be delivered to the engine. The traditional way to accomplish this is with a carburetor, which is still found in many vehicles. It has been replaced in later model cars by fuel injection systems.

In a carburetor system, a choke valve is used to control the flow of air. The choke valve is closed when the engine is starting from cold, to provide a fuel-rich mixture. Once the engine is running, the choke valve opens up, allowing more air into the mixture. The throttle valve controls the flow of air-fuel mixture according to the pressure applied on the accelerator pedal by the driver. The air-fuel mixture is fed into the engine through the intake manifold.

In a fuel-injection system, pressurized fuel is sprayed either directly into the cylinders or, more commonly, via the intake manifold. The manifold is

This mechanic is testing the performance of an automobile engine with the aid of a computer.

also fed by an air induction system, and the air-fuel mixture is created there. Early fuel-injection systems were mechanical, linked to pumps driven by the engine. Modern electronic fuel-injection systems use computerized sensors to monitor the amount of oxygen in the exhaust gases and adjust the fuel mixture so that it burns cleanly (see FUEL INJECTION).

Lubrication

Moving parts, such as those in an automobile engine, generate a great deal of friction. This friction causes surfaces that are rubbing together to heat up and eventually develop scuffed and worn areas. An engine without lubrication will eventually seize up: the heat of friction causes either its parts to expand so that they will no longer move or metal-to-metal contact that welds the rubbing surfaces together.

Automobile engines are lubricated with motor oil, a refined petroleum product that contains additives such as detergents to help keep the engine clean. An oil pump provides the circulation between the oil pan and the moving parts, such as bearings and pistons. Over time, contaminants such as dirt and bits of metal accumulate in the oil, so both the oil and the oil filter must be replaced periodically.

Motor oil is generally classified in terms of its viscosity (thickness). A standard scale is used so that different oils may be compared. Light oils that can be used at temperatures down to 0°F (−18°C) have a *W* after their viscosity rating. Heavy oils that are suitable for higher temperatures, up to 210°F (99°C), are designated by a viscosity number alone. Most modern oils have polymer additives that allow high- and low-temperature use (see LUBRICANT).

Cooling system

The temperature of the burning gasoline in a modern automobile engine is more than 4000°F (2200°C). Only one-third of the heat of combustion is turned into work. About another third is dissipated in the exhaust gases. If the remaining heat were not removed, the engine would get too hot. The excess

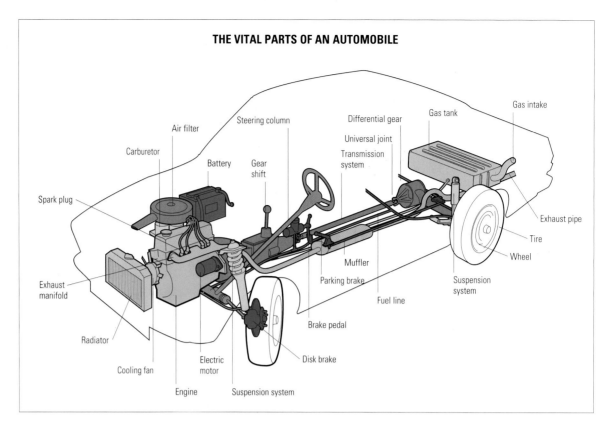

THE VITAL PARTS OF AN AUTOMOBILE

heat could cause the oil to decompose chemically so that it would no longer be able to lubricate the engine parts effectively.

To prevent this from happening, most automobiles use a liquid cooling system. A coolant is pushed by a water pump through passages in the engine block and carries the heat out into a radiator, where it can be dissipated into the surrounding air. Despite the name of the pump, the coolant is not water alone. This is because water freezes at 32°F (0°C), and if the coolant were not able to circulate, it could not carry away the heat. For this reason, water is mixed half and half with ethylene glycol (antifreeze) to give a coolant that has a higher boiling point and lower freezing point than pure water. The cooling system is pressurized to allow the coolant to work at even higher temperatures without boiling away.

Exhaust system

Waste gases are produced whenever fuel is burned. In the automobile, these exhaust gases, which are hot and toxic, must be carried away from the passenger compartment. The exhaust system also serves to reduce noise and the emission of pollutants.

The exhaust gases from the engine are channeled into the exhaust manifold, and from there to the rest of the exhaust system. The entire system must be designed so that it will not restrict gas flow, or back pressure will result, opposing the cylinders' exhaust stroke and reducing the engine's efficiency. Some automobiles have twin exhaust systems to offer more capacity for exhaust gas flow. Others use headers—special manifolds with pipes of different lengths leading from each cylinder, so that the exhaust-gas pulses from the cylinder heads join the exhaust stream at regular intervals and reduce back pressure.

Catalytic converters reduce the amount of polluting gases in the exhaust by converting toxic hydrocarbons and carbon monoxide into carbon dioxide and water. At the same time, nitrogen oxides that contribute to acid rain are turned into harmless nitrogen. Catalytic converters came into widespread use in the United States in the 1970s, when tougher emissions-control legislation was imposed on all new cars. Emissions reduction requires tight controls on the air-fuel ratio and ignition timing. Early emissions-controlled vehicles exhibited some performance problems as a result. Modern computer-controlled fuel injection, timing, and emissions systems have assisted in solving these problems.

The muffler is the part of the exhaust system that reduces the noise caused by the flow of exhaust gas. In the reverse-flow muffler, the gases are made to change direction so that the sound waves cancel each other out. In the straight-through muffler, the sound is deadened by metal baffles, packed fiberglass, or steel wool (see ACOUSTICS AND SOUND). The tailpipe routes the exhaust gases from the muffler into the outside environment.

Electrical system

Although most automobiles run on gasoline, many of their systems would not operate without electricity. Electricity is required to start the car and operate the fuel injection system, the electronic gauges and sensors, the various lights, the audio system, and many other devices. Small electric motors may be used to open and close windows, convertible tops, sunroofs, and vents; and to raise and lower the radio antenna. The electricity source for all these devices is a large 12-volt battery that is recharged while the engine is running by a type of generator called an alternator.

The alternator converts some of the mechanical energy of the car's motion into electricity. It is driven by a belt as the crankshaft of the engine turns. In the alternator, an electromagnetic field coil (or rotor) spins, which causes current to flow in a stationary coil called the stator. The alternator uses a pulley system to multiply the rotation speed of the crankshaft and produce electricity to charge the battery. The amount of electricity generated by the alternator is controlled by the voltage regulator (see BATTERY; ELECTRIC MOTOR AND GENERATOR).

One of the most important uses of electricity in an automobile is for starting the engine. As described earlier, the ignition switch activates a system that creates sparks to ignite the fuel. But this is not the only thing that happens when the ignition key is turned. The ignition switch also allows the battery to supply electricity to the starter, an electric motor that causes the crankshaft to start turning and thereby starts the cycle of fuel induction, compression, combustion, and exhaust. Once the engine is firing, the starter is disengaged. Before starter motors were used, early automobiles had to be cranked by hand, a process that can be seen in some old movies.

From the battery, wiring is run throughout the automobile to operate its various systems. For ease of installation and maintenance, the wires are generally run in groups, bunched together in wiring harnesses. Some equipment, such as the pumps that provide pressurized hydraulic fluid to operate power-steering and power-braking systems, does not need to be powered up unless the vehicle is moving; the wiring for these is often routed through the ignition switch. Other wiring is run directly from the battery so that devices such as lights can be used even when the ignition is switched off. Fuses are used to guard against short circuits that could otherwise damage the electrical system.

Transmission system

The purpose of an automobile transmission is to apply the mechanical energy of the engine to the axle which is used to move the wheels. Turning the axle under different conditions requires different amounts of torque (turning force). More torque is required to begin moving from a standstill or to go uphill than is needed for proceeding at constant speed on a level surface. Torque is adjusted in the transmission by means of gears. In low gear, plenty of torque is available, but the axle cannot be turned very fast. In high gear, the axle can turn very fast but this motion is supplied with only a small amount of torque (see GEAR).

Automobile transmissions may be manual or automatic. In a manual transmission, the clutch, when operated with a pedal, disengages the transmission from the engine. This allows the gears to be shifted with a lever operated by the driver. A synchromesh unit smoothes the transition between different gears to prevent clashing or grinding. Most manual transmissions have four or five speeds plus a reverse gear.

Automatic transmissions are so called because they shift automatically between different gear ratios to produce the appropriate torque for the vehicle's speed and loading. In order to ensure smooth transitions between gears and reduce mechanical stress, the engine's power is delivered to the transmission via a torque converter rather than a mechanical clutch. The engine's crankshaft drives an impeller (a type of pump) that directs a light, oily transmission fluid at a turbine. The impact of the transmission

FOUR-WHEEL DRIVE

Four-wheel-drive vehicles are designed to cope with driving in adverse conditions.

Four-wheel-drive vehicles have become increasingly popular because of their suitability for driving in wet or muddy conditions, or on snow or ice. The advantage of four-wheel drive comes from the ability to deliver traction through both axles: if the front wheels lose their grip, power is transferred to the rear axles and vice versa.

Whereas two-wheel-drive vehicles have a differential assembly on one axle to spread the power between the two powered wheels, four-wheel-drive vehicles have differential assemblies on both axles. They also have a transfer case that splits the engine power between the front and rear axles according to conditions.

Some vehicles are set up to operate in four-wheel drive all the time. Generally, part-time four-wheel-drive vehicles are powered to the rear wheels but have a transfer case that can be engaged to power the front wheels as well when this is necessary.

A CLOSER LOOK

The stylish dashboard of a red Chevrolet incorporates a steering wheel and speed indicators.

fluid produces a torque on the turbine, which is connected to the wheels via the transmission. The important feature of the torque converter is that it delivers torque from the engine to the transmission without requiring the impeller and turbine to rotate at the same speed. This tolerance of different impeller and turbine speeds is known as slip (see MECHANICAL TRANSMISSION).

In a rear-wheel-drive car, a driveshaft must pass underneath the car between the transmission output shaft and the rear axle. This accounts for the hump on the floor of the passenger compartment of rear-wheel-drive cars. A universal joint (a device that can transmit rotational motion between shafts that are not parallel) provides the flexibility necessary for the driveshaft to traverse bumpy roads without breaking. The axle assembly includes a differential gear, which provides power to both wheels while allowing them to turn at different speeds when the car is turning a corner. Automobiles with front-wheel drive also use differential gears, but since no driveshaft is required to power the rear wheels, the

transmission and front axle mechanism, including the differential, are housed together in an assemblage called a transaxle.

Steering system

The steering system must allow the driver to turn the automobile by pointing its front wheels to either side. While it must be sensitive to the driver's actions, it must not transmit road shocks back to the driver. This requirement is called nonreversibility.

The steering system works whenever the driver turns the steering wheel, which is mounted on the steering shaft. The shaft is attached to a steering gear, which multiplies the torque that is applied. The spindle assembly and steering arms are attached to the suspension system and are the parts of the system that directly turn the wheels. These subsystems are joined using the steering linkage—either the traditional parallelogram linkage still used on many large cars and trucks, or the rack-and-pinion linkage, which has fewer moving parts and is now used on most small and midsize automobiles. Either type of linkage may be augmented with hydraulic power steering systems (see STEERING SYSTEMS).

Brakes

The function of the brake system is to stop or slow the vehicle. When the driver pushes the brake pedal, a hydraulic system employing brake fluid changes the pressure on the pedal into pressure in the fluid and activates a piston that applies friction pads to the wheels. In most modern automobiles, power brakes are used. These have a booster system that allows the driver to apply the brakes with a lighter force on the pedal. In disk brake systems, the friction surface is a disk bolted to the wheel hub. The brake pads are pressed against the rotating disk when the brake pedal is pressed, resulting in a frictional force between the surfaces. In drum brake systems, a rotating drum assembly, which is connected to the wheel axle, encloses a nonrotating pair of brake shoes. When the brake is applied, the brake shoes press against the drum, preventing further rotation of the drum and thereby stopping the wheel (see BRAKE SYSTEMS; HYDRAULICS AND PNEUMATICS).

Safety systems

There are two basic categories of safety systems: those designed to prevent accidents, and those designed to protect the occupants and the vehicle itself if an accident does occur. Antilock brake systems, which are found in many modern automobiles, are an example of the former. These prevent the wheels from locking up and causing the car to skid out of control during hard braking. Antilock brake systems cause the brakes to be applied in a pulsing motion if their sensors indicate that the wheels are beginning to lock. Drivers are taught to pump the brake pedal in wet, icy, or hard-braking conditions to achieve a similar effect. However, antilock brake systems achieve a higher pulse rate than is possible by pumping, and they can act on individual wheels.

SUPERCHARGERS AND TURBOCHARGERS

Superchargers and turbochargers are used to push more of the air-fuel mixture into the engine cylinders, so generating more power. In the supercharger, a drive belt turns a compressor that pumps in the air. The output of the supercharger is thus dependent on engine speed. In the turbocharger, the pressure is provided by using the exhaust gases leaving the engine. The exhaust gases cause a turbine to spin, and this, in turn, makes the compressor rotate (see TURBINE).

With higher pressures in the engine comes the need for caution. If the pressure created by a turbocharger becomes too high, it could cause engine damage or overheating. A waste gate is used so that the exhaust gases bypass the turbine if the intake manifold pressure rises past a particular predetermined point. Modern superchargers and turbochargers use electronic controls in order to monitor the level of waste gas spillage. This helps to maintain an appropriate level of pressure in the cylinders.

A CLOSER LOOK

THE COMPUTERIZED CAR

In the 1980s, onboard computers began to appear in automobiles. Modern vehicles have many functions that are controlled by computer, from basic operations such as the ignition and fuel systems to complex adjustments such as those required for emissions control, and to peripheral systems including antitheft devices and temperature control in the passenger compartment. In many cases, the onboard computer consists of a single microprocessor that coordinates the various electronic subsystems (see COMPUTER).

Onboard computers are also used for diagnostic support, producing defined trouble codes when put into test mode. Efforts are under way to standardize these codes so that technicians need not learn or look up a different set for each automobile make or model. Another important development in automotive computing is the computer guidance system, which can display the current location of the car and recommend directions. This information is based on a combination of stored geographic data, information from ground-based transmitters, and data from Global Positioning System satellites (see SATELLITE).

A computer is used for navigation in some BMW cars.

A CLOSER LOOK

Bumpers and protective moldings that absorb the impact force can protect the car from the kind of minor impacts that are common in parking lots. In a more serious accident, protection of the passengers must be the paramount consideration. If an automobile comes to a sudden stop, as in a head-on collision, the passengers' inertia keeps them moving at the speed they were traveling before impact. They may strike the interior of the automobile at high speed, or even be thrown from the vehicle, which can result in serious injury or death. Passenger restraints, such as seat belts, reduce the likelihood of such tragedies. Modern vehicles are equipped with air bags, which inflate during a collision, cushioning the impact. These are generally found in the steering wheel and above the glove compartment, where they protect front-seat passengers in head-on collisions. Some automobiles are also equipped with side air bags (see AIR BAG). In addition to passenger restraints, strengthening of the frame around the passenger compartment can help to prevent injuries caused by crushing (see SAFETY SYSTEMS).

Heating and cooling

One of the most important features of a passenger compartment is the provision of temperature control sufficient to guarantee a reasonable degree of passenger comfort. Heat is relatively easy to provide, since the engine generates so much of it. The radiator cools the engine by dissipating the heat carried to it by the hot coolant leaving the engine. When heat is required, the hot coolant also flows through a heater core. Instead of shedding the heat to the outside, the heater core warms air that can be blown into the passenger compartment.

The air conditioner cools the passenger compartment using a refrigeration system not unlike those found on the back of a refrigerator, and discharges excess heat to the outside air. Until recently, a refrigerant called R-12, or dichlorodifluoromethane, was used in automotive air-conditioning systems. However, it was found to harm the ozone layer, the protective layer of Earth's atmosphere, and its production was banned by an international treaty. As supplies of R-12 diminish, older air-conditioning systems must be retrofitted so that they can accept a substitute refrigerant, R-134a or tetrafluoroethane (see AIR CONDITIONING AND VENTILATION; HEAT EXCHANGER; HEATING SYSTEMS; REFRIGERATION).

S. CALVO

See also: AUTOMOBILE, HISTORY OF; FUELS AND PROPELLANTS; MILITARY VEHICLE; RACE CAR.

Further reading:
Janicki, E. *Cars Detroit Never Built: Fifty Years of American Experimental Cars.* New York: Sterling Publishing Company, 1995.
Lord, T. *Amazing Cars.* New York: Random House, 1992.
Riley, R. *Alternative Cars in the 21st Century: A New Personal Transportation Paradigm.* Warrendale, Pennsylvania: Society of Automotive Engineers, 1992.

AUTOMOBILE, HISTORY OF

Automobiles have developed from the first "horseless carriages" to today's streamlined and efficient models

This photograph from 1895 shows the winner of the first auto race, from Chicago to Evanston, Illinois. Frank Duryea drove the automobile that he and his brother, Charles, built together.

CONNECTIONS

● Car inventors Benz and Daimler both worked on **RAILROAD LOCOMOTIVES** before turning their knowledge to car manufacturing.

● Catalytic converters are used to reduce the amount of **POLLUTION** that automobiles produce.

The true father of the automobile, in the sense of building a automobile practical enough to be sold to the public, was a penniless German tinsmith named Karl Benz (see the box on page 128). At the same time, his rival and future partner, Gottlieb Daimler, was working on his own gasoline-powered vehicle. Whereas Benz designed his automobiles from scratch, Daimler began fitting engines to existing vehicles. He bought a horse-drawn carriage from a local coach-builder, redesigned the axles, and fitted an engine under the floor; the engine drove the rear wheels, thereby producing a working automobile.

Early automobiles used large, spoked wheels with wooden rims. Certain types of automobiles seated the driver and passengers facing one another, as in an open carriage, with a central steering wheel. In the United States in particular, automobiles needed high wheels and strong springs to cope with rough and deeply rutted country roads.

By 1900, however, the basic layout and design of the automobile had developed into a form still recognizable today. Spoked wheels were fitted with pneumatic (air-filled) tires (see TIRE). Engines were usually mounted at the front and connected to the rear wheels through a clutch, gearbox, propeller shaft, and differential gear. These devices, many of which had initially been developed for railroad vehicles, made the automobile a more practical and reliable means of transportation.

Restriction and opposition

Solving engineering problems with the design of the automobile was easier than winning its public acceptance. Expensive automobiles were seen as playthings

CORE FACTS

■ After the first American motor race in November 1895, the winning car was bought by Barnum and Bailey's Circus as a major attraction.

■ The Detroit auto industry was established by Ransom Eli Olds, with his 1901 Oldsmobile Curved Dash runabout.

■ The 1906 Rolls-Royce Silver Ghost was so smooth and reliable, it ran the 400 miles (644 km) from London to Edinburgh in top gear and was turned into a highly successful armored car in World War I.

■ When Henry Ford's Model T first appeared in 1908, it sold for $850. Nineteen years later, mass production had brought the price down to less than $300 each.

■ By 1927, when its production ceased, more than 15 million Model Ts had been produced.

for the rich or useless curiosities. When the first U.S. motor race was held between Chicago and Evanston in November 1895, only two automobiles started, and of those, only one finished. This was built by the Duryea brothers, Charles (1861–1938) and James Frank (1869–1967), the United States' first automobile builders, and was bought by Barnum and Bailey's Circus as a circus attraction.

When automobiles were first introduced in Britain at the start of the 20th century, they were only allowed on the roads if a person walked in front carrying a red flag. (New York had a similar law for steam carriages, but sensibly avoided using the system for gasoline-powered vehicles.) In November 1896, this requirement was removed, but automobiles were limited to 12 mph (19 km/h), and speed limits were strictly enforced.

In some locations in Chicago, open warfare broke out because so many people were speeding. On Chicago's North Shore Drive, a popular high-speed run, police used ropes, chains, and wooden balks to stop speeding drivers; they finally resorted to opening fire on those who tried to escape.

Mass acceptance and mass production

Improvements in design and the switch to mass production methods caused automobile prices to drop. Wider automobile ownership made more people aware of the benefits of the automobile. An engineer named Ransom Eli Olds (1864–1950) started building automobiles in a small town named Detroit near the Canadian border. He designed a small, simple gasoline-powered runabout vehicle in 1901 to sell for around $300, but his partners wanted bigger and heavier automobiles for higher prices. However, when his factory was destroyed in a fire, all that was saved was the prototype runabout.

Put into production as the Curved Dash Oldsmobile, the automobile became highly successful. Since Olds could not make all the parts until his factory was rebuilt, he signed up local companies to make components. This established the core of the Detroit automobile-manufacturing industry and turned the Oldsmobile into a mass-produced automobile well ahead of Henry Ford's Model T (see the box on page 129).

Engineering improvements

The first decade of the 20th century brought a number of changes to the automobile. Improvements were made to the ignition systems for starting automobiles, which originally had to be cranked by hand (see IGNITION SYSTEM). Engines revolved faster and burned fuel more quickly because of a more efficient valve mechanism, which allowed them to deliver more power (see VALVE, MECHANICAL). All quality automobile models at this time were sold as bare chassis (the basic structure of the automobile). Cars were eventually made more comfortable, especially in bad weather. Coach builders were employed to add doors, hoods, and windows to shield the passengers from the wind and rain.

An advertisement from 1906 for the first mass-produced automobile, the Oldsmobile.

Over the years, performance improved and reliability followed. In Britain, Charles Rolls (1877–1910) and Henry Royce (1863–1933) decided to develop an automobile using conventional engineering of the highest quality, and a large engine. In 1906, the Rolls-Royce Silver Ghost established its reputation by running the 400 miles (644 km) from London to Edinburgh in top gear. So rugged was the design, it became an armored car in World War I (1914–1918), and was used by T. E. Lawrence (1888–1935), known as Lawrence of Arabia, in the fighting against the Turks.

After World War I, the automobile market boomed. Ideas used in wartime airplane engines were employed in automobiles. In Britain, between the wars, road tax was based on the power of the engine, measured in horsepower. This formula compelled automobile manufacturers to design inefficient engines with narrow cylinders and longer strokes in order to reduce the level of tax. However, this also limited the speed and performance of the automobiles. In Italy, a road tax was imposed that was based on engine capacity (the total volume of the cylinders that the pistons move through in a cycle). This caused the automobile manufacturers to build smaller engines and cars than overseas equivalents—a tradition that has continued in Italy with automobiles such as today's Fiat 500.

Cars in the United States developed very differently. Trips were usually longer, roads and streets were wider, and gasoline was much cheaper than in Europe. Production automobiles grew in size and performance and included large engines that had plenty of power and high reliability. When the 1921 Highways Act was passed, most long-distance routes were well-engineered modern highways rather than

the winding roads of Europe. This meant that the suspension systems on U.S. automobiles were developed more for ride comfort than for cornering capability and road handling.

During the 1920s and 1930s, ferocious competition made U.S. automobile manufacturers provide quality engineering to make their products more attractive. Features included six- and eight-cylinder engines for smoother performance, hydraulic brakes on all four wheels, hydraulic shock absorbers, and full-pressure engine lubrication (see HYDRAULICS AND PNEUMATICS; LUBRICANT).

Between the wars

Thanks to innovations like these, and the mass market success of the Ford Model T, the United States took to the automobile more enthusiastically than any other country in the world. By 1920, there were eight million automobiles owned in the United States, and ownership continued to increase. Because automobiles lasted longer, manufacturers stressed fashion in their advertising, and styling became much more important to the automobile consumer. Standardized, pressed-steel bodywork became the norm and hand-crafted coachwork was confined to the most luxurious models. Annual restyling of automobile models became a popular marketing ploy to boost mass sales.

By the time of the 1929 stock market crash, the three largest automobile producers in the United States were Ford, General Motors (which took over Oldsmobile), and Chrysler. Demand for luxury automobiles dwindled sharply during this time, but the economic recovery of the late 1930s produced a burst of innovation. Styling moved from square-rigged 1920s bodywork to sleeker, more streamlined designs (see AERODYNAMICS). Under the shell of these automobiles were further technological developments ranging from gearshifts mounted on the steering column to fully automatic transmissions.

Postwar advances

Soon after World War II (1939–1945), the U.S. automobile industry resumed full production. However, the first truly postwar models only appeared at the end of the 1940s as straightforward developments of the last pre-war automobiles. In time, integral body-chassis combinations replaced chassis frames that carried a separate body. The resulting lighter, faster, and more economical automobiles had larger windows than earlier models and were also safer and more comfortable.

European makers tried various other engine designs such as the Wankel rotary engine (see INTERNAL COMBUSTION ENGINE). However, problems from poor sealing and poor fuel economy restricted its potential in countries where gasoline was expensive. Because European automobiles lacked the power of their U.S. equivalents, acceleration was limited. However, road handling was vital on the more winding roads of Europe so that curves could be taken more quickly to maintain high average speeds.

KARL BENZ AND GOTTLIEB DAIMLER

Karl Benz and his family pose with two of their early automobiles from 1891.

Karl Benz (1844–1929) was the son of a German railroad engineer, who was killed in an accident when Karl was two years old. Fascinated by machinery, Karl worked in a locomotive factory. In 1872, he set up his own business as a tinsmith, working in his spare time on a gasoline engine. By 1880, the engine was running well, even though his business had collapsed and he could barely afford to eat.

After another five years, the first Benz car was running at night to avoid curious onlookers. In 1888, Benz's wife Berta took their two young sons for the first auto trip in history, from Mannheim to her old home in Pforzheim, 31 miles (50 km) away. After Benz exhibited the car at the 1889 Paris World's Fair and found new financial backing, sales began to increase, and by 1899 his factory was producing nearly 600 cars a year.

Gottlieb Daimler (1834–1900) was technical director of the locomotive works where Benz had worked. In 1882, he set up an automobile research laboratory where he developed a faster and more efficient engine that he put in a two-seat car for the 1889 Paris World's Fair. This set him on the road to success, and other car manufacturers built his engines under license for their own vehicles.

In 1901, a wealthy Austrian customer ordered 36 Daimlers to sell to friends in France. Convinced the French were anti-German, he insisted the cars be named after his daughter Mercedes, hence Mercedes-Benz models. For years Daimler and Benz continued as competitors until they merged in 1926 to form the Daimler-Benz car, truck, locomotive, and aircraft-engine giant.

PEOPLE

HENRY FORD AND THE MODEL T

The Model T Ford was offered in several styles, including this two-seater version.

Henry Ford (1863–1947) helped put the world on wheels. He fitted a steam engine to a horse-drawn buggy but decided the danger of boiler explosions made it unsuitable (see STEAM ENGINE).

In 1903, Ford set up the Ford Motor Company in partnership with the Dodge brothers (John and Horace), who would eventually form their own, separate company. Ford's first cars were relatively expensive, but he decided success would come from producing huge numbers of cheap and simple cars.

The best-selling Model T appeared in October 1908. Though it looked fragile, the Model T was made from vanadium steel for lightness and strength and stood up to the toughest conditions. It was produced on a moving assembly line, adapted from overhead trolley systems used in the meat-packing industry.

The Model T had a 177-cubic-inch (2898-cc) engine, which gave a top speed of 40 mph (64 km/h). The two-speed transmission was controlled by a pedal instead of a gearshift. At first, the price was $850. More than 15 million Model Ts were produced over 20 years, by which time the price was less than $300.

PEOPLE

As more and more European sports automobiles appeared in the United States, drivers came to value their agile cornering, their economy, their compactness, and their individuality. By 1963, more than 400,000 foreign automobiles were imported to the United States each year, and four years later, one U.S. buyer out of 15 chose a foreign-made vehicle.

Soon European family automobiles, such as the unmistakable Volkswagen Beetle (see the box on page 130), were taking an increasing share of the U.S. market, prompting U.S. automobile manufacturers to develop rival vehicles. These compact automobiles included the air-cooled, rear-engined Chevrolet Corvair, which used the basic layout of the Beetle, including its independent rear suspension system (see SUSPENSION SYSTEM).

Unfortunately, an inherent problem with this suspension system was a tendency to cause the vehicle to oversteer and spin whenever corners were taken too quickly. This problem caused a number of accidents. A crusading attorney named Ralph Nader took up the cause of safer automobile designs, and a new consumer movement was born that provided an additional challenge for car manufacturers.

Prices, pollution, and safety

Safety concerns produced new legal requirements, like safety belts, to keep occupants in place during a crash. Each new model was subjected to a series of crash tests to simulate a major impact. This produced vehicle components with crumple zones, designed to absorb the energy of a collision before it reached the passenger compartment. Parts like engines and steering columns were designed to be deflected clear

of the occupants. Eventually air bags were introduced to provide further protection (see AIR BAG; SAFETY SYSTEMS).

All these safety systems are examples of passive safety designs. These are features that make the effects of accidents less severe. At the same time, other design improvements, referred to as active safety systems, began to be employed to make accidents easier to avoid. Disk brakes gave improved braking performance on the older drum-brake system. Improved suspension provided more predictable road handling. Antilock brake systems, which helped to avoid skidding, were developed

The classic Italian sports car, the Ferrari, is renowned for its high speed and stylish design.

THE PEOPLE'S CAR

Adolf Hitler and other Nazi leaders inspect a model of the Volkswagen.

In the late 1930s, German dictator Adolf Hitler (1889–1945) was determined to build a Volkswagen (people's car) that would be affordable for the working classes. Designed by Professor Ferdinand Porsche (1875–1951), it had an air-cooled engine with four horizontally opposed cylinders, adapted from one of his designs for a World War I aircraft engine. The engine was mounted at the back, driving the rear wheels. The sloping bodywork was designed for maximum strength and minimum weight and wind resistance, and months of engineering development testing gave it legendary reliability. But war came before any vehicles were delivered, and it was only after the fighting was over that the Beetle went into mass production.

In all, more than 20 million Beetles were made, and the car took a leading role in the European invasion of the U.S. market. Clever advertising made the most of its virtues. For example, one poster showed a parking lot full of snow-covered cars, with one gap and a set of tire tracks leading out of the picture. The caption consisted of the words "The one that got away" and the VW symbol, stressing the car's easy starting and good traction on snow and ice.

HISTORY OF TECHNOLOGY

The impetus for reducing air pollution started with California's first limits in 1959 and continued in the Clean Air Acts from 1970 on. Tighter regulations require engines to burn fuel more completely and filter exhaust gases through catalytic converters (see CATALYTIC CONVERTER).

The modern automobile

In many ways, the layout and design of today's automobiles would be familiar to the pioneers. Power is still supplied by a multicylinder internal combustion engine burning gasoline or diesel fuel. The engine power is then transferred to the transmission via a clutch for manual transmissions or a torque converter for automatic transmissions (see MECHANICAL TRANSMISSION). The output shaft from the transmission is connected to a differential gear, which sits in the middle of the drive axle and automatically adjusts the amount of power delivered to each wheel when the car turns. The driver controls the automobile through a steering wheel, an accelerator pedal, a brake pedal, and a gearshift. The wheels are connected to the body through a suspension system.

However, a number of details have boosted efficiency, reliability, safety, and performance out of all recognition. For example, carburetors for mixing, metering, and supplying the fuel-air mixture to the cylinders have been progressively replaced by fuel-injection systems. In these, the fuel-air mixture is made to swirl on its way into the combustion chambers, which ensures more complete combustion and produces maximum power from the minimum amount of fuel, (see FUEL INJECTION).

Engine management computers monitor all the engine's vital functions to ensure efficient running and warn of problems. An output signal from these systems can be analyzed by diagnostic equipment in maintenance workshops to identify how the engine is running and which functions need attention. Synthetic oils protect moving parts and reduce wear.

Some steering systems use all four wheels for more reliable cornering. Adaptive suspension gives a soft ride at constant speed in a straight line. If the driver brakes, accelerates, or enters a corner, suspension sensors respond to changing conditions and shock-absorber settings switch to the stiffer and more precise response needed for road handling.

D. OWEN

See also: AUTOMOBILE; BATTERY; BRAKE SYSTEMS; DESIGN, INDUSTRIAL; ENGINE; FUELS AND PROPELLANTS; RACE CAR; ROAD BUILDING; ROAD SYSTEMS AND TRAFFIC CONTROL; ROAD TRANSPORT, HISTORY OF; STEERING SYSTEMS; WHEEL.

from airplane brakes, and four-wheel-drive systems made automobiles more controllable on poor or slippery road surfaces.

The biggest pressure for automobile design changes came from the rapid rise in world oil prices after the Arab-Israeli War of 1973. As the United States became more reliant upon foreign oil, domestic gasoline prices began to rise. Imported cars, because they were smaller and more efficient, were taking 30 percent of the U.S. market by 1978, and automobile manufacturers responded by making new automobile models that were smaller, more economical, and more responsive. Design features such as front-wheel drive were adopted from European compacts, and tighter suspensions, which produced more accurate steering, were incorporated to make U.S. automobiles more appealing and thereby counter the threat from imported cars.

Further reading:
Batchelor, R. *Henry Ford, Mass Production, Modernism, and Design.* Manchester, New York: Manchester University Press, 1994.
Coffey, F., and Layden, J. *America on Wheels: The First 100 Years: 1896–1996.* Los Angeles: General Publishing Group, 1996.

BAKING INDUSTRY

Baking is a dry-heat cooking process used to prepare products made from ground cereal grain

Freshly baked loaves of bread are removed from an oven at a small-scale bakery in Forfar, Scotland.

Baking is one of the oldest cooking methods known to humankind. It is well documented that prehistoric people baked a form of bread on rocks in the sun. Today, bread is still the most common bakery product and is the world's most widely eaten food.

GRAINS

Almost all bakery products are prepared from flour or meal (a coarse-ground powder) derived from some sort of cereal, or grain, which is harvested from plants of the grass family. Most grains are made up of three distinct parts. The embryo, or germ, is the part of the grain that produces the new grass plant. The main part of the grain, called the endosperm, serves as food for the germinating seed and forms the raw material from which flour is made. The endosperm is primarily composed of starch, which is a complex carbohydrate made up of many molecules of glucose, and protein. The endosperm and embryo are protected by layers of husk, which form the third component of the grain.

Wheat is probably the most important type of grain used for baking. It can be either hard or soft. Hard wheats, grown in the United States and Canada, yield excellent bread-making flour because they contain high quantities of gluten, a protein found in most cereal grains. Gluten is a semi-elastic protein and, for example, gives bread its spongy texture. Soft wheats, grown mainly in Europe and Australia, possess excellent qualities for the production of cakes and cookies, but they are also used to make a rich variety of breads.

The grains of other grasses, such as corn, barley, rice, and rye, contain less gluten than grains of wheat. As a result, doughs made with flour from these other grains are less elastic than wheat dough and are less well suited to bread making.

Milling grain

To separate the nutritious endosperm from the husk and embryo, milling the grain is essential. Grinding grain between stones or similar devices is the most primitive milling method. Used for thousands of years, grinding grain is a dry milling process. In parts of Asia, for example, rice is milled using a mortar and pestle worked by hand or foot. Windmills and water mills, once commonly used to power grindstones in the developed world, are now being used to increase the efficiency of milling in developing countries (see WATER POWER; WIND POWER).

Modern industrial techniques employ wet milling processes. The first step is to screen the grain to remove impurities. Water is added if the grain is too

CORE FACTS

- Although it is known that prehistoric people made bread, the ancient Egyptians are generally credited with developing modern baking techniques.
- Flour is vital to the baking industry. It is made by milling grains such as wheat.
- Leavening agents are added to dough to make it rise. They include microorganisms such as bacteria and yeast, chemical substances such as baking powder, and foaming agents such as egg whites.
- Bread is the most common bakery product. In industry, it is usually made in a process known as continuous bread making.

CONNECTIONS

- The **BREWING INDUSTRY** also uses microorganisms to produce alcoholic **BEVERAGES** by fermentation.

- Bakery products are kept from spoiling by the use of **FOOD PRESERVATION** techniques.

- **HARVESTING MACHINERY** is used to collect the grains that are processed to make bakery products.

A woman grinds grain between two grindstones in Kweichow, a particularly rural area of China. Milling grain in this way is called dry milling and has been practiced for thousands of years.

Treating flour

Flour is graded according to the content of endosperm material. Patent flour is the purest flour, having a low mineral content and only traces of bran and other substances. Flours with a high bran and mineral content may undergo further milling treatments and air purification to yield purer flour.

Natural colorants in endosperm give even the purest flour a yellowish color. Bleaches such as chlorine dioxide can be used to make flour whiter, but their use is controversial and unbleached flour is becoming more popular.

During the milling process many of the essential vitamins and minerals are discarded along with fiber from the husk. Today, whole-wheat products such as brown bread are a popular alternative to products made from white flour, and they use the entire wheat grain. Whole-wheat products retain most of the natural vitamins and minerals in the grain, all of which are essential to a healthy human diet.

Although white flour is high in protein—ideal for the baking process—vitamins and minerals are often added to increase the nutritional value of the flour.

dry; if it is too damp, the grain is gently dried to avoid damaging the gluten. The grain is then directed through a series of steel cylinders, which have grooved surfaces rotating at different speeds. Here the grain is crushed in what is called the first break roll. The resulting product—the chop—is sieved into three separations. The first, called first break flour, consists of endosperm material in the form of a fine flour. The second, called semolina, consists of fairly coarse pieces of endosperm. The third contains large pieces of endosperm still attached to the husk.

All the separations except for the first break flour undergo further break rolls to release more endosperm as semolina. An air-assisted sieving process called purification is used to separate the bran (fibrous material from the husk) from semolina. The resulting semolina is reduced to fine flour by a series of grindings between smooth steel reduction rolls. As much bran as possible is removed by sieving between each roll. The final flour may contain up to 75 percent of the weight of the original grain.

THE BAKING PROCESS

Most bakery products are made from a mixture of flour or meal and water. Other ingredients, such as leavening agents, shortening agents, salt, and sweeteners, can be added to change the appearance, flavor, and texture of the final product. The ingredients are combined in what is known as dough.

Leavening agents. Most bakery products require the addition of leavening agents. Leavening may result from fermentation (metabolic degradation of sugar by microorganisms) or by chemical reactions. Bread is usually leavened with baker's yeast, *Saccharomyces cerevisiae,* which ferments starch and sugars in the dough and produces carbon dioxide gas and ethanol. As carbon dioxide is released, it becomes trapped in the elastic network formed by hydrated gluten (formed as the dough is mixed), forming bubbles and causing the bread to rise.

Cookies and many other products are leavened using baking powder, which is a mixture of sodium bicarbonate (the leavening agent) and an acid such as calcium phosphate, which accelerates carbon dioxide production and maintains a palatable flavor. Sponge cakes and similar products are leavened through vigorous beating and require foaming agents such as egg whites as leavening agents.

Shortening agents. Shortening agents, or fats and oils, are used to modify the color, texture, and flavor of the product.

Sweetening agents. Sugar is added to sweeten baking products and provide an extra source of fermentable material for the yeast. Crust color is also related to the amount of sugar present in the dough.

Yeast-leavened bakery products

Bread is the most common yeast-leavened product. There are two processes used to make dough into yeast-leavened bread. Conventional bread making is

THE HISTORY OF BAKING

The Egyptians are credited with inventing modern baking techniques. By 2600 B.C.E., they were baking leavened doughs in clay ovens, varying the shape and adding poppy and sesame seeds. However, the Romans heralded baking as an industrial process. Wealthy Roman families used slaves as professional bakers who organized themselves into guilds, with various rules and regulations enforced by legislation. The first mechanical dough mixer was of Roman origin and consisted of a large stone basin in which horse-powered wooden paddles kneaded the dough.

During the Middle Ages, technological improvements began to accelerate. The purity and quality of the ingredients used to make the dough increased, and equipment was developed that reduced the need for individual skill. Gradually, automation of the mixing, shaping, fermentation, and baking processes meant that they could be carried in an unbroken sequence, eventually leading to the continuous operations in use today. Enriching bread with vitamins and minerals remains a major achievement of the 20th-century baking industry.

HISTORY OF TECHNOLOGY

used by most domestic bakers and smaller bakeries. This process has remained relatively unchanged for hundreds of years. Continuous bread making is highly automated and is used only by the largest bakeries. Today, many yeast-leavened sweet goods, such as Danish pastries and doughnuts, are made from mixtures similar to bread doughs, although they contain other ingredients such as eggs and sugar.

Conventional bread making. The first step in bread making is to mix the dough by either the sponge-and-dough method or the straight-dough method.

The sponge-and-dough method comprises two stages. In the first stage all the yeast and about three-quarters of the flour are mixed with enough water to make a stiff dough. This mixture is called a sponge and is left to ferment until it begins to decline in volume. The time required for this process, called the drop, depends on variables such as temperature and the amount of yeast added. The remaining ingredients are then mixed with the sponge, after which another period of fermentation is required.

The straight-dough method is more straightforward than the sponge-and-dough method but requires more space for fermentation. All the ingredients are mixed in one step and the dough is left to ferment. Once again, the time depends on the variables such as temperature.

After either of these fermentation processes, the dough is divided into pieces and molded into the required shape. It is then fermented again for a short time in a process called proving, which restores the dough's pliable structure. After proving, the dough is baked in loaf pans or on trays. Oven temperatures vary from 375°F (190°C) to 475°F (246°C) according to the type of bread.

Continuous bread making. Bread made using the continuous system relies on a continuous flow of ingredients into a device that mixes them into a smooth, elastic dough. After a fermentation period of around three hours, the mixture is fed into a huge dough pump, which regulates the flow and delivers the mix of ingredients into a dough developer. Continuous kneading for around 90 seconds results in about 100 lb (45 kg) of dough with the desired structure, after which it passes from the developer into a device that extrudes the dough into loaf-sized pieces. After proving, the pieces of dough are transported to a gas-heated oven. Most bakeries use a tunnel oven, which transports the pieces of dough on a metal belt through a series of connected baking chambers. Another common oven, the tray oven, has a rigid baking platform carried on chain belts.

The continuous process produces a more consistent quality of bread. The grain, or structure, of the bread is usually small, and the loaves are uniform in appearance. However, the flavor is often considered blander than conventionally made bread.

Marketing bread. After baking, bread is often sliced. The still-warm loaves are carried through parallel arrays of slicing saws with blades that are coated to prevent sticking. After slicing, most breads are wrapped in plastic packaging material.

Chemically leavened bakery products

Products such as certain cakes, cookies, and muffins are a large and important class of chemically leavened bakery foods. These products are designed to have a softer, crumblier texture and, therefore, do not require high-protein flour to make an elastic dough. However, considerations such as flavor and taste require other ingredients such as vanilla, cocoa, and eggs to be added.

Many domestic and small-scale bakeries use preprepared mixes, but industrial production mixes ingredients in a similar way to the bread-making process, albeit geared toward specific products.

Shaping the dough. The shape of cakes results mainly from the container in which the dough (called batter in the case of many sweet products) is baked. However, the dough of other products, such as cookies, passes through rollers, forming sheets of uniform thickness; the desired shape is cut in the sheet by embossed rollers or by stamping pressure. Any scrap dough is removed for reshaping.

Unleavened bakery products

Pie crusts, crackers, tortilla chips, and chapatis are all unleavened (they do not rise). They are made from flour, water, salt, and shortening, but do not contain any yeast or chemical raising agent. Desirable qualities include flakiness, which is often related to the type of shortening used. Milk is often added to pie-crust dough to improve browning and flavor.

L. GRAY

See also: ARABLE FARMING; MECHANICAL HANDLING; PACKAGING INDUSTRY; PRODUCTION ENGINEERING AND PROCESS CONTROL; STOVES AND OVENS.

Further reading:
Bennion, E., and Bamford, G. *Technology of Cake Making.* 6th edition. New York: Blackie Academic & Professional, 1997.
Technology of Breadmaking. Edited by S. Cauvain and L. Young. New York: Blackie Academic & Professional, 1998.

This picture shows a selection of bakery products made at a small bakery in Cumbria, Britain. Cakes and pastries are baked using chemical leavening agents. However, bread is baked using the yeast Saccharomyces cerevisiae (baker's yeast) as the leavening agent.

BALLOON AND AIRSHIP

Balloons are unpowered and drift with the wind, whereas airships are powered to steer a controlled course

The first successful hot-air balloons were made by French paper manufacturers and brothers Joseph Montgolfier (1740–1810) and Jacques Montgolfier (1745–1799). These balloons were shaped like open, upturned bags. When held over a fire, the balloon's envelope (the bag containing the gas) trapped the rising hot air. Since the hot air in the envelope weighed less than the air displaced by the balloon, it began to rise. On September 19, 1783, the Montgolfiers launched a balloon carrying a rooster, a sheep, and a duck. On drifting away from the fire, the trapped air cooled and the balloon sank slowly to the ground. Its occupants were unharmed.

On November 21, 1783, French scientist Jean-François Pilâtre de Rozier (1756–1785) and French army officer Marquis François Laurent d'Arlandes (1742–1809) made the first flight across Paris's Bois de Boulogne. However, it was not long before balloons with closed envelopes filled with hydrogen, rather than air, became more popular. Since hydrogen is lighter than hot air, and no additional heat source is needed, hydrogen-filled balloons performed much better.

The development of balloons

Because of its availability in the 19th century, coal gas was used as a fuel instead of hydrogen. In the United States, ballooning began with coal-gas balloon flights by a series of self-styled "professors." In 1859, the balloonists Professor John Wise (1808–1879) and Professor La Mountain (1830–1880) flew 804 miles (1290 km) from St. Louis to Henderson, New York, but abandoned a proposed crossing of the Atlantic Ocean. Professor Thaddeus Lowe (1832–1913) also built a balloon to cross the Atlantic. It was held aloft by the coal gas in its envelope and was to be propelled by a 30-ft- (9.1-m)-long steam engine that was suspended beneath its gondola. However, the balloon was so huge (to support the weight of the steam engine) that the New York Gas Company failed to inflate it completely. It was taken to Philadelphia, but 30 minutes before departure, a weather squall tore apart the partly flaccid—and therefore vulnerable—balloon and destroyed it.

The French balloon, *Le Géant*, was even larger. Holding 212,000 cu ft (6000 m^3) of gas, it had a gondola with an open upper deck over sleeping berths, storage rooms, a lavatory, a dark room, and a printing press. On its first flight, in October 1863, it carried 15 people. Two weeks later, *Le Géant* flew 400 miles (645 km) with nine passengers before the enormous balloon burst upon landing.

CORE FACTS

■ The first passengers on a balloon flight were a rooster, a duck, and a sheep, all of which survived unharmed.

■ A 19th-century U.S. balloon designed to cross the Atlantic Ocean carried a 30-ft- (9.1-m)-long steam engine below its basketwork gondola.

■ Count Ferdinand Zeppelin realized the potential of military airships while serving in the Union Army in the Civil War. Zeppelin airships were later used to bomb London and Paris during World War I.

■ When the German airship *Hindenburg* caught fire while mooring at Lakehurst, New Jersey, in 1937, two-thirds of those on board survived the blaze; 36 were killed.

Some balloons were used for spying on enemy movements in the American Civil War (1861–1865) and World War I (1914–1918).

Today, balloons have two main uses. Weather balloons ascend into the upper atmosphere with recording instruments. Balloons are also used to carry passengers to record heights. For example, Captain Joseph Kittinger Jr. (1928–) reached 102,886 ft (31,277 m) in 1960 with a U.S. Air Force Skyhook balloon.

Balloons remain popular for leisure flying. The Gordon Bennett races, inaugurated by James Gordon Bennett (1841–1918) of the New York *Herald* in 1906, ran intermittently until 1938. These races involved the use of hydrogen balloons, but when sports ballooning became popular again after World War II (1939–1945), it revived the hot-air balloon with new technology. The cumbersome furnaces used to create the hot air for lift were replaced by lightweight propane burners. In addition, the balloon materials of paper, silk, or animal membranes gave way to light, durable, and fire-resistant synthetics. New designs replaced the classic hot-air balloon, and now various advertising symbols are placed on the balloons. Today, balloon meets attract hundreds of entrants and thousands of spectators.

The introduction of airships

Astute observers of early balloon realized that their usefulness would be increased by the addition of a power unit and steering gear to make them more controllable. This observation resulted in the development of the airship.

The first successful airship was built in 1852 by French engineer Henri Giffard (1825–1882); it was propelled by a small steam engine and the near spherical shape of unpowered balloons was replaced by a more easily steered torpedo shape. Like airships made by other pioneers, including Brazilian Alberto Santos-Dumont (1873–1932), Giffard's balloon was kept in shape by the pressure of the gas inside it.

Longer distances and heavier loads created a need for bigger airships, and light aircraft alloys allowed huge, rigid frameworks to be built to contain the gas bags and support the gondola. These were used in the first rigid airship, built in 1900 by Count Ferdinand von Zeppelin (1838–1917), a German volunteer officer in the Union Army. During World War I, Zeppelins bombed London and Paris. After the war, even larger airships were built by Germany, Britain, and the United States.

At best, airship travel offered unrivaled smoothness, luxury, and range. Due to these advances, airships were crossing the Atlantic Ocean long before passenger airplanes. However, their very size made them vulnerable to bad weather. U.S. Navy airships could store, launch, and retrieve their own aircraft. They could also lower observers in baskets on ropes to look for enemy warships while the airship hid in the clouds. With several lost in storms, however, the Navy switched to smaller, nonrigid airships for antisubmarine patrols.

RETURN OF THE AIRSHIP?

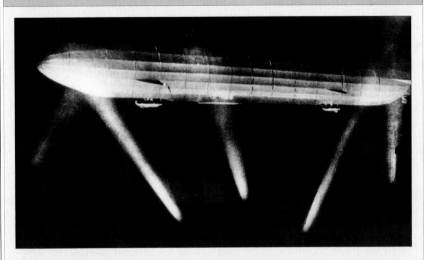

A German Zeppelin airship is caught in searchlights during a bombing raid in 1916.

Since World War II, small airships have been used for advertising, as camera mounts, and for leisure flights. The combination of polyurethane skins with helium gas makes them very safe, and their small size makes them more stable—especially in gusty wind conditions—than their larger predecessors.

More recently, work has begun on larger, rigid airships using modern technology. One South African project is a passenger airship the size of a Boeing 747. The structural framework is to be made with a light, carbon-fiber composite and the finished airship—named *Nelson* after South African President Nelson Mandela—is designed to carry up to 60 passengers. A subsidiary of the Zeppelin company has already built a prototype rigid airship—the first since the *Hindenburg*—and a second German consortium is developing the CargoLifter—an airship with twice the capacity of the prewar Zeppelins. The CargoLifter is designed to transport freight to remote areas far from existing ports and airfields; it is planned to go into service in the early 21st century.

Finally, companies in Japan and the United States plan to use nonrigid airships to relay telecommunications signals without incurring the launch and maintenance expenses associated with satellites.

LOOKING TO THE FUTURE

Because of the U.S. embargo on supplying Nazi Germany with nonflammable helium, German airships continued using hydrogen, in spite of the fire risk. In 1936, the huge *Hindenburg* made ten round-trip Atlantic crossings and seven round-trip voyages to Rio de Janeiro, Brazil. On the second of 18 planned 1937 Atlantic crossings, it caught fire while mooring at Lakehurst, New Jersey. Although two-thirds of the passengers and crew survived, 36 were killed. As a result of this disaster, the *Hindenburg* was the last luxury airship used to carry passengers (see ACCIDENTS AND DISASTERS).

D. OWEN

See also: FUELS AND PROPELLANTS; GASES, INDUSTRIAL; HEAT, PRINCIPLES OF; STEERING SYSTEMS; UNPILOTED VEHICLES AND AIRCRAFT.

Further reading:
Belleville, C. *Flying in a Hot-Air Balloon.* Minneapolis: Carolrhoda Books, 1993.

BATTERY

Batteries are made in various shapes and sizes. The output voltage and energy content of the battery depend on the number and type of cells in the battery.

D evices driven by electricity figure prominently in modern life; batteries are portable power supplies that allow these devices to be used more flexibly. They also provide backup power in case of electrical outages.

Primary and secondary cells
A primary cell is a battery that is not designed to be recharged and is thrown away when exhausted. A secondary cell or battery is designed to be repeatedly charged. The most familiar type of secondary battery is the lead-acid battery used in automobiles.

When a battery contains more than one cell, the component cells may be connected in series or in parallel. In series connection, the positive pole of one cell is joined to the negative pole of the next and so on. Joined in this way, the total voltage available is the sum of the voltages of each cell, but the current that can be drawn is no greater than the current that would be delivered by a single cell.

In parallel connection, the positive poles of all the cells are joined together to form one pole and all the negative poles are joined to form the other. The total voltage available is that of one cell, but the current that can be drawn is the sum of the currents available from each cell. Simultaneous high voltage and high current can be achieved by connecting in series banks of cells that are joined in parallel.

Dry cells
There are numerous kinds of dry cells. All of them are primary cells in which the electrolyte—the solution that conducts the electricity—is prevented from spilling by being absorbed onto a suitable material.

Almost any pair of dissimilar conducting materials immersed in an electrolyte can act as a source of electricity. The first electrical battery was the voltaic

pile made in 1800 by Italian physicist Alessandro Volta (1745–1827). It consisted of copper and silver disks separated by pasteboard that had been soaked with salt water or vinegar.

The first practical dry cell was the zinc-carbon or Leclanché cell, developed by French engineer Georges Leclanché (1839–1882). Leclanché's first version, made in 1865, was a wet cell in which a carbon electrode dipped into a solution of ammonium chloride (the electrolyte) in a zinc can, which acted as the other electrode. Leclanché later developed the wet cell into a dry cell by including an absorbent to soak up the electrolyte. The Leclanché cell has been in extensive use for well over a century.

How cells generate current
All types of chemical cells generate current by electrochemical reactions. In the case of the zinc-carbon cell, zinc has a tendency to dissolve in the electrolyte, forming positive zinc ions and free electrons in the process. The electrons flow into the zinc electrode and give it a negative charge. The zinc ions in solution give up their charge to the ammonium ions in the electrolyte and yield ammonia and hydrogen ions. The hydrogen ions migrate to the carbon electrode, where they pick up electrons to form hydrogen gas. The carbon electrode becomes positively charged as a result of the electrons it gives up to the hydrogen ions. The reactions are:

$$Zn \rightarrow Zn^{2+} + 2e \qquad \text{(zinc electrode)}$$
$$Zn^{2+} + 2NH_4^+ \rightarrow Zn + 2NH_3 + 2H^+ \quad \text{(electrolyte)}$$
$$2H^+ + 2e \rightarrow H_2 \qquad \text{(at carbon electrode)}$$

When an electrical connection is made between the electrodes of the cell, a current of electrons will flow though the external circuit from the negative zinc electrode to the positive carbon electrode (see ELECTRICITY AND MAGNETISM).

Modern cells
The original Leclanché cell suffered from an effect known as polarization, whereby hydrogen produced at the carbon electrode formed bubbles on its surface that blocked the electrolyte from making contact with the carbon. After a time, the voltage would diminish as the carbon electrode became covered in

CONNECTIONS

● Batteries are the main source of power for some types of **ELECTRIC ROAD VEHICLES**.

● Atomic batteries convert **NUCLEAR ENERGY** into electrical energy.

CORE FACTS

■ Most commercial batteries store energy in chemical form and release it on demand as electrical energy.
■ Primary cells provide a limited total energy and are discarded when exhausted.
■ Secondary cells can be recharged from an external power supply.

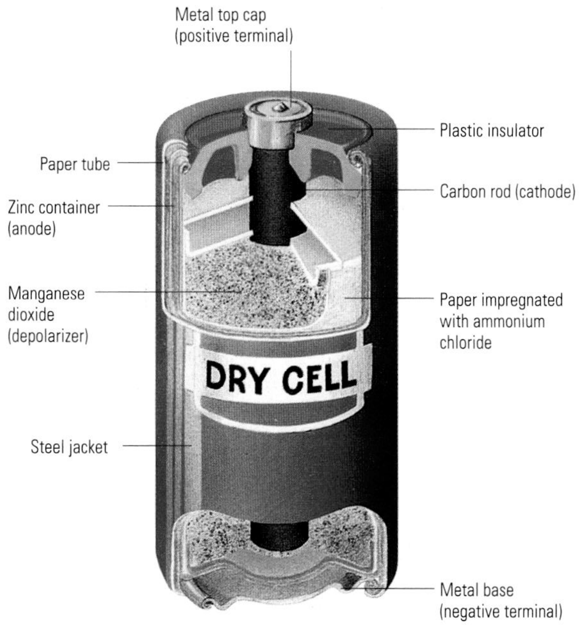

A DRY-CELL BATTERY

Metal top cap
(positive terminal)

Paper tube

Zinc container
(anode)

Manganese
dioxide
(depolarizer)

DRY CELL

Steel jacket

Plastic insulator

Carbon rod (cathode)

Paper impregnated
with ammonium
chloride

Metal base
(negative terminal)

Dry-cell batteries, such as the one illustrated above, are simply refined versions of the original Leclanché cell.

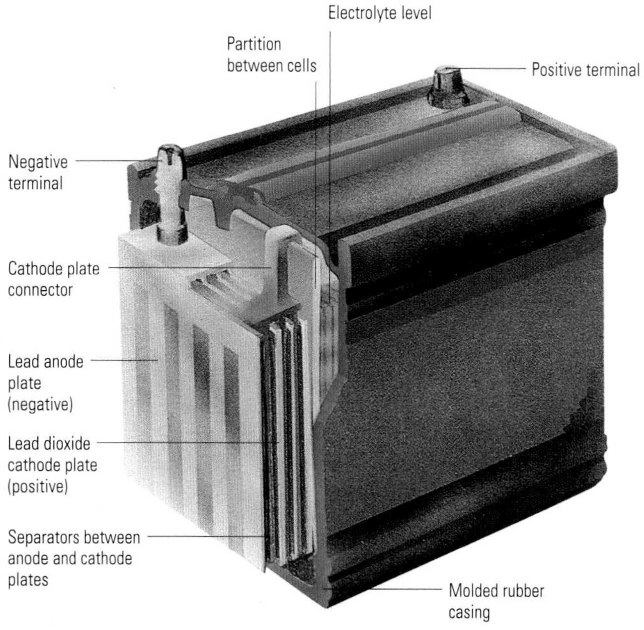

LEAD-ACID BATTERY

Electrolyte level

Partition
between cells

Positive terminal

Negative
terminal

Cathode plate
connector

Lead anode
plate
(negative)

Lead dioxide
cathode plate
(positive)

Separators between
anode and cathode
plates

Molded rubber
casing

Lead-acid batteries are commonly used in automobiles to provide energy for starting the engine and for electrical equipment.

bubbles. Older zinc cells used manganese dioxide paste to prevent the accumulation of hydrogen gas at the carbon electrode and maintain the voltage.

The most popular primary cell is now the zinc-alkali-manganese dioxide cell, which provides a longer service life and shelf life and better performance at low temperatures. Importantly, the container for the alkaline cell is a steel can, which is not involved in the electrochemical reaction. The negative electrode is still zinc, but this is used in powder form (which is more active) inside the can. The positive electrode, instead of being a carbon rod, is a compacted blend of graphite and manganese dioxide. The alkaline electrolyte is a solution of potassium hydroxide, which conducts electricity better than the ammonium sulfate electrolyte of the earlier zinc-carbon cell. Note that neither sulfate nor hydroxide ions take part in the battery reactions.

Other forms of primary cell include magnesium cells, zinc-mercuric oxide alkaline cells, silver oxide alkaline cells, cadmium-mercuric oxide cells, and a wide range of cells with lithium anodes. Note that solar cells, although sources of electricity, are not batteries. Their energy is derived from light energy (see SOLAR POWER).

How a secondary cell works

The lead-acid secondary cell consists of plates of lead immersed in strong sulfuric acid. The negative plate is sponge lead and the positive plate is coated with lead peroxide. When current is drawn from the battery, there is a reduction of the oxide at the positive electrode and oxidation of lead at the negative electrode. This reaction can be reversed—and the

battery recharged—by applying a reverse voltage and forcing a current to flow in the opposite direction to the discharge current. A great deal of electrical energy can be stored in this type of battery.

R. YOUNGSON

See also: ELECTROLYSIS.

Further reading:

Crompton, T. *Battery Reference Book.* New York: Oxford University Press, 1990.

THE ATOMIC BATTERY

A number of radioactive isotopes, such as hydrogen-3 (tritium), krypton-85, or strontium-90, are emitters of beta rays. Beta rays are streams of high-speed electrons that make the source positively charged as they are emitted. If the beta-ray source is placed next to a metal object, the object will take in some of the beta particles and become negatively charged, thereby producing an electric cell. This system generates high voltages but very little current.

Low-voltage, high-current atomic cells can be produced in various ways. Thermoelectric nuclear batteries use the heat of a nuclear reaction to produce electricity from thermocouples (devices that produce a current when heated). Isotopes such as polonium-210, strontium-90, or plutonium-238 can be used.

The gas-ionization nuclear battery uses beta-emitter isotopes to break a gas such as argon into ions. Ions are charged particles, and if an electric field is applied, the ions will start to move, producing a current.

Beta particles can cause phosphors to glow, as in television and computer screens. Light from glowing phosphors can cause photocells (devices that produce an electrical current from light) to produce electricity.

A CLOSER LOOK

BEVERAGES

This worker on a tea plantation in Kerala, India, is selecting and picking tea leaves by hand.

While it is true that people need only drink water to survive, other beverages are consumed for nutrition, for their varied tastes and for stimulation. There are many examples of beverages, including those made by infusion with hot water, such as tea, coffee, and cocoa; those containing alcohol, such as distilled spirits, wines, beers, and ales (see BREWING INDUSTRY); soft drinks, such as mineral water and cola; and fruit juices.

INFUSED DRINKS

Tea

The most common forms of teas are made from the dried leaves of the tea plant (*Camellia sinensis*), although other herbal teas, made from other plants such as rosehip, are gaining in popularity.

Legend has it that tea has been drunk in China since 2700 B.C.E. However, the first known account of tea processing came from Chinese records that date from the fourth century C.E.

Teas are classified according to their country of origin, by the size of the processed leaf, and by the manufacturing process. Of these classifications, the manufacturing process is the most important. Three categories of tea—fermented, or black, tea; unfermented, or green, tea; and semifermented, or oolong, tea—exist in the latter classification.

Processing tea. The main stages of tea processing are withering, rolling, fermenting, and drying, all of which serve to dry the tea leaf and allow chemicals in the leaf to develop a flavor unique to each type of tea.

The best known chemical in tea is the stimulant caffeine, but the most important are polyphenols, which give the tea its bitter taste.

Black tea. As soon as the leaves are plucked from the tea plant, they begin to wither. Traditionally, the leaves were laid on large trays and left to wither for up to 20 hours. Today, withering is an automated process, and continuous withering machines move the leaves on a large conveyor and subject them to hot air in a chamber. The conveyor discharges withered leaves as fresh leaves are added.

The second process is rolling, which twists the leaves into their distinctive shape. Leaf cells also burst in this process, and enzymes are released that will eventually give rise to the familiar reddish color and flavor of the drink. Traditionally, leaves were rolled by hand, but, once again, rolling is now an automated process.

CONNECTIONS

- The **BREWING INDUSTRY** uses fermentation to make beer.

- Many beverage producers rely on **REFRIGERATION** to keep their products from spoiling during transport.

CORE FACTS

- As many as 40 different teas are blended and sold as loose leaves.
- The world's biggest coffee producer is Brazil, and many developing countries are reliant on coffee exports as a vital source of income.
- The carbon dioxide resulting from the fermentation of champagne is unable to escape from the bottle and gives the wine its trademark sparkle.
- Malt whiskey is made from barley; bourbon is made from corn.

After they have been rolled, the leaves undergo a series of chemical reactions known as fermentation (not to be confused with the fermentation of sugars into alcohol by yeasts), whereby an enzyme called polyphenol oxidase converts polyphenols in the leaves into chemicals called theaflavin and theabrugin. Theaflavin is associated with the taste of brewed tea. Theabrugin is associated with its strength and color. In total, fermentation takes up to four hours, as long as the environment is carefully aerated under optimum conditions of temperature and humidity.

The leaves are then dried, primarily to stop fermentation. A large automated drying machine blows hot air onto the leaves as they pass down the machine on a series of descending conveyors.

Green tea. Green tea is prepared in the same way as black tea, but as soon as the leaves are picked, the polyphenol oxidase is destroyed by roasting the leaves in hot iron pans prior to rolling. Consequently, the theabrugins and theaflavins do not develop, making the tea taste weaker than black tea.

Oolong tea. Oolong tea is fermented for about half the time that black tea is. Fermentation is stopped by heating the leaves in an iron pan, and the leaves are rolled and heated until they dry.

Packaging and brewing. Tea is first graded by size, shape, and cleanliness, usually using mechanical sieves. Undesirable particles in the tea are removed by hand or by a mechanical extractor. Once the tea is graded, it is packed into airtight containers to prevent loss of flavor. The containers are then packed into chests, ready for transportation. As many as 40 different teas may be blended and sold as loose leaves. Alternatively, tea bags made from a porous paper are used to pack broken-grade teas.

Coffee

Coffee is made from the roasted and ground seeds (beans) of two species of coffee plant: *Coffea arabica*, which produces arabica beans, and *Coffea canephora*, which produces robusta beans. The origin of coffee is unknown, although many people believe it came from Africa and was first drunk around 1150 years ago. Coffee drinking became popular in Europe in the 16th and 17th centuries. Today, the biggest coffee producer is Brazil, and many developing countries rely on coffee as a vital source of income.

There are two processes that enable the skin and pulp of the coffee fruit to be removed—the wet process and the dry process. In the wet process, a pulping machine is used to remove the red skin and pulp of the fresh fruit. It consists of a rotating drum that presses the fruit against a sharp-edged plate. Any remaining pulp left on the seed is loosened during a 72-hour fermentation period. The seeds are washed to remove all traces of pulp and are then left to dry in the sun, or they are placed in automated driers. The dry skin around the seed (the parchment) is mechanically removed to reveal the green coffee beans.

In the dry process, the fruits are placed in direct sunlight, or in hot-air driers. Once the beans have been dried to 12 percent of their original moisture content, they are placed in a mechanical hulling machine, which removes the skin and parchment to leave green beans.

Grading the beans. After the skin and pulp have been removed, the green coffee beans are tested to provide information about the quality of the product. In warm, humid countries, green beans are prone to infection by molds and parasites, so coffee supplies in these regions are exported as soon as possible.

Processing the beans. Before the beans are roasted, they may be treated to remove their caffeine content. In the most common decaffeination process, steam is used to make the caffeine dissolve and rise to the surface of the bean. The beans are then washed with an organic solvent to remove the caffeine, treated with steam to remove traces of solvent, and then dried.

Roasting develops the aroma and taste of the coffee during the later brewing stage. At temperatures of up to 440°F (230°C), chemical transformations occur in the beans, which turn a deep brown and become crumbly. Roasting is usually performed in gas-heated, rotating drums. Rapid cooling ensures that the aroma of the coffee is preserved.

Some beans are packaged immediately so they can be ground later. However, many beans are ground immediately by rolling them between serrated metal rollers. Ground coffee is often a blend of several different beans, and blending is monitored by experienced coffee tasters. Both ground and whole coffees are vacuum-packed in airtight containers that prevent the oxidation of fats in the coffee, which would spoil its flavor.

Instant coffee. Instant, or soluble, coffee is made by removing water from a liquid concentrate of coffee that is prepared using boiling water. In the most common drying technique—freeze-drying—the coffee concentrate is frozen and then crushed, ground, and sieved to the desired granule size. The frozen granules are spread on trays and gently dried in a vacuum chamber, which causes the water content to sublime (evaporate from frozen). The gentle conditions used

Workers in Malaysia turn cocoa beans that have been spread on the ground to dry in the sun.

in the freeze-drying process help preserve the flavor of the coffee. Since the granules readily absorb moisture, freeze-dried coffee must be vacuum packed.

Cocoa

Cocoa is believed to have originated in Central America and introduced to Europe in the late 17th century. Cocoa beans are the seeds of the cacao tree, from whose misspelt name the word cocoa derives. The beans contain a large quantity of fat. The aim of processing is to remove the excess fat and then produce a fine powder. At first, the beans are fermented and dried as soon as they have been harvested from the tree. Then they are roasted and hulled. Roasting darkens the beans and increases the strength of the final beverage.

The process used to remove the fat, which is called cocoa butter, from the beans depends on how much needs to be removed. Essentially, the cocoa beans may be crushed, dissolved in a base (alkali), and washed, or steamed and pressed. The resulting cake is ground and sieved to give cocoa powder. An edible wetting agent called soy lecithin is added to the powder to make it easier to disperse in milk. The cocoa powder is then suitable for consumption.

WINE

Wine is an alcoholic beverage made by fermenting the juice of the fruit of *Vitis vinefera* (usually a European grape vine) or of *Vitis labrusca*, which is native to the Americas. Egyptian records mention that grapes were used to make wine in 2500 B.C.E.

Winemaking involves two processes: viticulture, which refers to the cultivation of the grape, and vinification, which is the process by which the grape is used to make wine. Italy and France are the world's major producers of wine, but recently many countries from the Southern Hemisphere, such as Chile, South Africa, and Australia, as well as the United States, have become involved in winemaking.

Viticulture

Viticulture is a complex process. Careful control is needed to insure a successful harvest of grapes suitable for vinification. Heavy pruning is particularly important in the winter months, since a small yield of grapes on each vine yields grape juice of a higher quality. Also, careful spraying with fungicides and pesticides prevents losses caused by infection. About 100 days after the vines have flowered, the grapes ripen and are ready for harvesting.

Vinification

The juice inside red or white grapes is basically colorless; it is the skin of red grapes that gives red wine its color. Consequently, the process used to make red wine is different than for white wines.

Red wines. After harvesting, the stalks are removed from the grapes, which are crushed in a mechanical crusher-presser, though many smaller vineyards still use traditional wooden wine presses.

The crushed grapes are fermented with their skins. The fermentation takes place using yeasts present in the skin of the grapes, along with the yeast *Saccharomyces cerevisiae*, to convert sugars present in the grapes to alcohol. As fermentation continues, more color is extracted from the skins. During fermentation in vats made from wood, steel, fiberglass, or concrete, the temperature must be kept as constant as possible, usually around 77°F (25°C). This is to facilitate yeast growth and to extract sufficient flavors, such as tannin, and colors from the skin.

After sufficient coloration, usually a period of 10 to 14 days, the juice (or must) is separated from the skins. The skins are pressed further to produce more wine. The sediment resulting from the fermentation is separated from the wine, which is run off into wooden barrels.

MATURING AND BOTTLING WINE

A man fills huge wine barrels in a cellar in the Alsace region of France.

The flavor and bouquet of many wines improve during barrel and bottle storage. Wines are usually matured in oak casks, which allow oxygen to enter and water and alcohol to escape. The wood also contributes to the flavor of the wine. The maturation period varies from 18 months to 2 years, during which time the barrels are regularly topped off to make up for evaporation. The exact period of maturation depends on the grape used, among other factors.

Before bottling white wine it is normal to remove any suspended solids by adding an albumin-containing substance, such as egg white. This process, called fining, makes the wine clear and bright. Different wines may also be blended. Often it is desirable for the wine to mature further in the bottle. Generally, white wines are matured less than reds. Today, white wines are usually matured in the bottle and should be drunk as soon as possible after opening.

Red wine is usually matured in oak casks so that the acids, sugars, and tannins blend properly. However, if a wine is matured for too long, it will lose its pleasant taste and the color will fade. As a result, wine that is being matured or stored should be placed in a room at constant temperature, ideally between 54 and 61°F (12 and 16°C), so that the maturation time is well defined.

The bottle is sealed by the use of a cork, although screw caps are common for wines that do not require further bottle fermentation. A seal is placed over the cork, a label is added, and the wines are cased.

A CLOSER LOOK

One new method in the production of red wine involves fermenting the grapes in a carbon dioxide atmosphere. This kills plant material in the grape skins and enables the color to dissolve into the juice more quickly, considerably shortening the red wine vinification process.

White wines and rosés. White wines are stalked and crushed in a horizontal press, where two wooden or metal plates gradually draw together and squeeze the juice from the skins of the grapes. The juice, called the free run juice, is collected, and the skins are left behind. Rosé wine is normally obtained from red grapes, and the juice is allowed to remain in contact with the skins for just enough time to absorb the desired color. The juice is then fermented using *Saccharomyces cerevisiae.* Sugar can added at this stage to increase the proportion of alcohol in the wine.

Following the fermentation, the wine is matured in barrels or bottles (see the box on page 140). In both red and white grapes, a secondary fermentation process is often necessary to convert malic acid into lactic acid, thereby reducing the acidity of the wine and improving its flavor. This is usually performed after a few months of maturation but can be done right after the first fermentation.

Champagne and other sparkling wines. Champagne, exclusive to the Champagne region of France, and other sparkling wines are made by the *méthode champenoise.* After the initial fermentation, sparkling wines are given a second fermentation in the bottle, which is turned upside down during the process so that the sediment is deposited on the cork stopper. The carbon dioxide resulting from the fermentation is unable to escape from the bottle and gives the wine its familiar sparkle. After the fermentation is complete, the neck of the bottle is frozen, the cork is removed (along with the sediment), and a new cork is inserted and wired to the neck of the pressure-resistant bottle.

Two other methods are used to make sparkling wines. The *cuve close* method is, in principle, the same as the *méthode champenoise,* but it takes place in a huge vessel called a vat. Although this is more economical, the bubbles don't usually last as long once the bottle is opened. An even cheaper method is to inject still wine with carbon dioxide.

DISTILLED SPIRITS

Spirits are alcoholic beverages in which the concentration of alcohol has been increased above that of the original fermented mixture by a method called distillation. Alcoholic distillation is thought to have originated in China around 800 B.C.E. Commercial distillation has only been performed for around the last 400 years.

The principle of distillation is based upon the different boiling points of ethyl alcohol (173.3°F or 78.5°C) and water (212°F or 100°C). If a mixture containing water and ethyl alcohol is heated to between 173.3°F and 212°F, the vapor that boils off contains a greater percentage of alcohol than the original liquid.

The still

Distillation is usually performed in a still. The best known is the pot still, which resembles a large copper kettle. A condenser is attached to the still, which cools the spirit-containing vapor and restores it to the liquid form. The design of the pot still depends on both the spirit being distilled and on local traditions and regulations.

The other type of still is called the patent still, which performs a continuous distillation. Continuous distillation may be used to produce spirits in vast quantities, and the exact conditions of continuous distillation can be controlled to produce a spirit that is often stronger than that obtained from a pot still.

Whiskey

Whiskey is first recorded in Scottish history, around 1494. Malt whiskey is made from barley malted (soaked) in water. When the barley germinates (sprouts), it is dried and peat smoke is allowed to permeate it. The barley is then ground and added to water, and from the resulting mash a sweet liquid called wort is drawn off and cooled. The wort is run into large vats, where it ferments under the action of *Saccharomyces cerevisiae.* The resulting alcoholic wash is distilled twice. The first distillation produces a weak, rough spirit called low wines. This is distilled in a pot still for a second time to produce a spirit that contains a higher percentage of alcohol and fewer impurities—the malt whiskey. High-quality malt whiskey is often matured for up to 12 years.

Grain whiskey is produced in a similar way, but corn is added to the malted barley mash. Grain whiskey is often mixed with malt whiskey to produce blended scotch whiskey, which is by far the most popular whiskey in Europe.

Bourbon is the most popular whiskey in the United States. It is produced from a mash containing at least 51 percent corn, and is matured in oak casks, which contribute to the characteristic taste of the final product.

This machinery is used in the distillation of Scotch whiskey.

This machinery is part of an orange processing plant. The transparent pipes contain freshly squeezed orange juice.

Other spirits

Other spirits include brandy, gin, vodka, and rum.

Brandy. Brandy is distilled from wine or a by-product of wine. There are many forms of brandy, but the finest quality brandy is cognac, which is made in France. Cognac is produced by double distillation, and it is matured in oak casks.

Gin. Gin is produced from purified grain spirits by redistilling it in a pot still in the presence of juniper berries. Other flavorings added to the still include, for example, coriander and lemon peel, depending on the brand.

Vodka. Vodka can be made from the distillation of potatoes, sugar beets, wheat rye, or a mixture of them all. After the distillation process, the resulting spirit is filtered through charcoal, diluted with water, and then bottled without maturation. Today, many vodkas are flavored with extracts of citrus fruits, pepper, chili, and even chocolate.

Rum. Rum is obtained by fermenting various sugar-containing by-products of sugar refining and distilling the alcoholic brew that results. In a typical process water is added to molasses—a residue of cane-sugar production—and natural yeasts start an extremely quick fermentation procedure. Distillation results in an exceptionally clean spirit called cane spirit. Dark rum is made by adding caramel (partly burned sugar) to cane spirit.

SOFT DRINKS

Soft drinks are a class of nonalcoholic beverages that contain a natural or artificial sweetening agent, edible acids, natural or artificial flavors, sometimes juice, and usually carbonation (dissolved carbon dioxide gas).

Production of soft drinks

To produce soft drinks, water is most often taken from the main supply and treated to insure a consistent, high-quality finished product. However, the production of specialist mineral waters often requires a particular spring water. The water used in these cases may be mineral rich or possess some other quality. Carbon dioxide (CO_2) is supplied to the manufacturer in solid form, called dry ice, or in liquid form under extremely high pressures. Carbonation takes place by chilling the water and cascading it over a series of plates in an enclosure containing the pressurized carbon dioxide.

Flavorings are usually added to the carbonated water in the form of a syrup, which contains a sweetener, an acid, the flavoring, and often a preservative and colorants. The ingredients are added in a precise order and then the mixture is diluted with carbonated water, cooled, and filled into bottles or cans. The blending stages of soft drink manufacture are almost always automated. Noncarbonated drinks such as still fruit-flavored drinks are made using plain water instead of carbonated water. Some soft drinks are pasteurized after filling to protect from spoilage (see FOOD TECHNOLOGY).

FRUIT JUICES

Fruit juices form a group of beverages that are enjoyed for their nutritious value and freshness as well as for flavor. Fruit juices are made from a growing variety of fresh fruits, either as freshly squeezed juice or as longer-lasting concentrate mixes. By far the most popular juice is made from oranges. Florida is the main orange-juice-producing region in the United States.

Oranges are monitored during their growth to insure that they are suitable for juice production. The juice is hand-squeezed from a sample of the orchard and is tested for two main attributes—soluble sugar content and acidity. Consequently, the ratio of sugar to acid content of the juice can be calculated: it is this property that determines the flavor of the juice.

Following harvesting, oranges are separated by size and sent to the juice extractors. The peel is pricked to release its essential oils (which can be sold for use in flavorings and fragrances), and then the juice is extracted. The pulpy juice is passed through a screen called a finisher, where the pulp and seeds are removed. From there, the juice may be sent directly to a pasteurizer, after which it is packaged.

A large proportion of the juice is sent to an evaporator, which removes most of the water from the juice by a vacuum and by heat. The concentrated orange juice is heated and then chilled to yield frozen concentrated orange juice. Most of the frozen concentrate is sold to juice packagers, who blend the concentrate with water, various essences, oils (recovered before juicing), and preservatives.

L. GRAY

See also: BREWING INDUSTRY; DAIRY INDUSTRY; FOOD PRESERVATION; FOOD PROCESSING; PACKAGING INDUSTRY.

Further reading:

Lipinski, R., and Lipinski, K. *The Complete Beverage Dictionary.* New York: John Wiley & Sons, 1997.
Lipinski, R., and Lipinski, K. *Professional Beverage Management.* New York: John Wiley & Sons, 1996.

INDEX

abacuses **11**
ABCs of emergency medical care 67, 71
abrasives **12–3**
ABSs (antilock braking systems) 124,
129–30
accidents and disasters **14–8**, 70, 135
acetic acid 20
Acheson, Edward Goodrich 12
acid rain 122
acids and alkalis **19–20**
acoustics and sound **21–6**, 30, 72–3
acupuncture 76
adhesives **27–8**
aerodynamics **29–32**
agricultural science **33–6**
agricultural transport and maintenance
machinery **37–8**
agriculture, history of **39–44**
air ambulances 70
air bags **45**, 125, 129
air conditioning and ventilation 24, 31,
46–7, 125
aircraft 25, 52–3
design and construction **50–5**
military 49, 53, 54–5
supersonic 22, 30
wings 29–30, 51, 52, 53
See also airliners and commercial
aircraft.
aircraft carriers **48–9**
aircraft engines 30, 52, 53, 54, **56–7**
airliners and commercial aircraft 18, 25, *50*,
52, 55, 71
airports and airfields 16, **58–60**
air traffic control 18, **61–2**
alloys 54, **63–6**
all-terrain vehicles (ATVs) 37
alternators, in automobiles 122–3
aluminum, alloys of 54, 63, 65
amalgams, dental *63*
ambulances and emergency medical
treatment **67–71**
ammonia 20, 94
amplifiers 24–5, **72–3**, 87
amplitude, sound wave 21, 22
amplitude modulation (AM) 88
anesthetics **74–6**
animals
breeding 43, **77–80**, 96, 110
domestication 40, 77, 81–2
animal transport 41, **81–3**
animation **84–6**
antennas and transmitters **87–9**
antiaircraft weapons **90**, 118
antibiotics **91–2**, 93, 96
antifreeze 122
antiseptics and sterilization **93–4**
aquaculture 34, 44, **95–6**
arable farming **97–101**
archaeological techniques **102–6**
armor 82, **107–8**
Armstrong gun 116, *117*
Arrhenius, Svante August 19
artificial insemination and fertility treatment
36, 79, **109–10**
artificial intelligence (AI) **111–4**
artillery 90, **115–8**
automobiles 129–30
air bags **45**, 125, 129
design and construction **119–25**
history of **126–30**
noise reduction inside 25
auxins 35

Babbage, Charles 11
bacteria 34, 91, 94
Bakewell, Robert 43, 77, 80
baking industry **131–3**
ballistas 116
balloons and airships 56, **134–5**
barbed wire 44
barley *35*, 39, 41
Bassi, Agostino 91
batteries 121, 122, 123, **136–7**
behavior, animals and farming 35
Belugas 50
Bennett, Gordon 135
Benz, Karl 126, 128
beverages **138–42**
bicycles 32
biofeedback 76
biological control *34*, 35–6, 100
biotechnology, and medicine 91
bleeding, emergency control of 68
Boeing 747s (jumbo jets) *50*
bone, chemical dating 105
bookbinding 28
bovine spongiform encephalopathy (BSE) 36
bows and arrows, bows, and armor 107
brake systems 124, 129–30
brass 63, 65, 66
breeding, animals 41, **77–80**, 96
bridges, disasters 31
bronze 63, 65
buildings, noise reduction in 24
building techniques
and acoustics 23
and aerodynamics 30–1

calcium hydroxide *19*
cameras, focusing 25
cannonballs 115
carbonated drinks *20*, 142
carborundum 12
carburetors 121, 130
cardiac arrest 69, *70*, 71
Carver, George Washington 36
catalysts 20
catalytic converters 122, 130
catapults 49, 115, 116
cattle 35, 41, 79, 110
cavalry 82, 108
cavitation 25
cementite 65
cereals 39, **97–100**
Chain, Ernst 92
Challenger (space shuttle) 16
chamber process 20
Chapman, Colin 32
chess computers *112*
chickens 35, 78
childbirth, and anesthesia 76
chromosomes 78
cleaning agents 12–3, 94
cleaning systems, ultrasonic 25
cloning 35, 77, 80
clutch, automobile 123, 130
cocoa 140
coffee 139–40
Coke, Thomas 43
Cold War, submarine detection 26
collars, horse 41, 42
combine harvesters 44, 100
computers 11, 86
contact process 20
control systems, aircraft 53–5
cooling towers 46, 47

copper 64, 65
corn 39, 42
corn pickers 44
corrosion 66
cotton 36
CPR (cardiopulmonary resuscitation) 67–8,
70, 71
cranberries *44*
crash dummies 45
Creutzfeldt-Jakob disease, new-variant 36
crops 39–41, 101
rotation 41, 42–3, 100
crossbows 107, 116
cultivator-drill combination 99
cultivators (harrowers) 98

Daimler, Gottlieb 126, 128
dating 104–6
decibels 22
Deere, John 43
defibrillators 69, 71
dendrochronology 106
diamonds 12, 13
dichlorodiphenyltrichloroethane (DDT) 35,
44
dioxin 17
diseases, and microorganisms 91
disinfection 93, 94
Disney, Walter (Walt) 84
distillation, of spirits 141, 142
ditches, digging/clearing 38
diving technology, and archaeology 104
Dodge, John and Horace 129
dogsleds 83
Domagk, Gerhard 91
domestication
of animals 40, 77, 81–2
of plants 40
drinks, soft 20, 142
drugs (medicinal), fertility 109–10
ductility, of metals 65
duralumin 65
Duryea, James Frank and Charles *126*, 127

earthquakes 14–5
Ehrlich, Paul 91
electric oscillations 87
electrocardiographs 69
electromagnetic theory 87
Ely, Eugene 48
embryos
transplants in animals *78*, 79–80
tubal embryo transfer 110
emergency rooms (ERs) 70–1
endorphins 75, 76
engineering, agricultural 34
engines
cooling 121–2
internal combustion 24, 56, 57, 120,
121, 128, 130
environmental engineering *19*
epidural anesthesia 75–6
ether 74, 75
exhaust systems, automobile 122
expert systems 112, 114

Faraday, Michael 87
fast Fourier transform (FFT) 26

fermentation 91, 132, 139, 140, 141
ferries 17
fertilizers 34, 43, 99, 101
field guns, antiaircraft 90
firefighting and fire protection 15, 16, 49
first aid 67–8
fish, diseases of 96
Fleming, Alexander 91, 92
flight 22, 29–30, 59
flight data recorders (FDRs) 18
Florey, Howard 92
fly-by-wire controls 54–5
Ford Motor Company 129
Model T 128, 129
formic acid 19–20
fortress guns 118
four-wheel drive vehicles 123, 130
frequency
fundamental 24
wave 21, 72, 87
frequency modulation (FM) 88
fruit juices 142
fuel injection 121, 130
fuel pumps 121
fungicides 35, 36, 100
fuses (for explosives) 90, 118

gasoline 121
gas turbines 56, 57
gears 123, 124, 130
genetic engineering 35, 80, 96
geographic information systems (GIS) 104
geostationary equatorial orbits (GEOs) 89
Giffard, Henri 56, 135
glass, etching 13
GPS (global positioning systems) 61, 125
grapes, cultivation of 140
grinding wheels 12
Groening, Matt 84, 85
ground stations 89
GRP (glass-reinforced plastic) 54
Gulf War, and newsgathering 89
gum arabic 28
gunpowder 45, 116

Haber, Fritz 20
Hall, Jim 32
halogens, as disinfectants 94
hardness, mineral 13
harvesting *43*, 100, 101
head-up displays (HUDs) 55
hearing, human 21, 22
heat exchangers 47
heating systems, and air conditioning 47
helicopters 57, 70
helmet-mounted symbology system (HMSS)
55
hemorrhage, emergency control of 68
heredity, and genes 77–8
hertz 72, 87
Hindenburg (airship) 135
honeybees 40
hormones, plant 34–5, 99
horse-drawn transport 37, 41, 81
horsepower 120, 127
horses 38, 82–3
armor 82, 107
howitzers 115, *117*

Page numbers in **boldface** type refer to main articles and their illustrations. Page numbers in *italic* type refer to additional illustrations or their captions.

hybrids 35, 79
hydrochloric acid 20
hydrofluoric acid 13
hydrophones 26
hydroponics 44

ignition systems 121, 123
image recognition systems 114
indicators, acid/alkali 20
Information Processing Language (IPL) 112
infrasound 22, *22*
instrument flight rules 62
instrument landing system (ILS) 60, 62
Integrated Pest Management (IPM) 100
Intelsat 89
intermetallic compounds 65
Internet 69, 106
Invar 66
in-vitro fertilization (IVF) 80, 110
iodine, as a disinfectant 94
iodophors 94
iron 41, 107
irrigation 39, 41, 101
isopropyl alcohol 94

Jabir ibn Hayyän 20
Jackson, Charles 75
joint strike fighters (JSFs) *54*

Kevlar *54*, 120
Kittinger, Joseph, Jr. 135
Krupp, Alfred 117

lactic acid 20
lakes, acidified *19*
language, and artificial intelligence 113–4
Lawrence, T. E. (Lawrence of Arabia) 127
Leclanché cells 136–7
Leeuwenhoek, Antonie van 91
legumes 100
Leonardo da Vinci 46
Libby, Willard F. *105*
lidocaine 75
Lindbergh, Charles 59
Lister, Joseph 91, 93
LISt Processing (LISP; computer language) 112
livestock farming 35, 36, 38, 43, 80, 92
Lockerbie airplane disaster 18
longbows 107
long-range navigational (LORAN) systems 62
loudness, sound 22, 26
Lowe, Thaddeus 134

McCarthy, John 112
McCreery, Joseph 46
Mach number 22
mad cow disease 36
magnesium, alloys of 54, 65
maintenance machinery, farm 37–8
manors 41
martensite 66
Maxwell, James Clerk 87
mechanical transmission 123–4, 130
megahertz 73
metals *64*, 65
microorganisms 91, 93–4
microphones 23, 26, 72
minimal tillage systems 98, 99
mining, and ventilation 46
missiles 90, 118
modulation, AM and FM 88
Mohs' scale 13
molds, and antibiotics 91
Montgolfier brothers 134
mortars 115
Morton, William Thomas 75
mulching 34, 98

Murdoch, Sir Thomas Octave *55*
musical instruments 24, 72

Nader, Ralph 129
natural language processing 113–4
navigation, aircraft 62
neural networks 112
neutralization reactions 19
newsgathering, electronic 89
nickel, alloys of 64
nitric acid 20
nitrocellulose 28
nitrogen-fixing plants 34, 36, 100
nitrous oxide (laughing gas) 74, 75
noise (sound), reduction 24, 25
nuclear quadrupole resonance 103
nuclear weapons, battlefield 118

Ohain, Hans von 57
O'Hare International Airport (Chicago) 18, 60, *62*
oil, crude, spillages 17–18
oil, motor oil 121
Olds, Ransom Eli 127
op amps (operational amplifiers) 73
opiates 75
ores, detection 114
organic farming 101
outbreeding 79
overtones 24

Pan-American airlines flight 103 disaster 18
paramedics 68
Park, Nick *84*, 85, 86
passenger terminals, airport *58*, 59–60
Pasteur, Louis 34, 91
Perspex 54
pesticides and herbicides 17, 35, 44, 98, 100
pewter 66
phonemes 113–14
photography
    aerial 102
    time-lapse 86
photoperiodism 34
pH scale 20
Pilâtre de Rozier, Jean-François 134
plants
    breeding and propagation 35
    growth regulators 99
    physiology 34–5
plastics 54
plowing 97
plows/plowing *33*, 34, 39–44
polyvinyl acetate 28
Porsche, Ferdinand 130
potatoes 40, *43*, 101
power-steering 123
power-takeoff systems 44
preamplifiers 72–3
predicate logic 113
Priestley, Joseph 20
procaine hydrochloride 75
progeny testing 78, 79
PROSPECTOR system 114

race cars 31–2
radar 90, 102
radiocarbon dating *105*, 106
radio communications 58–9, 62
radio-frequency amplifiers 89
radio receivers 89
radio waves 88
ramjets 57
Räzï, ar- 20
relay stations, microwave *87*
remote sensing, from spacecraft 102
resonance 24

resonant-tuned circuits 87
rice 39, 42, 100–1, 131
rifling 116, 117
robotics *111*, 114
rocket engines, for aircraft 57
Roebuck, John 20
Rolls-Royce 57, 127
RO-RO carriers 17
Rosenblatt, Frank 112
Royce, Henry 127
rule-based systems 113

Saccharomyces spp. (yeasts) 132, *133*, 140, 141
safety systems 45, 124–5, 129–30
salts 19
Salvarsan 91
sandblasting 12, 13
sandpaper 12
Santos-Dumont, Alberto 135
satellites 89, 102
Searle, John 112
seat belts 125, 129
seeds
    pesticides for 36, 98
    sowing 43, 98–9
Semtex explosive 18
servometers 54
Seveso disaster 17
sheep 43, 77, 80
shot blasting 13
sick building syndrome 47
silicon carbide 12
silver, sterling 63
Simpsons, The (cartoon show) *84*, 85
sirens 23, 25
slash-and-burn agriculture 42
slaughterhouses 35
sodium azide 45
sodium hydroxide 20
soft drinks *20*, 142
soil 34, 97–8, 99
soldering 65
solid solutions 64, 65, 66
sonar 23, 26, 103, 104
sonic booms 30
Sopwith Camels 54–5
sorghum 39, 44
sound barrier, breaking 22, 30
sound reflectors 22–3
soybeans 44
space shuttles, *Challenger* 16
spark plugs 121
spirits, distilled 141–2
stacking, aircraft 62
standing waves 24
stealth aircraft technology 53
steam plows *42*, 44
steel 66, 107, 108
    alloys of 65, 66
steering systems, automobile 124, 130
sterilization (microorganisms) 93–4
STOL aircraft 53
stratigraphy 105
submarines 26
sulfuric acid 20
superalloys 65
superbugs 94
supercarriers 49
superguns 118
super jumbos 55
surgery, aseptic 93
surrogacy 110
suspension systems, automobile 119–20, 130

tack, horse 82–3
Tacoma Narrows Bridge (civil engineering disaster) 31

tanks, anti-tank artillery 118
tea 138–9
telemedicine systems 69
television 73, 88, 89
terraced agriculture 41, 42, 99
test-tube babies 110
tetrachlorodibenzodioxin 17
thermionic valves 73
thermoplastics 28
thermosets 28
tillage, soil 97–8, 99
tin, alloys of 65
tinnitus 22
tires, automobile 120
tissue culture, plant 35
Titanic (ship) 16–17
titanium, alloys of 63, 65, *66*
tone 24
tools, agricultural 40
torque converters 123–4, 130
Torrey Canyon (tanker) 17
tourniquets 68
Townshend, Charles 42–3
tractors 37, 38, 44, *98*, *99*
trailers, farm 37
transistors *72*, 73
transmission systems, automobile 123–4
transplant surgery 80
trisodium phosphate 94
tubal embryo transfer 110
tuboplasty 110
Tull, Jethro 43
turbofan engines 52, 53, 54, 57
turboprops 53, 57
Turing test 112
TWA flight 800, explosion 18

ultrahigh frequency (UHF) 88, 89
ultrasound 22, 25, 103, 110
universal joints 124
unmanned combat aerial vehicles (UCAVs) 55

valves, thermionic 73
ventilators (respirators) 69, 76
ventricular fibrillation 69
videophones, in ambulances 69
virtual reality 50, *54*, 86, 106
voice recognition and synthesis 55, 114
voice throttle and stick (VTAS) 55
Volkswagon Beetles 129, 130
Volta, Alessandro 136
voltaic piles 136
VRML (virtual reality modeling language) 106

wagons 37, 41
Waksman, Selman 91
Warren, John 75
wave motion 21, 88
weather balloons 135
weeds 36, 98, 99–100
Wells, Horace 75
wheat 39, 41, 97–100, 131
wheels 82, 120
Whittle, Frank 57
Whitworth gun 117
windmills 42, 131
wind tunnels *29*, 31–2
wine 140–1
Wright brothers (Wilbur and Orville) 31, 56

yeast, baker's 132, *133*

zeppelins 135
zoetropes 85
zygote intrafallopian transfer (ZIFT) 110